HIGH PERFORMANCE IN THE 90s

LEADING THE STRATEGIC AND CULTURAL REVOLUTION IN BANKING

HIGH PERFORMANCE IN THE 90s
LEADING THE STRATEGIC AND CULTURAL REVOLUTION IN BANKING

Cass Bettinger

BUSINESS ONE IRWIN
Homewood, Illinois 60430

Project editor: Margaret A. Schmidt
Production manager: Diane Palmer
Artist: Benoit Design
Compositor: Eastern Graphics
Typeface: 11/13 Century Schoolbook
Printer: Arcata Graphics/Kingsport

Library of Congress Cataloging-in-Publication Data

Bettinger, Cass.
   High performance in the 90s : leading the strategic and cultural
revolution in banking / Cass Bettinger.
     p.   cm.
   Includes index.
   ISBN 1-55623-425-2
   1. Bank management. 2. Banks and banking—Planning. 3. Public
relations—Banks and banking. 4. Banks and banking—Personnel
management. 5. Corporate culture. I. Title.
HG1615.B47 1991
332.1′068′4—dc20   90–41580

Printed in the United States of America
1 2 3 4 5 6 7 8 9 0 K 7 6 5 4 3 2 1 0

To Thelma Ferguson Bettinger (1910–1986)
with love and appreciation.

FOREWORD

Banking has changed. No longer can a bank survive and thrive by borrowing short and lending long. Our volatile interest rate structure has made this the certain path to oblivion. And, maybe the difficulty of this policy can be summed up by the sign in an investment department of a bank that reads: "GOOD NEWS AND BAD NEWS. FIRST THE BAD NEWS: WE CAN'T PREDICT INTEREST RATES. NOW THE GOOD NEWS: WE FINALLY REALIZED IT."

With the traditional source of profits gone, banking must turn inward for its revenues. And here is where Cass Bettinger's new book shines.

No securitization, immunization, interest rate swaps, and the like. Just plain common sense is included in this volume, with the emphasis on making a plan for the bank that cuts costs and augments revenue both through more efficient handling of traditional functions and through development of more noncredit income sources. Turn inward, pleads Cass, and if you work on your corporate culture and rituals, you will be far better off than if you chase after that quixotic goal of profitable, rapid growth.

Bankers who read this volume will understand why human resources and marketing are so important today. No CEO can make it without having a dedicated, loyal, and effective staff behind him or her. Bettinger tells how you can improve your people resources in all three areas.

Marketing is a key. But this means returning to relationship banking—looking at a customer as a friend whom you serve in handling both profitable and unprofitable business. No more of taking the good stuff and saying "The other banks participating with me turned this deal down" when the customer wants something not completely to your liking.

How do you know when you are doing a good job? Cass Bettinger gives lots of ideas here, but my favorite is when the employees, in talking to the customers, take the bank's side and not the customer's side. Nothing is worse than a bank in which the CEO talks about the bank and uses the term "I" instead of "we," unless it is employees who talk about their bank and instead of saying "we" say "they." To describe the policy makers and goal setters in this manner indicates that they have no say or no interest in how the bank performs.

Keeping your goals in focus is what this book is all about. And to Bettinger, as well as to most observers of banking today, this means quality—not price. As John Glenn, the astronaut, was reputed to have replied when asked what it was like flying around in his capsule: "All I could think was that there were 862 moving parts, each of which was built by the low cost bidder." The public wants service, recognition, quick answers, and more than a loan at an eighth of a percent lower cost.

But, to this writer, the most happy aspect of Cass Bettinger's new and different book on banking is that he stresses SHAREHOLDER VALUE! Far too often the people who provide the capital and make the bank possible are treated as an afterthought, if anyone thinks of them at all. This volume stresses that without shareholders and their capital, there would be no bank, and that it is up to all employees to remember this and work to make them as happy as possible.

If the reader finishes this quick reading volume keeping only this and the emphasis on quality over price in mind, he or she will have well spent the time that it will take to do this book justice.

Paul S. Nadler
Professor of Finance
Graduate School of Management
Rutgers University and
Contributing Editor
The American Banker

PREFACE

By constantly altering the rules which govern success or failure, the forces of external change are forever challenging our most cherished conceptions of how the world works. None of the institutions, public or private, created by humanity to meet its diverse needs is immune, as demonstrated so dramatically by the recent events in Eastern Europe.

Commercial banks, like other financial intermediaries, enjoyed a long period of relative stability and preferential treatment. Favorable tax laws, reasonably moderate interest rate volatility, fixed raw materials costs, and regulatory barriers to competition from inside and outside the industry all combined to make the intermediary function extremely lucrative for those who adhered religiously to the rules of prudent banking.

The pace of external change, however, intensified in the 1970s and accelerated dramatically during the 1980s, in the process invalidating many traditional banking practices and creating a series of unprecedented new challenges for America's bankers. Users and providers of funds found cost-effective ways to deal with each other directly. A wide variety of substitute products was created by a host of new competitors. Borrowers and depositors became more sophisticated and discriminating. The financial markets, in light of the additional risks, demanded that banks provide a higher return on capital. Success was no longer inevitable—and the possibility of failure became increasingly real for those who were unable or unwilling to adapt.

As bankers enter the last decade of the 20th century there is one overriding and compelling reality which cannot be ignored: *because there isn't enough quality business to go around not everyone will survive!*

Having worked with over 1,000 bank and bank holding company CEOs over the past decade, first as the implementor and manager of Sheshunoff's High Performance Affiliation Program for Sheshunoff and Company, Inc., and currently as a private consultant, I have learned firsthand the nature of the challenges which today's CEO faces, as well as the dramatic and painful changes which must be made to survive and prosper during the 1990s and beyond.

I have written this book for those commercial bank CEOs, senior managers, and directors who recognize that external change is inevitable and irreversible, that yesterday's solutions are inappropriate for today's realities, and that high performance in the 1990s will require the courage to discard obsolete paradigms, the vision to conceptualize new ones, and the unwavering commitment to remain steadfast in the never ending battle against ignorance, complacency, and resistance to change. They are the leaders of the strategic and cultural revolution in banking—and the purpose of this book is to help them achieve and sustain high performance in the 1990s.

ACKNOWLEDGMENTS

During my fifteen years as a commercial banker, first with Citicorp in New York, Latin America, and Asia, and later with Commercial Security Bank in Salt Lake City, I was fortunate to work with many outstanding bankers who always had the time to share their knowledge and expertise. I am especially indebted to Bob Simmons, Will C. Wood, Ignacio Perez Guerri, Rhees Ririe, and Bob Bischoff.

When, in 1982, I joined Sheshunoff and Company to implement and manage the High Performance Affiliation Program, I had no idea that I would come to know, and work with, well over 1,000 of America's top CEOs over the next six years. I think of them often and am appreciative of the wisdom and knowledge which they so willingly shared with each other—and with me. Naturally, I am deeply grateful to Alex Sheshunoff and to all the other outstanding professionals at Alex Sheshunoff and Company—Mike Morrow, Bill Meredith, Tom Macready, Jack Jacobs and Ed Pace—all of whom contributed immensely to one of the most rewarding periods of my life, both personally and professionally.

To those exceptional CEOs and industry specialists who contributed their perspectives to this project—Mike Higgins, Harold Brewer, Bob Walters, Linn Wiley, Bob Zullinger, Tony Abbate, Rick Parsons, Mike Ryan, and Carl Carballada—I am particularly thankful. Their friendship and support is greatly appreciated.

Finally, I am grateful to my partners at Matrix Funding Corporation and Bettinger Isom and Associates for their support of this project. Special thanks go to my administrative assistant, Linda Pearce, for all the long hours spent in preparing the manuscript, Michelle Bettinger, who served as my research assistant, and to my wife, Connie, for her tireless review of each and every draft.

Cass Bettinger

CONTENTS

Epigraph   xvii

SECTION I
INTRODUCTION:
INVENTING THE FUTURE

The Key Questions Affecting Bank Survival in the 1990s   2

Focus and Scope of Chapters 1–6   2

Sources of High Performance Strategy   4

1   THE FORCES OF CHANGE   6

Changing Paradigms and Paradigm Paralysis   6

  Technological Discontinuity   9

The S&L Industry: A Case in Point   11

  Industry Viability and Shareholder Value   16

Banking and the Forces of Change   17

Porter's Model of Industry Attractiveness   20

2   MASTERING THE PROCESS OF STRATEGIC CHANGE   24

Challenging the Traditional Paradigm   24

  The Importance of Honest and Open Communication   26

The Six Key Steps in Mastering the Change Process   27

  A New State of Mind   28

  Enlightened Leadership and the Strategic Vision   34

  Defining what Business(es) the Organization Is In   35

  *Upgrading from Strategic Planning to Strategic
  Management and Planning*   46

  Strategic Focus   49

  A Strategically Supportive Culture   63

SECTION TWO
REALIZING THE STRATEGIC VISION

3   FINANCIAL PERFORMANCE AND SHAREHOLDER VALUE
OPTIMIZATION   69

Creating Shareholder Value   69

Generic Growth and Profitability Strategies   70

The Growth Component: Internal and External Growth Strategies   71

*The Earnings Component: Economic Value, Cash Flow, and
Earnings*   74

The Profitability Dynamics of Return on Equity   78

The Profitability Dynamics of ROE   83

The Profitability Dynamics of Return on Assets   85

The Profitability Dynamics of Interest Income   90

The Profitability Dynamics of Interest Expense   98

The Profitability Dynamics of Noninterest Income   101

The Profitability of Overhead (Noninterest) Expense   105

The Profitability Dynamics of Asset Quality   119

The Sixth Dynamic Variable of ROA: Taxes   124

4   HIGH PERFORMANCE LEADERSHIP AND CULTURE   127

What Is Corporate Culture?   128

Leadership and Cultural Change   130

Employee Reaction to Cultural Change Initiatives   131

The Cultural Change Process   133

*Changing the Corporate Culture: Step 1, Comprehensive
Analysis of the Existing Culture*   136

*Changing the Corporate Culture: Step 2, Definition of the
Characteristics of the Desired Culture*   174

*Changing the Corporate Culture: Step 3, Prioritization of the
Specific Areas Requiring Cultural Change*   177

*Changing the Corporate Culture: Step 4, Ongoing
Management of the Cultural Change Process*   177

Corporate Culture and Human Resource Management and
Development   182

Key Issues in HRMD   183

Corporate Culture and Employee Motivation   189

5   MARKET POSITIONING STRATEGY: CREATING
    COMPETITIVE ADVANTAGE   193

    What Is Marketing?   194

    Developing the Marketing Plan   194

    Marketing and the Bottom Line   196

      Marketing Focus: Segmentation   197

      Market Research: Needs Analysis   208

      Creating a Differentiated Benefits Package   213

      Promotion and Delivery   229

      Creating, Implementing, and Managing a Sales Culture   238

6   A MODEL FOR CREATING AND SUSTAINING HIGH
    PERFORMANCE   246

    Enlightened Leadership and the Strategic Vision   248

    Strategic Management and Planning   251

      Opportunity Identification and Prioritization   254

      Developing the Strategic Plan   263

      Implementation and Execution   263

      Management and Strategic Refocus   264

      Quality of Leadership, Management, and Supervision   265

      Strategic Focus and Accountability   271

      *The Individual Employee: The Keys to Superior Individual
      Performance*   272

      Teamwork: Quality of Implementation   277

      *Quality and Strategic Value of Individual and Organizational
      Performance*   278

      Consequences and Reinforcement   278

Endnotes   295
Index   305

There are times when the atmosphere is thick with the potential for change, and works of genius or madness have their best chance for a friendly reception. A disproportionate number have occurred when an aged century was about to give way to a new one . . . a powerful spur to the accomplishment of tasks long neglected.

Marvin Cetron and Owen Davies
Omni October 1989

HIGH PERFORMANCE IN THE 90s

LEADING THE STRATEGIC AND CULTURAL REVOLUTION IN BANKING

SECTION I

INTRODUCTION: INVENTING THE FUTURE

Businessmen go down with their businesses because they like the old ways so well they cannot bring themselves to change. . . .

—Henry Ford

American Commercial Banks have a choice: they can change, or they can die.

—Suzanna Andrews
Institutional Investor

The overriding reality in the financial services environment of the 1990s is that an ever greater number of increasingly innovative and aggressive banks and nonbanks are competing for a finite supply of quality business. The best customers of every financial intermediary are being targeted by a seemingly endless variety of financial service providers, many of which have competitive advantages the individual commercial banking institution simply cannot match.

The implications of this reality include significant industry overcapacity, severe price competition, increased risk, concerned and increasingly less tolerant shareholders, regulatory

1

alarm, and, inevitably, massive strategic restructuring and consolidation.

Market share warfare is, in such an environment, a zero-sum game. Increases by one player are invariably at the expense of one or more other players. Clearly, not everyone will survive; there simply isn't enough profitable business to go around. In recognition of this grim reality, and the additional risks it implies, the financial markets are demanding that banks deliver consistently higher returns on capital.

THE KEY QUESTIONS AFFECTING BANK SURVIVAL IN THE 1990s

The key questions which must be addressed successfully in order to survive and prosper in the final decade of the 20th century are these:

1. How specifically are the forces of change affecting the profitability and shareholder value dynamics of the financial services industry, and of the individual firm, and what are the strategic* implications of those changes?
2. What must the leadership of the individual bank or bank holding company do *now* to gain mastery of the change process, thereby ensuring successful adaption?
3. What specific strategic and cultural initiatives must be undertaken to enable the individual bank to achieve and/or sustain superior performance in the 1990s?

FOCUS AND SCOPE OF CHAPTERS 1–6

The focus of this book will be directed toward these three critically important questions, with the greatest emphasis on ques-

---

*The Oxford American Dictionary defines strategic as "giving an advantage." Throughout this book strategic will refer to those initiatives designed to give the originator competitive advantage in support of specific objectives, most notably the creation of shareholder value.

tion number three. First, I will examine the forces of external change and the specific ways in which the nature of the financial services business is being altered. Because so many bankers have been unable or unwilling to accept and/or understand the strategic and cultural implications of change and/or continue to define their business(es) incorrectly, their chances of survival are poor unless they take the difficult, painful, yet liberating actions necessary to take control of their destinies.

Second, I will discuss the six key steps that bankers must take *immediately* to achieve mastery of the process of strategic and cultural change. Change, which one writer defines aptly as "the impetuous forward motion of history,"[1] is, after all, neither good nor bad; it is simply inevitable. The challenge, of course, is quite clear: either we master the dynamics of the change process and use change to our advantage, or we become its victims.

Those businesses which survived and prospered during the 1980s bear little resemblance to the companies of the previous decade which carried the same names. As the forces of external change have redefined market realities, the adaptive organizations have, in turn, redefined their businesses in terms of those realities.

Sadly, however, many companies seem either unwilling or unable to let go of old ideas and outdated perceptions of reality. Change represents the unknown and, as such, is feared and, all too often, ignored altogether until it is too late. Albrecht and Zemke write: "The history of organizations as adaptive entities is anything but impressive. It is all too common for a company to experience a radical change in the structure of its industry and yet utterly fail to mobilize its resources to cope with the change."[2] As we will see in Chapter 1, the S&L industry is a classic example of the validity of this observation.

According to Toffler: "Some firms are already beyond rescue; they are organizational dinosaurs."[3] This can, in fact, be said of entire industries, and even societies. Many, for example, are already predicting the demise of the United States as the world's leading economic power as Japan continues its impressive growth and the European Economic Community integrates its considerable resources in preparation for 1992. Per capita GNP in the United States has already fallen behind that of several countries, including Japan, West Germany, Switzerland, Denmark, and Sweden.[4]

Firms, industries, and civilizations decline, not because of external factors, but rather because of what historian Arnold Toynbee calls "an internal hardening of ideas"[5]—a mentality that is trapped in the dogma of the past rather than inspired by the dreams and possibilities of the future. After all, just as yesterday's seemingly impossible dreams have become today's reality, the reality of tomorrow will emerge from the dreams and visions of today.

The real threats to survival are rarely external, since change is an inescapable element of everyday existence. Throughout recorded history, in fact, the downfall of institutions and their leaders has almost invariably resulted from their inability or refusal to accept that the rules they have worked so hard to master, and on which their success has been based, have changed, and that they must not only master new rules, but must take an active part in their creation. Furthermore, change, and the new rules which change mandates, are not random and devoid of direction and purpose. They are driven for the most part by those seeking to gain competitive advantage of one kind or another by inventing a more accommodating future through the exploitation of new external realities.

The multiplicity of external forces at work to bring about change in the last decade of the 20th century is unrelenting, and the pace and pervasiveness of that change is accelerating. The competitive challenges facing the individual financial institution are very real, and will not be overcome by clinging to outdated perceptions of reality and rules which are no longer valid. Those who cannot or will not change, and the institutions for which they are responsible, will not survive to welcome the new millennium.

SOURCES OF HIGH PERFORMANCE STRATEGY

Once the six steps necessary to gain mastery of the change process have been discussed, including the five key strategic initiatives or critical success factors for high performance in the 1990s, I will focus on the three primary sources of high performance strategy, each of which plays a critical and indispensable role in achieving and/or sustaining excellence. The first is what I call Financial Performance and Shareholder Value Optimization and is based on mastering the changing profitability and shareholder value dynamics of the business. These will be addressed comprehensively in Chapter 3. The second is Leadership and Corporate Culture. In Chapter 4, 34 specific cultural issues in seven key component areas will be discussed and evaluated, as will appropriate culture modification strategies. Emphasis will be given to cultural and leadership characteristics traditional to banking that represent an impediment to successful strategic adaptation and to the leadership initiatives that are necessary to bring about cultural change. Using actual examples, specific characteristics of high performance cultures will be compared to those typically found in poor performing organizations.

The third area receiving special attention will be Market Positioning Strategy, the subject of Chapter 5. Marketing will be precisely defined, and the key steps needed to create, implement, and manage a successful high performance marketing strategy, based on sustainable competitive advantage, will be detailed.

Finally, A Model for Creating and Sustaining High Performance will be presented in Chapter 6 which integrates (*a*) mastery of strategic and cultural change, (*b*) financial performance and shareholder value optimization, (*c*) corporate culture assessment, modification, and management, (*d*) enlightened leadership and human resource management and development, and (*e*) market positioning strategy into a comprehensive framework which, if followed, will result in sustainable superior performance in the next decade and beyond.

CHAPTER 1

THE FORCES OF CHANGE

When the group or a civilization declines, it is through no mystic limitation of corporate life, but through the failure of its political or intellectual leaders to meet the challenge of change.

—*Will and Ariel Durant*
The Lessons of History

Every morning in Africa, a gazelle wakes up. It knows it must run faster than the fastest lion or it will be killed. Every morning a lion wakes up. It knows it must outrun the slowest gazelle or it will starve to death. It doesn't matter whether you are a lion or a gazelle. When the sun comes up you'd better be running.

—*The Economist*

CHANGING PARADIGMS AND PARADIGM PARALYSIS

Success or failure in any competitive endeavor results primarily from the quality of decision making over time. Decisions to act in a specific manner, or not to act at all, are generally based on certain assumptions and beliefs which comprise the perception of "reality" held by an individual or group. As the forces of change challenge, contradict, and eventually undermine many of these beliefs and assumptions, replacing them with new and unfamiliar concepts, there is almost always a tendency to resist, ignore, and/or disregard that which is threatening, uncomfortable, and/or does not fit the prevailing concept of reality. Worse, perhaps, is the tendency to judge or evaluate that which

6

is new based on what one "knows" to be true as a result of prior experience.

Einstein, for example, when attempting to apply the known laws of physics to the newly discovered world of the atom, was shocked and shaken to find that his prevailing concept of reality simply did not apply: "All my attempts to adapt the theoretical foundation of physics to this knowledge failed completely. It was as if the ground had been pulled out from under one, with no firm foundation to be seen anywhere, upon which one could have built."[1] Einstein's genius was his ability to overcome his shock and discomfort, discard a comfortable yet obviously flawed paradigm (from the Greek *paradigma*, or pattern), and create a totally new conceptual framework to accommodate the new realities he had discovered.

Peter Drucker, when inquiring as to why so many at IBM had failed to anticipate the tremendous success of the personal computer, received an answer which typifies paradigm paralysis: "Precisely because we *knew* that this couldn't happen, and that it would make no sense at all, the development came as a profound shock to us. We realized that everything we'd assumed, everything we were so absolutely certain of, was suddenly being thrown into a cocked hat, and that we had to go out and organize ourselves to take advantage of a development we knew couldn't happen, but which then did happen."[2]

Because our prevailing "view of the world," or paradigm, defines reality for us, establishes what is, and is not, possible, provides a groundwork for communication and understanding, and establishes parameters which help us to evaluate and predict behavior, it represents truth. Decisions, therefore, are almost always made within the confines of an existing paradigm.

Because the individual consciousness can only accommodate a small percentage of the stimuli to which it is subjected each day, those new ideas which are compatible with an established paradigm are accepted for consideration. Others, regardless of their value, are filtered out and rejected. Thus, while "reality" may certainly shape our perceptions, to an even greater degree our perceptions shape and define our reality. Consequently, anything which challenges the existing paradigm is by definition false, unreliable, and not to be trusted. The more strongly we hold our views to be sacred, and the more personally threatening we perceive the challenges to be, the more vigorously, and often irrationally, we will defend and protect the status quo. Because we have so much invested in the existing paradigm, there is always a considerable price to be paid, in terms of discomfort, inconvenience, and stress, in adopting a new paradigm—which, of necessity, forces us to discard the old one.

Thomas Kuhn referred to this movement from a prevailing paradigm to a new one as "paradigm shift" in his classic book *The Structure of Scientific Revolutions*.[3] In almost every case, those who continue to embrace blindly the old patterns inevitably go the way of the dinosaur, while those who have the capacity to accept and understand the forces of change, create and/or adopt a new paradigm, and adapt strategically, ultimately displace their less adaptive and innovative counterparts. *In other words, a seemingly safe, conservative, and paradigm-conforming mentality is, ironically, the riskiest and most life-threatening mind-set of all, especially during a period of rapid and pervasive change.*

In her ground breaking book, *The March of Folly*, Pulitzer Prize winner Barbara W. Tuchman chronicles humanity's remarkably consistent failure throughout recorded history to accept the challenges posed by unpleasant new realities. Much of the blame, according to Tuchman, is attributable to what she calls woodenheadedness, which "consists in assessing a situation in terms of preconceived fixed notions while ignoring or rejecting any contrary signs."[4]

Others refer to the inability of policy and decision making groups to cope rationally with change as "groupthink", the "nondeliberate suppression of critical thoughts as a result of internalization of the group's norms."[5] The more amiable the group, the stronger its esprit de corps, and the more threatening the change, the greater the likelihood that independent critical thinking will be subjugated to groupthink. In such cases the immediate need for harmony and mutual support overrides the seemingly less personal need to deal objectively with external threats, with potentially disastrous consequences.

A classic example was the January 1988 acquisition of Allied Bancshares by First Interstate Bancorp. According to published reports, First Interstate's Chairman, Joseph Pinola, and his top management team were so driven to consummate a major transaction after their failure to take over Bank of America that responsible and comprehensive due diligence was not allowed to dampen their enthusiasm. James E. Burns, an executive vice president, apparently voiced his opposition and was summarily "banished from the first rung of the negotiating team."[6] The transaction, as it turned out, not only dissipated shareholder value but cost Pinola his job and made First Interstate itself vulnerable to takeover.

Warren Bennis argues that the single greatest problem faced by the president of any organization is "getting the truth" and creating an environment where subordinates will resist telling the boss what he or she wants to hear rather than expressing honest feelings which may threaten the harmony of the group. "When banal politeness is assigned a higher value than accountability or truthfulness, the result is an Orwellian world where the symbols of speech are manipulated to create false realities."[7]

In today's rapidly changing environment, as banks attempt to conceptualize coherent and unique competitive strategies which will set them apart from their peers, groupthink cannot be allowed to inhibit the responsible consideration of unorthodox viewpoints that may challenge existing paradigms— and fragile egos. In fact, the articulation of such viewpoints should be encouraged.

Technological Discontinuity

In *Innovation*, Richard Foster refers to displacement of old ideas with new conceptual breakthroughs as "technological discontinuities" and provides examples such as the shift from vacuum tubes to semiconductors, the switch from propeller-driven planes to jets, and the displacement of cloth diapers by disposable diapers.[8] Other examples include the shift from the slide rule to the electronic calculator, which seemingly occurred overnight, and the displacement of electronic typewriters by sophisticated word processing systems.

Foster argues persuasively that because the "defender" has so much invested in the existing technological paradigm, the advantage generally goes to the "attacker," who is not constrained by an entrenched mind-set and, therefore, has greater innovative flexibility. A classic example is the Swiss watch industry which lost two thirds of the world market to those Japanese and American manufacturers who recognized and exploited the potential for discontinuity represented by digital technology. Ironically, the Swiss had the new technology first, but could not free themselves from their traditional world view in order that the technology might be exploited effectively. Groupthink prevailed, with predictably disastrous consequences.

The Swiss, however, have since staged an impressive recovery. Learning from their mistake, they have created a dramatic new paradigm of their own. In the past six years about 65 million low-cost Swatch fashion watches have been sold. Thanks largely to the astonishing success of Swatch, sales for Societé Suisse de Microelectronique et Horologerie (SMH), the holding company for the Omega, Tissot, Longines, and Swatch brands, jumped 16.2 percent in 1989 to $1.43 billion. Breaking sharply with tradition, Swatch designs its colorful watches in Milan, imports many of its parts from Asia, benefits from automation, uses novel and innovative marketing concepts, yet adheres religiously to the well-known Swiss penchant for quality.

Increasingly, the major impetus for paradigm shift has been technological advancement. For every entrenched defender there are numerous attackers who, through the application of emerging technologies, seek to upset the competitive equilibrium and establish sustainable competitive advantage.

Even in financial services, deregulation, which many identify erroneously as the principal source of industry disruption, is much more an effect than a cause. As large, innovative, and aggressive bank and nonbank financial institutions began to use new technology to develop new products, conduct highly sophisticated market research, conceptualize and implement direct marketing techniques to expand their geographic coverage, create and manage customer and customer prospect data bases, and expedite and accelerate the movement of funds, the old regulatory structure (the traditional paradigm) came to be increasingly inadequate as a meaningful and viable framework of reality. The geographic barriers had begun to fall long before the regulations were changed, and the elimination of Regulation Q was simply a response to new realities that had already become a fact of life in the financial marketplace.

The banker's world, and the rules governing its existence, were clearly undergoing revolutionary change throughout the early 1980s, and it became equally clear to anyone whose thinking ability had not been subjugated to the outdated logic of an obsolete paradigm that the big winners in the financial services business would be those who proved to be most skillful at determining (a) where the world was going, (b) how they might get there first, (c) what the new rules would be, (d) how those rules might be most effectively exploited and/or rewritten to their advantage, (e) what impediments to successful adaption might be imbedded in the cultural fabric of the organization, and (f) how they might be overcome.

Conversely, the losers would be those who were unwilling or unable to liberate themselves from the old paradigm (based on a stable, regulated, protective, low-risk, and noncompetitive environment), or who were inept in matching their strategic initiatives with the realities of the new paradigm, which we might characterize as volatile, deregulated, nonprotective, high-risk, and extremely competitive.

The 1990s, in other words, would become a time during which unprecedented opportunities would be created. As is always the case during a period of discontinuity or paradigm shift, a select few would accept—even welcome—the inevitability of change, and would override their fear of the unknown to play a role in shaping the future, thereby benefiting enormously. Many others would cling defiantly to the past and would die with it. The majority would be somewhere in between, performing somewhat better or worse than average, its future largely dependent on the tolerance of shareholders and on their relative attractiveness to potential buyers.

THE S&L INDUSTRY: A CASE IN POINT

The S&L industry is a classic example of what happens when reality is dramatically and irreversibly altered.

As shown in Exhibit 1–1, the traditional role of S&Ls was

EXHIBIT 1–1
Traditional Role of the S&L Industry

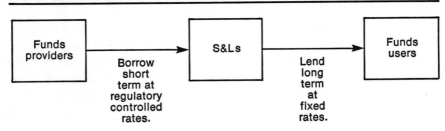

Funds providers — Borrow short term at regulatory controlled rates. → S&Ls — Lend long term at fixed rates. → Funds users

a fairly simple one: making long-term mortgage loans at fixed rates funded with short-term instruments, the price of which was controlled by regulation.

Over time, most S&Ls became reasonably efficient at performing these two functions, neither of which was highly competitive. Because their focus was specialized, operating expenses were low, especially since S&Ls were not burdened with a costly infrastructure to support demand deposits. Also, lower capital ratios were permitted vis-à-vis banks, thereby allowing a lower return on assets to generate an "acceptable" return on equity. This, in turn, encouraged less attention to pricing discipline, expense control, risk management, and the development of product benefit superiority. S&Ls, in other words, had the luxury of competing almost exclusively on the basis of price. Finally, since many S&Ls were mutuals, and unaccountable to shareholders, commonly accepted measures of financial performance were simply not used.

This traditional concept remained viable until the early 1970s, when a series of unprecedented discontinuities emerged: more aggressive competition for both deposits and loans, often from lower-cost providers; greater money market and interest rate volatility; more sophisticated secondary markets; and interest rate deregulation all combined to change the basic nature of the business. Extensive branch networks, established as funding mechanisms to support increased growth in mortgage loans, became extremely expensive as operating costs escalated. These costs, added to higher interest costs as markets became more competitive, resulted in total funding costs that made it difficult to invest in mortgage loans at spreads producing an acceptable return on capital.

Seeking to reduce funding costs, many S&Ls rushed into the checking account business, not realizing the high noninterest costs and unattractive economies of scale would, in many cases, actually increase total funding expense. Finally, of course, the heightened appreciation of the dangers of interest rate risk precluded prudently managed S&Ls from ever again doing what they had always done in the past—borrowing short and lending long.

At this critical juncture, instead of recognizing the pervasive and irrevocable nature of the new realities imposed by the forces of external change and adapting strategically to help create a viable new paradigm compatible with the new environment, Congress and the S&L regulators allowed basic accounting conventions to be modified, thereby effectively covering up the severity of the capital and earnings problems (a classic example of a temporary "solution" to a permanent problem), and allowed their constituents to enter a variety of higher risk businesses for which they had minimal expertise, experience, and/or exploitable competitive advantage. As S&Ls expanded into commercial lending, for example, bankers all over America sat back in disbelief as many of their weakest commercial borrowers were given larger lines of credit, at lower rates, by their new S&L competitors. Meanwhile, funded increasingly by expensive and volatile brokered deposits, S&Ls began investing in large commercial real estate projects, often as equity participants, in markets thousands of miles away, about which they knew virtually nothing. Finally, to hedge interest rate risk, many S&Ls experimented with exotic and complex hedging strategies which very few actually understood. In many cases financial problems were heightened considerably by these poorly advised actions. At the same time, the weakened capital positions of many S&Ls left them highly vulnerable to adversity.

Because the political and regulatory "solutions" were all made within the boundaries of an outdated paradigm, a world which no longer existed, they doomed their constituents to failure. Between 1980 and 1988, over 500 thrifts failed, more than three and a half times as many as in the previous 45 years combined. The costs of the entire S&L fiasco have been estimated conservatively at $1,000 per taxpayer, or in excess of $165 billion.[9] Others believe the total cost will exceed $500 billion. The real cost, however, is much higher. Because bankrupt thrifts, which should have been closed, continued to divert billions of dollars from prudently managed financial institutions, the taxable earnings of the latter were adversely affected, thereby contributing to the federal deficit. For example, between January 1987 and June 1988 the 28 percent of thrifts that were insolvent generated over $50 billion in new deposits to perpetuate their mismanagement at the taxpayer's expense.[10]

Prudently managed banks have been adversely affected in other ways as well. For example, at the very time when major U.S. banks need to be granted additional powers, such as securities underwriting, in order to compete on an equal footing with foreign banks in the global marketplace, Congress is understandably reluctant to open itself to additional criticism by expanding bank powers. The result is a significant competitive disadvantage for American banking institutions vis-à-vis their European and Japanese competitors.

The S&L crisis of 1989, in other words, was not a new crisis at all but rather reflected the inability of Congress and the regulators to create additional ways to hide and/or postpone the inevitable—as they had done so effectively in the past. In addition, many congressional leaders seemed to be far more interested in helping their financial supporters in the industry, thereby perpetuating the problem, than in safeguarding the public interest.[11] In this regard, I believe that the insights of Edward J. Kane, Reese Professor of Banking and Monetary Economics at Ohio State University, are extremely relevant. Kane's research reveals four highly dangerous regulatory propensities which go a long way toward explaining the undeniable contribution of both Congress and the regulators to the entire S&L debacle.[12]

The first, the "Ostrich Reflex," is the propensity to stay deliberately "uninformed about dangerous or threatening situations." This establishes a deniability option "when long-standing problems finally surface as public scandals." The second propensity is to use the power of their official office to force consent and cultivate groupthink. Kane calls this the "Denial or Trust Me Reflex." The third, called the "Coverup or Speak-No-Evil Reflex," is the propensity to conceal past mistakes and to discredit any critical observers, such as the media and academia. The fourth, and final, propensity is in many ways the most insidious. This, called the "Guilt Redistribution or Weasel Reflex," involves the search for convenient scapegoats and the wholesale attempt to rewrite history.

Sadly, the political and legislative solutions as of this writing continue to reflect the same myopia and lack of appreciation for the structural nature of the problem. Furthermore, they perpetuate the myth that individuals are at fault (Gray, Wall, et al.) rather than coming to grips with the inherent conflicts of interest, paradigm paralysis, and regulatory propensities which seem to be built into our political and regulatory structures.

While Congress, the S&L industry, and its regulators all persisted in ignoring reality throughout the 1980s, nontraditional competitors, who were not tied to the old paradigm, found more innovative and cost-effective ways to meet the needs of traditional thrift customers. General Motors Acceptance Company (GMAC), for example, became the second largest mortgage lender in the United States, with over $22 billion of commercial and residential mortgages outstanding, most of which were securitized, thereby minimizing funding and operating costs as well as capital requirements.[13]

Because most S&Ls today do nothing that cannot be done as well, if not better, by those who have adjusted their thinking to current realities, they are simply no longer needed. Only those that have reconceptualized their business and have created perceived added value and competitive advantage by differentiating themselves can justify their ongoing existence. Often that reconceptualization has involved going back to basics; that is, generating deposits cost effectively; staying away from costly activities, such as branch networks, demand deposits, ATMs, credit cards, and so forth; avoiding businesses where they have a significant competitive disadvantage, such as commercial lending; keeping operating costs extremely low; and providing exceptional service and added value in mortgage loan origination.[14]

Industry Viability and Shareholder Value

While it is true that 69 percent of the nation's thrifts earned a profit in 1988 and that 59 percent of the losses experienced by federally insured S&Ls were centered in Texas, thereby leading many to believe the crisis is self-correcting, profitability per se is but one of the issues.[15] As will be discussed in Chapter 3, *the ongoing viability of any for-profit enterprise is the extent to which value is created for its shareholders, largely a function of return on equity (ROE)*. ROE for the S&L industry as a whole was 4.69 percent in 1984, 9.57 percent in 1985, 3.16 percent in 1986, − 10.57 percent in 1987, and − 21.98 percent in 1988. By state, only one in 1988 showed an ROE for its S&Ls in excess of 15 percent—Hawaii at 15.59%. Two others, South Dakota at 12.78 percent and Nevada at 11.23 percent, showed ROEs above 10 percent. S&Ls in 18 states had an average ROE between 5 percent and 10 percent, in 10 states between 0 percent and 4.99 percent, and in 20 states S&Ls as a group experienced a negative ROE.

Because most enlightened commercial bankers have established a minimum ROE standard of 15 percent, with targets closer to 20 percent, the extent of the S&L problem becomes even more obvious, especially when the grossly inadequate capital base of the industry is considered. Regulatory capital as a percent of average assets for S&Ls was 3.8 percent in 1984, 4.4 percent in 1985, 4.6 percent in 1986, 3.9 percent in 1987, and 4.3 percent in 1988. Therefore, even with an equity multiplier of 23.26 in 1988 (100 divided by 4.3), twice that of the typical commercial bank, the industry as a whole still produced a negative ROE of 21.98 percent! When we look at a more meaningful and realistic capital ratio (equity less deferred losses and goodwill), the capital shortfall is even more apparent: 0.4 percent in 1984, 0.9 percent in 1985, 1.4 percent in 1986, 0.8 percent in 1987, and 1.7 percent in 1988.

As regards the industry's future, the questions that must be asked are these: In the 1990s, if S&Ls are required to maintain the same capital requirements as banks (and why shouldn't they?), will they be capable of generating returns on equity that will create value for their shareholders, thereby justifying their existence? Or will they continue to provide a return that is a fraction of what the same investment could earn in risk-free government securities? This is the issue which really determines industry viability. The answer, to this writer at least, is clear: while a few S&Ls will adapt strategically, thereby legitimizing their continued existence, the industry, for all intents, is no longer viable.

As one contemplates the new realities that have been created for America's S&L industry by the forces of change and the failure of the industry, including its regulators and Congress, to accept and understand the structural implications of those changes and to adapt accordingly, one cannot help asking the question: Could not the same fate be in store for America's banks? After all, no one is immune to the inevitability of change, nor is the continued viability of one industry any less threatened by an obsolete paradigm than is that of another. Furthermore, are not banks, as financial intermediaries, subject to many of the same discontinuities that have devastated the S&L industry, and that are adversely affecting both the insurance and brokerage industries?

BANKING AND THE FORCES OF CHANGE

Exhibit 1–2 illustrates the traditional role of banks in the U.S. economy. Banks, like S&Ls, are financial intermediaries, created for the purpose of bridging the gap between funds providers and funds users. As a result of Regulation Q, savings and CD customers were not paid a fair market rate for their deposits. This was especially true for the largest depositors, who in essence subsidized the smaller, less profitable deposit relationships. Meanwhile, large, low-risk borrowers paid rates that exceeded what was reasonable, given risk and cost considerations, thereby subsidizing the smaller, higher-risk borrowers. Given regulatory protection and a lack of viable alternatives for both low-risk borrowers and large depositors, the high cost of

EXHIBIT 1–2
The Traditional Role of Banks

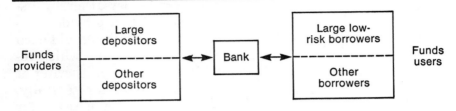

bank intermediation was accepted by both sides. Meanwhile, banks felt no need to evaluate the profitability of individual products or customer groups, no real pressure to control operating expenses, and little need to create added value that would justify the high costs of intermediation. In addition, because bank failures were relatively rare, the financial markets did not impose the same financial performance demands on banks as they did on other industries.

However, as with the S&L industry, discontinuities developed in the 1970s and carried through the 1980s which dramatically altered the nature of the business of banking.

As illustrated in Exhibit 1–3, advanced telecommunications, information and processing technology; direct marketing and market research techniques; a liberalized regulatory environment (deregulation); the monetary policy decision by the Federal Reserve Bank to allow interest rates to fluctuate; innovative new product development on the part of nonbanks; strategic marketing refocus on the part of retailers, brokerage houses, and insurance companies; changing demographic and lifestyle trends; more sophisticated financial markets; the penetration of foreign banks (mostly Japanese) into major urban markets; and better informed consumers and business leaders all contributed to the development and growth of a host of lower cost and/or more focused alternatives.

As banks' large depositors were targeted successfully by aggressive, lower cost nonbanks and as large, low-risk borrowers moved to lower-cost alternatives, such as the commercial paper market, bankers discovered that their unprofitable

EXHIBIT 1–3

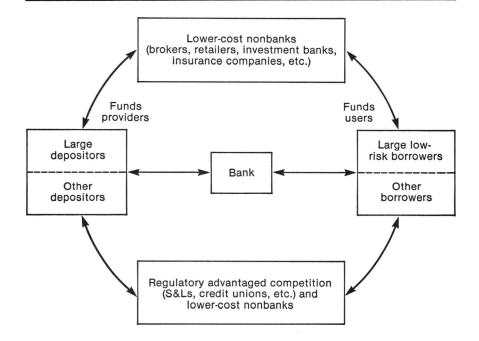

and marginally profitable customers were no longer being subsidized. At the same time, regulatory advantaged competitors, such as S&Ls, credit unions, and nonbanks all mounted successful attacks on commercial banking's deposit base through aggressive marketing oriented primarily around price. Suddenly bankers began to realize what they should have known all along—that as any market becomes more efficient and sophisticated, intermediation costs must be reduced and/or added value benefits created that transcend price. Sadly, this is a lesson that many bankers have still not learned.

Exacerbating the problems listed above, of course, were major discontinuities in other industries, such as energy, agriculture, and commercial real estate development. The impact of these negative trends had a devastating affect on those banks which, unwisely, had large portfolio risk concentrations in those industries.

PORTER'S MODEL OF INDUSTRY ATTRACTIVENESS

Michael E. Porter, in his best selling books *Competitive Advantage* (1985) and *Competitive Strategy* (1988), presents a comprehensive model for evaluating relative industry attractiveness and competitive equilibrium and for developing corporate strategy based on sustainable competitive advantage.[16] The application of Porter's model is particularly relevant to the financial services industry of the 1990s.

Porter argues persuasively that there are five powerful forces which interact to determine the profit potential of any industry: (1) the threat of new entrants, (2) the threat of substitute products, (3) the bargaining power of suppliers, (4) the bargaining power of buyers, and (5) intensity of rivalry.

Clearly, if entry barriers are low, thereby encouraging new entrants, the profit potential in that industry will be relatively weaker. The same can be said for the relative availability and potential acceptance of substitute products. Naturally, to the extent that suppliers and/or customers have a stronger bargaining position and are therefore better able to control the relationship, industry profitability will be adversely affected. Finally, the more intense the rivalry, the more likely it will be for competitors to use price as a weapon, thereby reducing profits for the industry as a whole. Also, as rivalry intensifies, the likelihood of casualties becomes increasingly greater. Furthermore, as failing institutions become more and more desperate, their pricing strategies tend to become increasingly irrational, thereby reducing industry profitability even further, at least in the short- to intermediate term. When Porter's model is applied to the industry we have traditionally called *banking,* there is ample cause for concern.

Whereas banks were once protected from outside competition, a more liberal regulatory climate has encouraged the proliferation of the new entrants we see today. Brokerage firms, insurance companies, retailers, and foreign banks have all made major commitments to meeting the financial service needs of both consumers and businesses. Because many of the strategies being pursued by these nonbanks are directed toward leveraging existing customer relationships and, given the superior resources, lower delivery costs, and specialized marketing expertise enjoyed by many of these new competitors, the threat should not be taken lightly.

Several years ago the author was privileged to speak to the West Virginia Bankers Association. On the same program was the head of product development for Prudential-Bache. His opening remarks were straightforward and alarming: "Bankers, your customers don't need you anymore!" Any audience skepticism was quickly dispelled as he discussed the innovative array of nonbank substitute products available or under development.

The IRA account is an excellent example of how substitute products can erode an industry's dominance. Whereas banks were once viewed as "the" source for IRAs, the multitude of specialized product options created and delivered by mutual funds, securities brokers, and insurance companies has taken billions of dollars from the nation's banks.

In banking, of course, the "suppliers" are the banks' depositors, and we have seen their relative bargaining power increase steadily over the past decade. They are much better informed, are more accessible to direct marketing, have far more choices regarding vendors and products, and, as a result of new technology, can manage their money far more efficiently and effectively.

Fidelity Investments published *The Fidelity Catalogue*, which discusses the features and benefits it provides to its customers.[17] Those listed include:

1. A 24-hour toll-free number—which is repeated on each page of the booklet.
2. Guidelines on developing an investment strategy, prioritizing goals and objectives, and creating an appropriately diversified portfolio.
3. Six different money market funds.
4. Checkwriting on any of the money market funds.
5. A list of over 50 Fidelity Investor Centers nationwide.
6. Automatic transfer from money market funds to savings.

7. Five different government bond funds.
8. Four different taxable bond funds.
9. Six different tax-free bond funds.
10. Nine different state-specific bond funds.
11. Eight different growth and income funds.
12. Ten different growth funds.
13. Six different international and global funds.
14. Thirty-five different industry-sector portfolio funds.
15. Discounts on commissions of up to 76 percent versus full-cost brokers.
16. CDs insured by FDIC or FSLIC.
17. U.S. treasuries.
18. Zero coupon bonds.
19. Corporate bonds.
20. Municipal bonds.
21. Unit Investment Trusts.
22. Fidelity USA Black or Gold VISA and Mastercard.
23. A free bimonthly investment oriented magazine called *Investment Vision*.
24. A variety of variable annuity and variable life insurance products.
25. IRAs, SEP-IRAs, Keogh Plans, and rollover IRAs.
26. A combined monthly statement.
27. Fidelity Automated Service Telephone (FAST), a Touch-Tone phone system providing price and yield quotes, account balances, and transferring capabilities.

Fidelity, which also offers home equity loans, may well represent the bank of the future—a new paradigm.

As we enter the last decade of the 20th century, the chilling reality is that commercial banks do not have a single generic deposit product which cannot be obtained elsewhere, quite often at a lower price.

A bank's borrowers are, of course, analogous to the customers in Porter's model, and their bargaining power has increased as well in recent years. Not only do they have nonbank alternatives, such as captive finance companies and the capital markets, they are also being pursued aggressively by foreign, money center, and/or regional banks. As a result, commercial banks' market share of the total financial assets held by financial institutions declined by almost 20 percent from 1975 through 1986.[18]

For example, McKinsey and Company estimates that as early as 1982 Goldman Sachs was providing as much financing to large corporate borrowers as was Citibank.[19] From 1980 to 1988, the commercial paper market grew from $124 billion to $357 billion. The junk bond market, which totaled $10 billion in 1978, by year end 1989 exceeded $200 billion or 25 percent of all outstanding corporate debt.

Meanwhile, captive finance companies, such as GMAC and Ford Motor Credit, have diverted considerable consumer loan business from the nation's banks. Less obvious, perhaps, is the fact that captive finance companies have also been established by most major manufacturers with an equally negative impact on quality loan demand, in this case on the commercial side.

This brings us to the fifth of Porter's five forces, intensity of rivalry. As deregulation allows banks and their nonbank competitors to enter new markets, a common strategy is to expand market share as rapidly as possible in order to leverage fixed costs. Aggressive pricing and marketing are, of course, the cornerstone of such a strategy, and that, too, has a dampening affect on industry profitability, at least in the short term.

In summary, the application of Porter's model to the banking industry reinforces the concerns expressed earlier. Therefore, as commercial bankers prepare for the 1990s three key questions must be considered:

1. Are the forces of change threatening the traditional economic viability of commercial banks—just as they did for the S&Ls?
2. Can banks adapt strategically to survive, prosper, and create value for their shareholders?
3. If so, how?

The answer to the first two questions is an emphatic Yes! The answer to question number three is what this book is all about.

CHAPTER 2

MASTERING THE PROCESS OF STRATEGIC CHANGE

Nothing is forever in this business. If you think the horse
you're riding now is going to be the same horse you will be
riding in ten years, you're crazy. The name of the game is
being awake enough to change with the times.
—*Richard Flamson III*
Chairman, Security Pacific Corporation,
as quoted in Forbes

Last year's strategy won't win us this year's championship.
—*Pat Riley*
Los Angeles Lakers

CHALLENGING THE TRADITIONAL PARADIGM

Nothing is more stressful and discomforting for an individual or
an organization than breaking away from the familiar patterns
and rules of an existing mind-set, regardless of how outdated,
inappropriate, and destructive they may be. However, Marilyn
Ferguson offers these words of encouragement: "Long after an
old paradigm has lost its value, it commands a kind of hypo-
critical allegiance. But if we have the courage to communicate
our doubts and defection, to expose the incompleteness, the
rickety structure, and the failures of the old paradigm, we can
dismantle it. We don't have to wait for it to collapse on us."[1]

Perhaps the most surprising and compelling example in recent years of the change process in action is Mikhail Gor-

bachev's *perestroika*, and the democratic revolution in Eastern Europe and the Soviet Union which it made possible. In a speech published in *Pravda* in July 1989, Gorbachev declared, "In a changing society, the party should change constantly and do it ahead of society." Recognizing the inevitability of resistance, he stated, "I want to stress again there will be no return to the good old times, although there are some who still experience nostalgia about them." Reinforcing the absolute need for change, Gorbachev warned, "If someone thinks they can manage the acute situation, the new processes by the old methods, they are mistaken."[2] Talk about challenging a deeply entrenched paradigm!

As the traditional paradigms of our industry are made obsolete by the indomitable forces of change, the implications in terms of required actions will often be distressing and unpleasant, challenging many of our most fundamental perceptions of reality. The temptation to ignore or discount the threat will be enormous, and bank leaders will find ample support for a policy of nonaction. This will be the moment of truth for those leaders who earnestly seek to become high performers in the 1990s.

Dismantling the old paradigm and creating an adaptive, innovative, and future-oriented organization will not happen overnight. It will be painful, and, unfortunately, many will be unable or unwilling to change, thereby becoming part of the problem rather than part of the solution. Exposing the failures of the old paradigm and initiating the required changes will be highly threatening, disturbing the comfort zones of most of the organization's human assets. Therefore, a period of resistance, turmoil, suspicion, and outright hostility should be expected. Virtually every area of the organization, including lending, marketing, human resource management, trust, data processing, the branch system, and accounting and finance, must undergo substantial, often radical, change. While leaders in these areas may express enthusiasm and support for the change process, and mean it intellectually, the fact is that in almost every case they will have great difficulty buying in emotionally, and will simply be reluctant to pay the price which meaningful change requires. Not surprisingly, the tough decisions which may be needed will be especially difficult for those managers who pride themselves on their people skills and who fear the loss of the informal authority which they have worked long and hard to earn. Their tendency will be to resist change in ingeniously subtle ways.

For these reasons, firm, unwavering, and consistent pressure from the top will become the key to success. Having worked with dozens of organizations to bring about strategic and cultural change, I know this to be the case. The organization's leader must become a true revolutionary, passionately and fanatically committed to the Strategic Vision—and to those changes upon which that vision depends.

Bank leaders in the 1990s must be far more visible, dynamic, and demanding. They must make sure that everyone understands beyond all doubt that their worth to the company in the future will be a function of their active and positive contribution to the process of strategic and cultural transformation. The fight will not be an easy one, and there will be casualties.

The Importance of Honest and Open Communication

The less the organization's human resources understand regarding the implications of change as it affects their jobs, and the relationship between failure to adapt and their own personal well-being, the more irrational they will consider management to be when strategic adaptation is undertaken. Therefore, well planned, honest, and enlightening communication is essential, especially with those who have the capacity to play a valuable role in the organization's future. Fortunately, the vast majority will fall into this category, and with candor, proper direction, and inspirational leadership will contribute greatly to the organization's renewal. Others, however, will be so intimidated by change, paralyzed with fear, and/or incensed with the unfairness of it all, that they will be compelled to test management's resolve at every turn. Because these individuals may have considerable formal and informal authority which might be consolidated in a last ditch effort to preserve the status quo, the potential threat should not be taken lightly. These individuals must be identified, and every effort should be made to make them active and positive participants in the strategic and cultural revolution. For the most part, these are good people, hard working and loyal. Unfortunately, the reality which commands their loyalty no longer exists. Consequently, those whose intransigence and negativism threaten to infect others must be dealt with decisively; they simply cannot be allowed to sabotage the process. Everyone in the company (with the all too frequent exception of senior management) will know who these people are, and the organization's commitment to the change process will be evaluated largely on the basis of whether or not their resistance is tolerated and accepted. The organization's future may very well depend on the signals sent by management at this critical time.

THE SIX KEY STEPS IN THE STRATEGIC CHANGE PROCESS

For an organization to liberate itself from an obsolete and destructive paradigm (which today's commercial banker *must do* to survive) and to master the process of strategic and cultural change, six key steps are necessary:

1. From top to bottom, a new, dynamic, innovative, change-oriented and paradigm-challenging state of mind must pervade the entire organization; it must begin with the unwavering commitment of the organization's leadership (the only viable alternative is *new* leadership), and must then extend to all levels.
2. Through enlightened leadership, a Strategic Vision must be created which is compatible with the new paradigm and which defines the organization of the future, including the fundamental ways in which that organization will differ from today's reality.
3. Consensus must be reached as to what business(es) the company is actually in, and how its business(es) will be defined.
4. Annual strategic planning must be upgraded to continuous Strategic Management and Planning, a process in-

volving the entire organization in an ongoing effort to adapt strategically to changing realities in pursuit of the Strategic Vision.

5. Strategic focus must be achieved among directors, senior managers, middle managers, and staff regarding key strategic priorities, and full accountability for results, including those relating to one's contribution to the change process itself must be established *at all levels*.

6. The existing corporate culture must be subjected to in-depth analysis in order to identify every cultural characteristic which is a reflection of the old paradigm, thereby representing an impediment to the process of strategic change. A new culture must then be created, building on the strengths of the existing culture, and replacing debilitating cultural characteristics with those that are strategically supportive.

A New State of Mind

Mastery of the change process begins with a state of mind that views reality as dynamic and in constant flux, rather than static and compartmentalized. In this regard, it is a mentality which tends to be more oriental than occidental in its focus. A fundamental tenet of Eastern thought, for example, is that most people spend much of their existence in a state of anxiety and frustration resulting from their unwillingness to accept the impermanent and transitory nature of all things—the inevitability of change as a constant. Because they want so desperately to hold on to things as they are—to preserve the status quo—they perceive most change as undesirable and threatening and have great difficulty coping when the future invades their lives—as it inevitably must.

In most organizations, especially those having enjoyed a long period of relative stability and regulatory "protection," the prevailing mentality tends to be passive and anti-change, and will doom the organization to mediocrity and eventual failure in an era of severe structural discontinuity.

Therefore, during a period of rapid and profound industry

change, a leader's most critical role is to inculcate throughout the organization a state of mind which accepts the inevitability of change, welcomes and embraces change as the source of all strategic opportunity, refuses to be constrained by the realities of the past (including the successes), challenges constructively all preconceptions and established ways of doing things, and becomes focused positively on a well conceived and articulated Strategic Vision of the future.

The effective and successful leader will be a powerful and relentless catalyst for change who challenges everything that is "known," inspires everyone else to do the same, and refuses to allow the nonparticipants to hold the organization back. According to Ted Leavitt: "The effectively functioning organization makes change its open ally. It keeps the barriers low. Its leaders know that survival depends on the regular euthanasia of the organization's regularities."[3]

Kanter refers to such organizations as integrative as opposed to segmentalist. "To see problems integratively is to see them as wholes, related to larger wholes, and thus challenging established practices—rather than walling off a piece of experience and preventing it from being touched or affected by any new experiences."[4] Most banks still tend to be segmentalist, highly compartmentalized, and held captive by "established practices." Therefore, they are finding the transition to be a difficult one. In my view, the single greatest problem in such cases is the lack of a daring and courageous leader to direct the assault against ignorance, complacency, resistance, mediocre performance, and obsolete concepts of how the world works. *The strategic and cultural revolution begins, and lives or dies, with the organization's leadership.* Like it or not, those leaders who cannot adapt to the demands of the new environment must, of necessity, be replaced by those who can.

Whereas comfort in the regulated past came from maintaining control and adhering rigidly to proven and well-defined patterns of behavior, comfort in the future will result from being in tune with the forces of change, foreseeing their implications, and having the vision, commitment, focus, and confidence to adapt rapidly and strategically to ever changing sets of circumstances. Whereas comfort once came from having guidelines provided by the regulators, comfort in the future will come from using innovative and nontraditional thinking to create totally new solutions to a never ending onslaught of unfamiliar challenges. Whereas the heroes of the past were those who conformed to tradition, the heroes of the future will be those who can dream, inspire others to share the dream, and then make that dream a reality.

Lateral or Right-Handed Thinking

Edward De Bono refers to the process of generating creative and nontraditional solutions as lateral as opposed to vertical thinking. "You cannot dig a hole in a different place by digging the same hole deeper. Vertical thinking digs the same hole deeper; lateral thinking is concerned with digging a hole in another place. Lateral thinking seeks to get away from the patterns that are leading one in a definite direction and to move sideways by re-forming the patterns."[5]

Many well-known writers and scientists in recent years have come to regard lateral or creative thinking as a product of the brain's right hemisphere.[6] Whereas the left hemisphere processes information deductively and sequentially, and seems to move methodically from Step A to Step B in an attempt to organize information into "logical" solutions and conclusions, the right hemisphere is irreverent and intuitive, visualizes the big picture, and may leap inexplicably from Step A to Step Z, in the process reaching insightful conclusions and solutions which cannot be explained in purely "rational" and "logical" terms. It is the hemisphere of creativity and invention, and is increasingly being recognized and appreciated as the key to developing the innovative new strategies needed to deal with new constructs of reality, regardless of the endeavor. According to Pascale and Athos in *The Art of Japanese Management:* "Most of the important executive skills are intuitive—that is, they are not consciously cognitive."[7] This observation is consistent with a McGill University study on successful managers, who tended to be more intuitive and less constrained by logic and tradition in their decision making.[8]

Kenichi Ohmae, in *The Mind of the Strategist*, agrees: "In

what I call the mind of the strategist, insight and a consequent drive for achievement, often amounting to a sense of mission, fuel a thought process which is basically creative and intuitive rather than rational."[9]

It is widely acknowledged that banking traditionally has been an industry dominated by left-hemisphere thinking, which was perfectly appropriate given the realities of the old paradigm. Because there was little substantive change from year to year, it made perfect sense to emulate successful strategies from past experience, and to create a control-oriented culture where challenging the rules was frowned on and people were rewarded for loyalty rather than performance.

Because creativity, innovation, and iconoclastic thinking were of little value, and in many cases were downright dangerous, they were not encouraged or rewarded. Highly creative people who become bankers, unless in an organization such as Citicorp or Banc One, generally moved on rather quickly to less constraining environments. Unfortunately, many bank cultures today continue to treat truly creative individuals with suspicion and distrust. Such people, after all, tend to have a bad habit of asking the most impertinent questions, such as "Why?" Their lack of devotion to "the way we've always done it around here" and their audacity in believing there might actually be different and better ways to get things done, is perceived as "rocking the boat," which tends to make them unpopular and disliked. Unless they have a powerful sponsor, and/or the culture is undergoing modification from the top via leadership commitment to the new state of mind described earlier, it takes an unusually courageous and persistent personality to challenge the status quo and then survive the almost inevitable coalition of opposition forces. Donald MacKinnon describes such courage as: "personal courage, courage of the mind and spirit, psychological or spiritual courage that is the radix of a creative person: the courage to question what is generally accepted; the courage to be destructive in order that something better can be constructed; the courage to think thoughts unlike anyone else's; the courage to be open to experience from within and from without; the courage to follow one's intuition rather than logic;

the courage to imagine the impossible and try to achieve it; the courage to stand aside from the collectivity and in conflict with it if necessary; the courage to become and to be oneself."[10] Such is the courage of the true revolutionary; the courage which will be required of bank leadership to survive and prosper in the 1990s.

Enlightened leaders, therefore, must not only be courageous and unwavering in challenging everything that may be strategically inappropriate in view of the new paradigm, and inconsistent with the strategic focus and vision of the company, but must also empower and motivate others to do the same. Creative and irreverent people who are strategically focused are essential to the transition, and they cannot survive without sponsorship. David Ogilvy, one of advertising's most brilliant and successful innovators, advises: "Make sure you have a vice president in charge of revolution, to engender ferment among your more conventional colleagues."[11]

Having worked with banks of all sizes throughout the United States in recent years, I am convinced that there is no subtle or delicate way to undertake the transition from a segmentalist culture, characterized by vertical, left-hemisphere thinking, to an integrative culture, energized by creative and enlightened leadership at all levels. To some extent, the comfort level of everyone in the organization must be disturbed. Because most people, especially in an industry dominated so long by regulation, become immobilized mentally by routine and habit, they fight subconsciously as well as consciously to preserve the status quo at all costs. *Therefore, the new state of mind must be directed toward putting every function, department, process, policy, value, strategy, and tactic on trial for its very life, and only a visionary and committed leader can make that happen.*

CEO's Perspective

Michael F. Ryan is the President of Irwin Union Bank in Columbus, Indiana.

Question:

Mike, in 1988 you recognized that radical changes were required to adapt Irwin Union to the competitive new banking world—and that you would have to lead the process. As you initiated that process, what was the message you delivered to your senior management team—and how have you reconceptualized your leadership role?

Answer:

A survey of our employee group, reinforced by some difficult discussions among senior management, forced me to recognize the need for change in two areas:

1. *In the way we managed:* we needed to become single-mindedly committed to high performance, and I needed to hold each manager accountable for upholding his or her contribution to high performance.
2. *In the attitudes of all our people:* no one felt especially committed to getting new business. In spite of an increasingly competitive environment, we had become willing to accept whatever share of new business naturally came our way.

We would need to accomplish these changes in the face of two handicaps: we had never exhibited and had no tradition of high performance. And, we had begun several short-lived efforts previously and would have to overcome a "here we go again" syndrome.

I felt the necessary changes were so fundamental and the handicap so severe that leadership could not be delegated to anyone else.

The message to our management and staff was fairly simple:

- Forget about the past; it doesn't matter anymore.
- It's no longer good enough to just "do as well as we can"; from now on, we must earn at least 15 percent ROE every year, no foolin'. All support systems—budget, bonuses, profit sharing—will be tied to this target.
- It's everyone's job to get new business, either through direct sales or referrals. Making a sale or referral is no more than recognizing the existence of a financial need and moving to satisfy that need. What could be more honorable?

- It is important for everyone to buy into this new culture. Those who can't or won't will begin to stand out and be increasingly uncomfortable. And that's OK! Those who can't or won't recognize needs and can't or won't work to satisfy them probably shouldn't be in the financial services business.
- Finally, to those of you who think this effort will eventually go away and that we can't sustain it—Just watch us!

I believe this message has now been heard by all and internalized by most. It has changed my role from operating manager into sales manager and spiritual leader. I like it!

Enlightened Leadership and the Strategic Vision

Once the organization's leadership has accepted the inevitability of change as a constant, and has committed itself to sponsoring throughout the organization a state of mind which refuses to be held captive by obsolete perceptions of reality, the process of conceptualizing a Strategic Vision can begin.

Only when the organization has embraced, earnestly and passionately, a state of mind which allows it to challenge and overcome successfully the constraining and destructive thought patterns of the past, can the organization's resources and energies be focused effectively toward the needs of the future. Specific and fundamental ways in which the organization of tomorrow will differ from today's organization can then be conceptualized and articulated.

The conceptualization of the Strategic Vision will generally take place in one or more board and senior management retreats designed to focus on key questions, such as the following:

- What external forces are at work which will change the conditions under which the industry operates, the firm competes, and competitive advantages and shareholder value are created?
- How will the future be different as a result of these changes? What specific offensive and defensive oppor-

tunities will be created, and what specific competitive advantages will most differentiate winners from losers? What impediments and obstacles are inherent in today's reality, given the implications of change?

- In light of the above, what general and specific changes must take place internally for the organization to survive and prosper? How must the organization be different than it is today to achieve and sustain high performance in the world of the future? What levels of profitability, shareholder value, and employee and customer satisfaction will be necessary?

Initially, the Strategic Vision will be fairly general with respect to many of these issues. Then, as the process of strategic and cultural change continues, lines of business become more clearly defined, and the process of Strategic Management and Planning produces more precise objectives and strategies, the Strategic Vision will become more sharply focused. Ultimately, it will articulate characteristics such as size, financial performance, organization structure, geographic coverage, internal and external growth, lines of business, mission, corporate culture and core values, leadership styles and priorities, target market segments, sources of competitive advantage, uses of technology, staffing, facilities design, and so forth.

High performance financial institutions in the 1990s will be significantly different than their contemporary counterparts in virtually all of these areas and *high performance leaders will be those who are most skillful at visualizing the required changes and leading and managing the strategic and cultural revolution needed to bring these changes about.*

Defining What Business(es) the Organization Is In

In *Megatrends*, John Naisbitt warns, "Unless banks reconceptualize what business they are in, they will be out of business."[12] Drucker, of course, has long argued that the first responsibility of top management is to define clearly what business(es) the

EXHIBIT 2–1
How Businesses Work

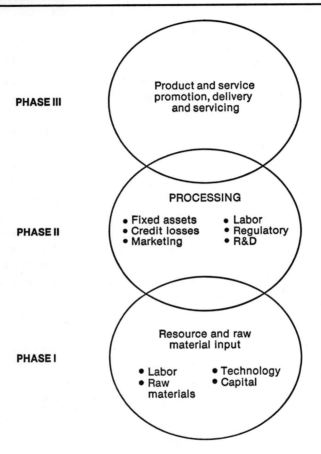

PHASE III

Product and service promotion, delivery and servicing

PHASE II

PROCESSING
- Fixed assets
- Credit losses
- Marketing
- Labor
- Regulatory
- R&D

PHASE I

Resource and raw material input
- Labor
- Raw materials
- Technology
- Capital

company is actually in.[13] And Ted Leavitt, in his essay "Marketing Myopia," presents several compelling examples of how defining one's business incorrectly, based on an invalid paradigm, can lead to failure.[14]

What, then, in the broad sense, is the business of banking? Within that framework, how might an individual bank go about defining its business in terms which set it apart from its competitors, and how will the forces of change influence that definition? And, once a bank has defined to its satisfaction the business(es) it is actually in, what implications does that definition have on the development of strategic priorities such as capital allocations; merger, acquisition, and/or diversification strategies; organization structure; human resource management and development policies; and marketing strategy? In other words, how must the bank define its business(es) in order to most effectively realize its Strategic Vision? The first step in defining the business is to understand how businesses actually work.

As can be seen in Exhibit 2–1, most businesses perform three basic functions. First, certain resource inputs (capital, ideas, labor, technology, raw materials, etc.) are absorbed. This stage involves costs, not revenues, and therefore is not the actual business which the company operates. Second, these resources are processed, value is added, and products and/or services are created which can be marketed. This stage, too, involves costs, and clearly fails to define the company's business. Third, the firm markets and delivers products and services, and manages customer relationships, thereby generating revenues that, hopefully, will allow the creation of shareholder value. Several distinct "businesses" may exist at this level within the same corporate entity. It is this stage, the generation of earnings, which serves to define the business(es) for a given industry and/or firm. Many executives err in attempting to define their business(es) on the basis of how costs—rather than earnings—are generated. Many bankers, for example, think they are in the deposit business. A firm's definition of its business(es) will, quite naturally, be more specific and precise than that of the industry as a whole.

Competitive advantage in the form of lower costs and/or added benefits can be created, enhanced, and/or sustained at each of the three phases. However, there are two sets of dynamics that influence any firm's ability to create competitive advantage, generate profits, and provide value to shareholders, customers, and employees.

The first set, external dynamics, are uncontrollable and include (a) technology and technological discontinuity, (b) competition and competitive disequilibrium, (c) macroeconomics, (*d*) geopolitics, (*e*) sociodemographics, and (*f*) the legal and regulatory environment. Because changes in these dynamics are constantly affecting the ability of an industry, and/or an individual firm within an industry, to create, enhance, and/or sustain competitive advantage in each of the three phases, *it is how well any firm, in any industry, performs these three functions that determines whether or not it will succeed, and remain successful.*

This explains, in fact, the fallacy of attempting to identify and emulate certain characteristics of "excellent" companies. There is only one true characteristic of the consistently excellent firm and that is strategically adaptive leadership in the face of relentless external change.

The second set of dynamics are fully controllable by the individual firm and represent the tools with which enlightened leaders will transform their institutions to conform to new realities. They include, (*a*) Strategic Vision and mastery of the change process (the focus of this chapter), (*b*) mastery of the key financial dynamics of profitability and shareholder value creation (Chapter 3), (*c*) leadership and corporate culture (Chapter 4) and (*d*) marketing and sales strategy (Chapter 5).

Strategic planning, therefore, which is covered in Chapter 6, might well be defined as "the process by which the firm's internal dynamics, which are controllable, are managed to best exploit changes in the firm's external dynamics, which are not, in order to create, enhance, and/or sustain competitive advantage leading to increased value for shareholders, customers, and employees."

The Business of Banking

Exhibit 2–2 presents the model from Exhibit 2–1 as it relates to the business of banking.

In the left-hand margin are the three stages from Exhibit 2–1; in the circles are the six income and expense components of return on assets (detailed in Chapter 3); and in the right-hand margin the income statement components are broken down into the two basic functions of banking: the creation and management of earning assets and fee-based services and funding. Based on this basic and general conceptualization of what

EXHIBIT 2–2
The Business of Banking

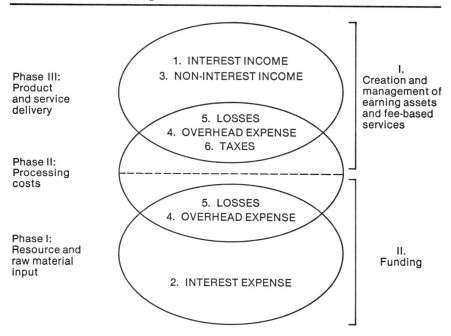

Phase III:
Product
and service
delivery

Phase II:
Processing
costs

Phase I:
Resource and
raw material
input

1. INTEREST INCOME
3. NON-INTEREST INCOME

5. LOSSES
4. OVERHEAD EXPENSE
6. TAXES

5. LOSSES
4. OVERHEAD EXPENSE

2. INTEREST EXPENSE

I.
Creation and
management of
earning assets
and fee-based
services

II.
Funding

the business of banking is really all about, the success of any bank will be determined by how well each of these two functions is performed. Poor financial performance can invariably be traced to weaknesses in one or both of these functions.

Given the above, one might well argue that the business of banking is "enhancing shareholder value through the creation and management of earning assets and fee-based services," since this is where earnings and cash flows are generated. Implicit in this definition is the notion that the customer relationships underlying both earning assets and fee-based services are being properly managed as well, and that value is being delivered to both groups.

An individual bank, then, will define its business(es) based on issues such as:

a. What it intends to do for its shareholders, and any other stakeholder groups to whom it considers itself accountable.
b. How external change is affecting the bank's ability to create, enhance, and/or sustain competitive advantage.
c. How capital will be allocated.
d. The specific markets and customer groups it will serve, and its position (existing and desired) within those markets and customer groups.
e. The specific types of earning assets it plans to create and/or acquire.
f. The specific fee-based services it intends to deliver.
g. The most appropriate sources of funding and how the funding process will be managed.
h. The specific customer needs it proposes to satisfy (tangible as well as intangible), for earning assets, fees, and funding customer groups.
i. The requisite core values on which its corporate culture will be built, and on which performance will be evaluated.
j. How it intends to set itself apart from its competitors in order to justify its existence and create sustainable competitive advantage.
k. How success will be measured.

It is the articulation of the firm's responses to issues such as these that enables its leadership to define the organization's business, mission, and/or purpose, justify its ongoing existance, and clarify and sharpen its Strategic Vision.

Decisions regarding these issues are analogous to the decisions that Ford Motor Company or IBM must make regarding the products or services they will create and deliver, the nature and sources of resource inputs, how best to process those inputs, the market segments to be targeted, how value will be created and delivered to customers, employees, and shareholders, and so forth.

Funding

Naturally, banks must fund the earning assets they create. Money is, after all, the basic raw material of banking. Funds acquisition, however, which generally is achieved through deposit generation, represents costs, not earnings. Banks are no more in the deposit business than General Motors is in the steel business, despite the fact that the acquisition and management of these raw materials is critically important.

Funding costs include interest expense, acquisition costs, and ongoing servicing costs. Many banks are marginally profitable not because their interest funding costs are too high but because their noninterest funding costs are excessive. Thus, interest expense alone is not a reliable indicator of funding effectiveness. Because many bankers believe erroneously that they are in the deposit business, and/or fail to properly measure and manage *total* funding costs from each source, they often make serious miscalculations regarding resource allocations, the relative attractiveness of alternative funding sources, and the profitability of alternative earning assets products.

Finally, a word about deposit-related noninterest income. Generally speaking, such income serves to recover a portion, and a small one at that, of total noninterest funding costs. Therefore, it is more realistically viewed, in most cases, as an offset to funding costs, rather than as income per se.

Funds Acquisition: Who's Buying and Who's Selling?

Another observation which may challenge prevailing perceptions is that funds acquisition actually involves "buying money" rather than "selling" CDs or checking accounts. This is an important distinction in terms of "sales" and marketing strategy, including product development, pricing, advertising, training, delivery, and so forth. After all, as Leavitt and others have pointed out so well, people do not buy products, they buy the expectation of benefits. The bank's sales and marketing efforts, therefore, must center around those benefits which can be added to a generic product, such as a checking account, thereby attracting sellers of funds away from alternative offers.

Given the dramatic increase in competitors for a finite supply of funds sources, it is the bidder/buyer making the most attractive offer who will prevail. *In other words, what the bank is actually selling is the superiority of its offers to buy money vis-à-vis those of its competitors.* This is a critically important distinction, the key to a bank's funding strategy, and will be discussed in more detail in Chapter 5.

While many sellers of funds will equate value received almost totally with price and will sell to the highest bidder, most will consider nonprice-related benefits in assessing the relative value of alternative offers. Issues such as location, friendliness of staff, accuracy, stability, safety, attractiveness of facilities, professionalism, and so forth, are all nonprice-related benefits that can produce value. Therefore, innovation in responding to customer needs with superior nonprice-related benefits is a vital key to success in generating viable funding sources. At the same time, those banks having lower noninterest funding costs can afford to pay a higher interest rate and still have a lower total funding cost. Therefore, it is extremely important to monitor and manage all funding costs.

Since different customer segments have different needs and value perceptions, banks, when structuring their offerings, will be more successful when they have added those benefits that best represent value to the specific segment(s) being targeted and that they have a competitive advantage in delivering. Therefore, market research (using techniques such as focus groups), market segmentation, competitor analysis, innovative "product" development that targets differentiated offers to specific segments based on the bank's competitive advantages, as well as benefits-oriented promotion strategies, are all critical success factors, as is the ability to measure and manage all funding costs.

In summary, any firm, to be successful, must have a clear conception of what business(es) it is actually in. When companies define their business(es) incorrectly, resources are poorly allocated, market opportunities are lost, human assets are not focused strategically, the wrong things are measured and rewarded, and the firm's very existence is threatened.

As external structural change affects the market and profitability dynamics of the financial services industry, and alters a bank's ability to create, enhance and/or sustain competitive advantage at each of the three phases of the business, many innovative and courageous bankers are challenging the traditional paradigm and are making an effort to reconceptualize what business(es) they are in. It is the thesis of this book that the basic business of banking is, quite simply, *building shareholder value through the creation and management of earning assets and fee-based services* (including their underlying customer relationships). A secondary function is funding, or the purchase of money to support the bank's earning asset portfolios. It is how well the individual bank defines what business(es) it is actually in, allocates resources, and performs these two functions, given the implications of external change, that determines its success.

As bankers attempt to reconceptualize and define their business(es) in light of new realities that affect their ability to create, enhance and/or sustain competitive advantage, thereby realizing their Strategic Visions, the following five critically important strategic initiatives (critical success factors) are essential, each of which must challenge and ultimately displace existing paradigms. Because the strategic solutions for most banks in each of these five areas will be outside the realm of traditional logic and experience, an outside catalyst may be required to help initiate and sustain the process.

Five Key Strategic Initiatives in Reconceptualizing the Business

A. *Banks must develop new fee-based lines of business, thereby reducing their vulnerability to disintermediation.* A bank's ability to generate earnings and create shareholder value strictly as an intermediary is being systematically eroded. That, plus the implications of risk-adjusted capital guidelines, forces banks to discover new sources of fee-based income. Many bankers view their business as an "8 to 5," five day per week, deposit gathering and lending activity, and because this paradigm will exclude consideration of anything that does not conform, it must be discarded—as must all other option-limiting mind-sets which constrain the ability of the organization's leadership to be creative strategically in identifying, prioritizing, and exploiting fee-income opportunities. (Options will be discussed in Chapter 5.)

B. *Banks must reconceptualize their relationship with funds users and must create, promote, sell, and deliver added value that transcends price.* Banks must reconceptualize their relationship with funds users, which involves issues such as the specific types of earning assets they elect to generate, hold, and sell; how earning assets will be acquired, serviced, and funded; how risk will be quantified, mitigated, and controlled; the nature of the relationship with earning-assets customers; how value will be added to the generic product; pricing; and how capital will be allocated and managed.

To provide but one example, in recent years equipment leasing has become a $120 billion per year industry as more and more corporations have elected to lease rather than own. Yet only a small percentage of banks have taken advantage of this tremendous strategic opportunity. Why? Because many lenders perceive their business to be lending—rather than financing. They are product-driven (the lending paradigm) rather than driven to understand the customer's business and satisfy his/her needs in ways that will create value for both parties (the financing paradigm). Because leasing does not fit their established mind-set, many bankers continue to allow highly profitable business(es) to go to someone else, and, more importantly, allow competitors to weaken their franchise. As more and more corporations seek financing solutions other than commercial loans, those bankers who continue to define their business(es) as lending rather than financing will find fewer and fewer quality earning assets available.

C. *Banks must reconceptualize the entire concept of funding, including their relationship with funds providers, and must create, promote, sell, and deliver added value that transcends price.* Banks must reconceptualize not only their relationship with funds providers, but the entire issue of funding as well. Many bankers, continuing to believe that they are in the deposit business, have been reasonably creative in satisfying the deposit customer and in meeting their production goals within the confines of that flawed paradigm. The result, in many cases, is a total funding cost (interest expense plus acquisition costs plus ongoing servicing costs) that makes the profitable deployment of those funds virtually impossible.

Having relied for many years on the regulators and data processors to tell them what they could and could not do with respect to deposit products, services, and pricing, many bankers are finding themselves ill-prepared to determine what the customer wants, what the competition is offering, and how to be brilliantly creative in formulating a superior offer at a cost that won't break the bank. Yet that is precisely what funding strategy is all about. Just as Ford has been forced to reduce its relative raw materials and processing costs in order to survive and compete, so must banks generate and process funding sources more cost effectively.

Here again, bankers must advance from vertical to lateral thinking in order to arrive at strategic solutions that are compatible with the realities of the 1990s, one of which may be the purchase of funds from newly created entities specializing in cost-effective deposit gathering.

D. *Banks must reduce substantially the costs associated with performing the intermediary function.* Unconstrained by "banking paradigms," nonbank competitors have anticipated the emerging opportunities created by change and have been innovative in developing new ways to meet the needs of both users and providers of funds more cost effectively. While banks, to survive, must reconceptualize their relationship with both of those groups, they must also find ways to meet the needs of these groups at a lower per-unit cost. Again, the solutions often lie outside traditional thinking, and will not result from the vertical, left-hemisphere-oriented approach which has dominated the industry in the past.

E. *The traditional "pooled capital" concept must give way to capital allocation and management based on return on equity and shareholder value considerations.* (This will be discussed in Chapter 3.)

These five strategic initiatives, each of which is based on breaking with existing views of how the world works, are essential for survival, and must be the cornerstone of the process by which a bank's Strategic Vision is conceptualized and achieved. They are, as such, critical success factors for the 1990s.

Chapters 3 through 6 will present a framework to facilitate the process by which these initiatives will be undertaken.

Upgrading from Strategic Planning to Strategic Management and Planning

The methodology by which the Strategic Vision is created and realized is generally associated with strategic planning, which addresses the questions· "Where are we now?"; "Where are we going?"; and "How will we get there?"

Unfortunately, however, most strategic planning, as currently practiced, seems to be based on vertical rather than lateral thinking, and is held captive by the parameters and constraints of the old paradigm. All too often, strategic planning is little more than an annual budget-related exercise; an end rather than the means to an end. The entire organization is disrupted for a few weeks in the fall and then everyone returns gratefully to what they were doing all along, secure in the knowledge that they have a full year to recuperate. Because it is perceived as essentially an analytical, left-hemisphere activity, it defines a future that is merely a logical extension of the past, devoid of conceptual or strategic creativity. Yet, in referring to successful strategic planning in Japan, Ohmae writes, "Insight is the key to this process. Because it is creative, partly intuitive, and often disruptive of the status quo, the resulting plans might not even hold water from the analyst's point of view. It is the creative element in these plans and the drive and will of the mind that conceived them that give those strategies their extraordinary competitive impact."[15]

The process by which the Strategic Vision is realized, therefore, must be viewed not as an annual event, but as an ongoing process that makes ample use of sound analytical practice, yet derives its real value from creative and original thinking that challenges the rules. Roger Von Oech writes, "Think about it: almost every advance in art, science, technology, business, marketing, cooking, medicine, agriculture, and design has occurred when someone challenged the rules and tried another approach."[16] Banking is no exception. To survive and prosper in the 1990s, bankers at every level of the organization must be motivated somehow to challenge the rules inherent in the traditional paradigm, explore a wide range of strategic alternatives, tap the initiative and creative energies of the entire organization, and conceptualize a vision which is much more than a logical extension of today's reality. That vision must not be the result of "digging the same hole deeper," but rather the product of digging in another place altogether.

Given the accelerated pace of change, new offensive and defensive opportunities can occur at any time, and may often be of limited duration. The organization must constantly monitor its external dynamics, recognize emerging opportunities in a timely manner, and respond in ways which are most appropriate strategically, that is, which enable the creation, enhancement and/or sustaining of competitive advantage. Because different levels of the organization are exposed to different environmental factors, the entire organization must be refocused in order to become actively involved in the process.

Strategic Management and Planning, therefore, involves the creation, implementation, and ongoing management of the process by which the Strategic Vision is to be realized; how the bank will get from "here" to "there" as well as the discipline needed to ensure that strategic and cultural change actually take place. Strategic Management and Planning consists of integrated strategy development *and implementation* in three key areas: Financial Performance Optimization, Leadership and Corporate Culture, and Market Positioning. Section II will deal with each of these key issues.

During the first year after the system of Strategic Management and Planning is implemented, the senior management planning team should meet monthly to review all strategic action plans (see box) and to make whatever adjustments are needed.

At the same time, all departments, branches, and other work groups must become actively involved in recognizing and reporting to the appropriate level of authority all relevant opportunities, problems, and needs which affect the organization's

---

Strategic Action Plans Will

1. Define the opportunity, problem, or need, including an analysis of how addressing it will enable the company to better achieve its financial goals, fulfill its mission, create, enhance and/or sustain competitive advantage, and realize its Strategic Vision;
2. Identify the key issues associated with this opportunity, problem, or need, including resource requirements;
3. Identify alternative approaches to exploit the opportunity, solve the problem, or meet the need;
4. Select and defend the recommended course of action;
5. Identify the primary impediments to successful implementation and detail the method(s) by which they will be overcome;
6. Determine who will be accountable and how success will be measured;
7. Outline the first step and the implementation date, as well as subsequent steps and the full implementation timetable.

---

ability to realize the Strategic Vision. Strategic action plans can then be developed, whenever appropriate, to deal with those issues and may, in fact, be initiated at any level of the organization. In most cases the senior planning team members will assume ultimate accountability for organizational strategic action plans (those which apply to the entire organization), even those which may be delegated to others. A similar process, however, must occur at the divisional, departmental, and/or strategic business unit levels.

Strategic action plans at each level should be numbered, and their ongoing management should become the primary focus of the monthly or quarterly meetings of that particular work group.

To encourage and support the active participation of all levels of the organization, positive reinforcement is essential, including liberal use of "the three Rs" of motivation: recognition, rituals, and rewards. In addition, it is important, especially the first year, that senior managers attend staff meetings at all levels to make sure the process is working: that everyone is focused strategically, actively involved in seeking opportunities for improvement, and generating innovative solutions which support organizational priorities.

Strategic Management and Planning, when implemented properly, becomes a continuous and proactive process of strategic readjustment and adaptation which focuses the entire organization on the Strategic Vision, separates planning from budgeting, rewards innovative strategic thinking, and replaces a disruptive, unpopular, and academically oriented annual burden with a process that is perceived as relevant to the priorities of every employee and to which each employee can contribute in a meaningful and rewarding manner.

Strategic Focus

Having worked with literally hundreds of banks and bank holding companies over the past decade, only occasionally have I found an organization with a strong and positive sense of strategic focus. Generally, this weakness results from fragmented leadership, the lack of a carefully conceptualized and clearly articulated Strategic Vision and/or the lack of a Strategic Management and Planning system to provide the discipline and accountability needed to maintain focus once it is achieved. In the typical bank, for example, regardless of size, there are only one or two people who are truly focused on creating shareholder value; everyone else operates from a private agenda, often with conflicting priorities and values. My experience convinces me that the primary reason many banks perform poorly, even when a substantial commitment is made to strategic planning, is because the organization and its management are not strategically focused on a Strategic Vision driven by shareholder value creation. They are often too concerned with doing things right—and not concerned enough with doing the right things— those that are needed to ensure survival and superior performance in a changing and increasingly competitive environment.

When strategic focus is weak or nonexistent, resources are rarely allocated appropriately, mixed messages proliferate, people at all levels confuse objectives with strategies, communication and teamwork are poor, individuals and functional areas

CEO's Perspective

D. Linn Wiley was formerly President and CEO of American National Bank, Bakersfield, California. As a result of that bank's acquisition by Wells Fargo Bank, Wiley is now Executive Vice President of that institution.

Question:

Linn, you have created one of the most strategically focused banks I have ever seen. What has your role been as the bank's leader to make that happen—and, in your view, how important has that focus been in the tremendous success the bank is enjoying?

Answer:

I felt that my primary responsiblity was to develop a plan and a strategic focus when I first joined American National Bank. This, in my opinion, was fundamental in addressing the changes required within the organization, as well as the dramatic changes occurring within the industry. It was simply the key to survival, and then to success in achieving high performance standards.

My belief is that management and leadership begin with planning. This does not mean that planning is the most important function of management, because planning is useless if the plan is not executed effectively. However, planning is the first step toward successful management and effective leadership.

Management success depends heavily on having a clear picture or *vision* of the results a leader or manager expects to achieve. Planning is at the heart of this process, because effective planning provides a systematic and orderly means for determining what management expects to achieve in every key aspect of the business. The objectives, which are established during the course of this planning process, integrate the plans of the entire organization. These objectives also determine the shape and character of the organization, and, when developed, communicated, and reinforced properly, serve as a source of motivation for the people in the organization.

A strategic focus is developed through the planning process as management carefully considers what has to be done to achieve its objectives, organizes the activities of the organization to ensure that they are constantly contributing to the desired results, maximizes the utilization of resources, provides direction and guidance to all personnel, and establishes control points which provide tangible measures for achievement.

My role, as the organization's President and CEO, was to first be a catalyst for developing a strong planning environment as part of our corporate culture and to develop a strategic focus through the planning process. Second, it was my responsibility to ensure that the plan was executed effectively. This involved frequent reference to our strategic focus; our three core values of *institutional strength, marketing focus*, and *cost-effective operation*. Third, it is my ongoing responsibility to ensure that this commitment to planning and to our strategic focus continues. There is always a tendency to relax and even become complacent when the objective has been achieved and success has become a reality. A true leader can never rest or relax; he or she must lead the way to even greater accomplishment.

The commitment to planning and the strategic focus, which was developed through our planning process, is the basis for our results and success today. These management elements have provided the framework for concentrating exclusively on our objectives and the means for achieving them, while avoiding the distractions that inevitably creep in without this discipline. However, the ultimate success is the effective execution of the plan and the strategic focus by people. Our bank has been blessed with an exceptional management and staff team who have proven themselves to be dedicated to the cause and equal to the task.

---

work at cross-purposes, and preserving the status quo becomes the priority of preference, simply because it is the safest. Without strategic focus, officers and employees don't realize for whom they are ultimately working (the shareholder), or what their jobs really are (contributing to the creation of shareholder value). Because they are devoting inordinate amounts of time to activities which fail to enhance shareholder value directly or indirectly, they are shortchanging not only the organization but themselves. I am convinced that this is a major shortcoming in most banks today, regardless of size, and one of the greatest impediments to superior performance in the coming decade.

Conversely, the strategically focused organization becomes energized by the tremendous power that is unleashed when a group of individuals become committed to the realization of a commonly shared vision—and to each other. Kenneth Labich, in a *Fortune* cover story, writes: "Don't underestimate the power of a vision. McDonald's founder, Ray Kroc, pictured his empire long before it existed, and he saw how to get there."[17] In other words, Kroc conceptualized a vision and then maintained absolute focus on the critical success factors underlying that vision. The vision, without company-wide focus, would have been meaningless.

Once an organization's leadership has truly accepted the inevitability of change, has expanded its consciousness (and that of the organization as a whole) to embrace a state of mind which is directed toward the future, has defined to its satisfaction the business(es) it is in, and has conceptualized and articulated a Strategic Vision, it is absolutely imperative that a strong sense of strategic focus be developed at all levels.

An excellent example in this regard is Peoples Bancorp of Worcester, Massachusetts, and its visionary president Woodbury C. Titcomb. According to Peoples' 1988 annual report: "Our strategy is focused and well defined: To provide quality, create value, and seize opportunities for the benefit of our community, customers, employees, and shareholders." The bank's mission? " . . . to create shareholder value by focusing on improving our performance and attempting to ensure that our performance translates into increased market value." You simply can't get much more focused than that!

Strategic focus exists when directors, senior managers, middle managers, and staff all share a common understanding regarding issues such as:

a. The paradigm-shattering implications of external change, and the absolute need for the organization to adapt strategically in order to survive and prosper.
b. The relationship between shareholder value creation, business continuity, and job security.
c. How competitive advantage will be created, enhanced and/or sustained at each of the three phases of the business.

d. The definition, mission, and purpose of the business.

e. Financial performance and shareholder value objectives.

f. Marketing focus, including target segments, sources of competitive advantage (added value), pricing philosophy, and so forth.

g. Their individual roles and accountabilities (including their positive participation in the strategic change process) as they relate to fulfilling the company's mission and achieving its objectives.

h. The need to place organizational priorities above personal ego gratification and the penalty for failing to do so.

i. The core values which will shape and sustain the organization's culture.

j. How individual, group, and organizational performance will be evaluated and rewarded.

Strategic Focus Begins with the Board and Senior Management

Strategic focus must first be established between the board and senior management, especially the CEO. All the key strategic issues must be addressed in an atmosphere which is open, honest, and unconstrained by "realities" that are no longer valid or relevant. Nothing should be so sacred that its viability cannot be challenged and discussed freely among those who are accountable for the organization's future. *Those whose egos and/ or insecurities are so pronounced as to impede the organization's ability to undergo a thorough and objective self-analysis inhibit the process of strategic change, and they themselves must change, be removed, or prepare to go down with the ship.* There is simply no way to overstate the importance of this point. A painful reality in all companies undergoing change is that one or more board members and/or senior managers may have skills and experiences which are well suited to the structure of a regulated past, yet may lack the creative insights, conceptual thinking, and adaptability that will be mandatory in the 1990s and beyond. They may simply be incapable of changing—and of becoming change agents themselves. Dealing constructively with this issue will not be easy, yet in most cases will be essential for survival.

Focusing Middle Management

Once strategic focus has been achieved among directors and senior managers, it is absolutely imperative that middle managers, those who influence daily the attitudes and behaviors of the vast majority of the organization's human resources, achieve a commensurate level of understanding and awareness. According to a *Fortune* article: "Yet getting those middle managers to embrace a new corporate vision is the most important step and the greatest challenge when a large company tries to reform itself, as so many are trying to do. They are asked to learn entirely different ways of behaving, and their worth to the company can suddenly depend on their ability or willingness to do something adults hate to do: change."[18] A subsequent *Fortune* article reported: "When Booz Allen, the consulting firm, surveyed 170 Fortune 500 companies, half the executives admitted that their middle managers—never mind the poor hourly workers—had no understanding of corporate objectives or only a partial grasp of them."[19]

Having worked with banks of all sizes throughout the country, it is my observation that most middle managers have a poor understanding of the organization's mission, objectives, and strategies. Because they lack insight into the pervasive implications of change, the serious threat to survival that is inherent in failure to adapt, the financial performance dynamics of the business, their responsibility to the shareholders, and the rationale underlying corporate strategy, they often feel alienated from the strategic direction of the firm. They have neither the focus nor the motivation to seek new and better ways to help the bank achieve its goals or to inspire their subordinates to do the same. In point of fact, they don't know what their jobs are! Furthermore, because they are not focused strategically, they cannot possibly focus their subordinates. Because they are not part of the solution, they become part of the problem.

For the most part, however, middle managers are not to blame. Until this middle management group is focused strate-

Weak Strategic Focus Exists When

1. Attachment to an outmoded paradigm by owners, directors, and/or senior management precludes innovative and strategic thinking and planning;
2. Management is not sure of the owner's and/or director's real objectives or priorities; no strategic vision and/or mission has been conceptualized and articulated;
3. Management does not really understand what business(es) the firm is in;
4. Certain topics or issues relevant to the organization's future are off-limits for discussion between directors and the CEO;
5. Management does not understand the implications of external change on the firm's ability to create, enhance and/or sustain competitive advantage;
6. Owners and/or directors are polarized into two or more groups with conflicting points of view;
7. A lack of consensus exists throughout the organization regarding the bank's core values, those which drive daily individual and group behavior;
8. No *real* communication exists on a regular basis between top management and employees regarding the bank's strategic vision, mission, objectives, strategies, values, performance vis-à-vis peers, pricing strategies, etc.;
9. The organization structure has simply evolved rather than having been designed strategically; it impedes—rather than supports—superior performance;
10. No quantifiable performance standards (quantity, quality, cost and/or time) exist for *all* positions which support the bank's strategic priorities; as a result:

    a) officers and employees aren't really aware of what is expected, and accountability at all levels is weak or nonexistent;
    b) supervisors have little objective criteria on which to evaluate performance; therefore "performance appraisal" ignores performance altogether;
    c) mediocrity is tolerated and accepted;
    d) exceptional performance is not reinforced;
    e) high achievers become bored and go elsewhere;
    f) compensation is not equitable and is not oriented to individual contribution;

g) few people perform anywhere near their potential.

11. A weak sense of teamwork (or worse) exists between key functional areas;

12. Marketing is not involved in strategic planning; no correlation exists between corporate objectives and marketing focus; therefore:

   a) no agreement exists as to which market segments the bank is targeting or why;

   b) the market position uniquely appropriate to the bank has not been identified and is not being pursued;

   c) the bank's products are like everyone else's; no value-added benefits have been created which transcend price;

   d) employees side with the customer rather than the bank regarding price considerations;

   e) the bank has no real image in the market which supports strategic priorities;

   f) no common understanding exists throughout the bank as to who the best customers are and what must be done to keep them.

gically by senior management and made accountable for becoming a creative and constructive part of the change process, even the best strategies and tactics will never be successfully implemented, and will die a mysterious death for which no one will accept responsiblity.

In many banking organizations today, middle managers represent one of the greatest obstacles to progress because they equate job security with preservation of the status quo. In the surviving, high performance banks of tomorrow, middle managers will be one of the most powerful forces for constructive change because they will come to equate *real* job security with their role as "change agents," that is, being innovative in finding better ways to (*a*) achieve personal performance goals, (*b*) deliver value to the customer, (*c*) contribute measurably to consistently superior financial performance, (*d*) enhance economic value for the shareholders, and (e) empower and motivate their subordinates to do the same.

A Common Example of Weak Strategic Focus

A common example of weak strategic focus in banking today, and one which can be easily quantified, relates to pricing strategy. Shown below, for example, are the responses to two pricing-related statements from a recently conducted corporate culture analysis in a large midwestern bank. Shown are the percentages of officers, nonofficers, and total employees selecting each of the response alternatives as well as the average response score. (Scoring and interpretation is covered in detail in Chapter 4.)

STATEMENT 1

"In my opinion, pricing policies on loans, deposits, and services are based on sound strategic thinking."

	Officers	Nonofficers	Total Bank
Strongly agree	19%	6%	10%
Agree	23%	25%	25%
Weakly agree	23%	25%	25%
Neutral	2%	0%	1%
Weakly disagree	14%	9%	11%
Disagree	9%	15%	13%
Strongly disagree	0%	6%	4%
Not relevant to my job	10%	12%	11%
Average response	2.09	.94	1.26

STATEMENT 2

"The rationale underlying our pricing strategy is clearly understood throughout the organization."

	Officers	Nonofficers	Total
Strongly agree	0%	6%	4%
Agree	15%	21%	19%
Weakly agree	21%	23%	22%
Neutral	2%	0%	1%

STATEMENT 2 (*continued*)

	Officers	Nonofficers	Total
Weakly disagree	15%	21%	19%
Disagree	15%	23%	20%
Strongly disagree	31%	0%	10%
Not relevant to my job	1%	6%	4%
Average response	(1.76)	.30%	(.39)

In tabulating the average for each question, points are given on the following basis:

Strongly agree	6
Agree	4
Weakly agree	2
Neutral	0
Weakly disagree	(2)
Disagree	(4)
Strongly disagree	(6)

In addition, employees may select "not relevant to my job." These responses are not included in the tabulation. However, because all the questions in the questionnaire are, in fact, relevant to every job in the strategically focused high performing company, the percentage selecting this response is also a reflection of a culture's relative strength or weakness.

Average response scores are interpreted as follows:

Strong positive	4.00 or above
Positive	2.00–3.99
Weak positive	0–1.99
Weak negative	(1.99)–0
Negative	(3.99)–(2.00)
Strong negative	(4.00) or below

In the example cited, only 65 percent of the bank's officers believed that pricing policies were based on "sound, strategic thinking." Of the remainder, 10 percent considered the issue irrelevant to their jobs while 23 percent disagreed. Nonofficer responses were even more negative with 30 percent disagreeing and 12 percent perceiving the issue to be irrelevant to their jobs. The average response score for the total work force of 1.26 falls in the weak positive range, an obstacle to high performance which must be corrected fairly quickly.

Clearly, a large percentage of the work force in this bank lacks confidence in senior management decision making when it comes to pricing. This, in turn, has a powerful impact on sales and on customer relations.

Responses to the second statement, however, are even more revealing. Fully 61 percent of the officers, along with 44 percent of the nonofficers, believe that the rationale underlying pricing strategy is not clearly understood. Only 45 percent of the total work force agrees with the statement. The total average score of (.39) falls in the weak negative range and indicates a fairly serious weakness requiring immediate action.

In dealing with customers on a daily basis, officers and employees, to be focused and effective, must believe that senior management is basing its pricing decisions on "sound, strategic thinking," understand and support the rationale underlying pricing strategy, and be ready and able to defend that rationale to the customer. *It should come as no surprise that a large percentage of the work force in this bank, as in the typical bank, sides with the customer against management on most pricing issues. Because the front line troops are not focused strategically, they have become part of the problem, rather than part of the solution.*

In my experience, while this lack of awareness regarding pricing strategy is one of the most acute problems in banking today, it is also one of the easiest to remedy and overcome. The solution is to take the steps necessary to focus the entire work force strategically, a key senior management responsibility. One bank that has done an excellent job in this respect is Evergreen Bancorp of Glen Falls, New York. Evergreen's highly respected chairman, William L. Bitner III, had this to say in the 1988 annual report: "High performing banks are not necessarily more innovative than others, nor do they usually have a unique marketplace that provides them with some mysterious advantage over their competition. Usually they simply are institutions that have convinced every staff member that profitable, quality service is the core ingredient for future success." Bitner is tireless in his efforts to educate and focus every individual in his organization on "profitable, quality performance."

Education and Awareness Sessions
An effective first step in focusing middle managers, supervisors, and staff may be a series of well organized and carefully planned education and awareness sessions. The bank's CEO must be viewed as the catalyst for these meetings, and his or

her active involvement is critically important. Senior managers should also be involved in a supportive role. Issues to be covered might include: the forces of change, new competitive realities, and their implications for the industry and the institution; how commercial banks make money (the profitability dynamics of commercial banking); the Strategic Vision; the key priorities and strategies on which directors and senior management have reached consensus; shareholder value and business continuity; the characteristics of the traditional paradigm and how they threaten survival; the bank's marketing strategy, including pricing; why more demanding standards of performance will be required of all personnel; and so forth. In addition, the implications for those who are unwilling or unable to become constructive agents for change must be communicated in terms which leave no doubt as to the commitment of senior management and the board to the change process.

These sessions, which need to become an integral part of the organization's culture, should allow for open discussion of all issues covered, and may also be used to involve middle management in the creation and/or modification of strategic action plans. Clearly, the more active their participation, the greater will be their sense of ownership and commitment.

Accountability: The Key to Successful Change Management

The next step, and an indispensable one, is to establish, for every middle management job, key results areas, those where the manager's performance, and the performance of those he or she supervises, have a direct and measurable bearing on the mission, objectives, and strategies of the company. For each key results area, quantifiable performance standards and targets must be established. Performance must then be monitored and rewarded based on contribution to the attainment of performance targets. This is what accountability is all about.

Empowerment, especially of middle managers, is a term which is receiving a great deal of attention these days. For true empowerment to take place effectively, middle managers must (a) become focused strategically, (b) understand what their jobs are and who they work for, (c) understand the profitability and shareholder value dynamics of the business, (d) become an integral part of the planning process, (e) have clearly defined key results areas and quantifiable performance standards, and (f) be evaluated—and rewarded—based on contribution to key goals. Anything less is superficial and meaningless. *Substantial change will only take place when not changing is viewed as more painful and less attractive than changing—and when the degree of compliance is measured and triggers meaningful consequences—both positive and negative.*

The Mission Statement or Statement of Purpose and Values

One extremely effective way of reinforcing the organization's Strategic Vision and Focus is to articulate a mission statement or what I prefer to call a statement of purpose and values.

To be effective, the statement of purpose and values should express what business(es) the company is in; how it intends to differentiate itself from other organizations, especially its major competitors; what values (such as Ray Kroc's "quality, service, cleanliness, and value") will drive the organization; and how success will be determined. It must be somewhat flexible so as not to inhibit the organization's adaptability yet at the same time not be so nebulous as to negate its value.

Whereas many companies publish their mission statements with great pride in their annual reports, and mention them once a year at the annual dinner, others recognize the importance and value of making the statement of purpose and values a daily reminder of what the organization stands for, where it is going, and what will be required to get it there. They view the creation of a meaningful mission statement not as an objective, but as a tool to help them accomplish their objectives. For example, Roy Nelson, President of the Bank of Utah, had plastic wallet size cards with the bank's mission statement made for all employees as a way to help reinforce the bank's mission and purpose. He also makes an effort to constantly refocus the organization by relating ongoing strategies and tactics to the bank's mission.

At American National Bank in Bakersfield, California (now Wells Fargo Bank), the mission statement, with which everyone in the organization was intimately familiar, was framed and placed in every office and department, a constant reminder to every employee of why they are there. D. Linn Wiley, the bank's charismatic CEO, never missed an opportunity to reinforce the bank's strategic focus as he made his regular visits throughout the bank's extensive branch system. Strategic focus continues to be a cornerstone of his highly effective leadership style in his position as Executive Vice President.

Bob Duggan, the dynamic President and CEO of Savings and Trust Company of Pennsylvania, uses their mission statement, shown below, to focus all employees on shareholder value—and how it is created.

It Is Our Mission To:

- Be the premier financial institution in the markets in which we operate.
- Create and deliver quality financial products and services which represent exceptional value to our customers.
- Provide a stimulating and challenging work environment which encourages, develops, and rewards excellence.
- Diligently serve our communities with integrity and pride.
- Through uncompromising dedication and commitment to the above, achieve consistently superior financial performance which creates value for our shareholders.

One of the most successful examples I have seen of a mission statement being used to focus an organization strategically is that of First National Bank of McCook (Nebraska). The mission statement is simple and to the point: "OUR MISSION is to deliver quality products to quality customers at a quality price." Denny Fargen, the bank's highly successful President, makes sure that everyone in the organization has a clear understanding of the relationship between the bank's mission and their day-to-day responsibilities. Each employee knows and accepts that (*a*) the bank has a clear market focus and is not interested in being all things to all people, (*b*) all products and services must be the best in town, which is largely a function of the quality of individual effort, and (*c*) pricing on loans, deposits, and services will reflect the high quality (and cost) of the product. Employees take great pride in delivering superior service, understand the costs required to do so, and don't apologize for not being the "cheapest bank in town."

A Strategically Supportive Culture

The final key to mastery of the change process is, in fact, one of the three key components in the successful realization of the Strategic Vision and the focus of Chapter 4. Because the existing corporate culture in most organizations is a product of the old paradigm, and has developed within itself powerful defense mechanisms to preserve and protect its existence, it is highly resistant to change and an impediment to superior performance in the 1990s. Every corporate culture has characteristics which impede successful adaptation. For the most part, these characteristics lie hidden and protected within the cultural framework of the organization and, if they are to be overcome, must first be exposed. Only then can they be challenged, evaluated, and modified.

No organization, especially in an industry undergoing rapid and explosive change, can truly adapt strategically without making fundamental changes in its corporate culture. In fact, on more than one project in which I have been involved, a severely troubled and negative corporate culture has forced management to put the development and implementation of external strategy on hold indefinitely until appropriate culture modification strategies might be created and implemented effectively.

SUMMARY

For decades, America's bankers operated confidently within the familiar confines of a banking paradigm characterized by protective regulation, fixed raw materials costs, limited out of market and/or nonbank competition, a monopoly on transaction accounts, relatively stable economic conditions, minimal latitude in product design and differentiation, low risk of failure, highly tolerant financial markets, and broadly shared accountability for results.

The realities of the traditional paradigm had a powerful impact on issues such as:

   a. Organizational standards of financial performance.
   b. Types of individuals recruited to—and attracted by—the banking industry.
   c. Leadership and management styles.
   d. Organization structures.
   e. Corporate culture values and characteristics.
   f. Distribution of authority and power.
   g. Individual "performance" expectations and appraisal.
   h. Compensation.
   i. Criteria for advancement.
   j. Customer service attitudes.
   k. External "strategy."
   l. Critical success factors.
   m. Management of costs and pricing.
   n. Training.
   o. Staffing.
   p. Usage of technology.

Beginning in the 1970s and accelerating through the 1980s, the relative stability and calm in the banking industry (as in all business sectors) was shattered as a series of unprecedented structural discontinuities transformed virtually every aspect of banking and challenged traditional practices in all areas listed above. Interest rates began to fluctuate wildly; the globalization of the U.S. economy, combined with severe turmoil in a multitude of world trouble spots and serious challenges from emerging economic superpowers such as Japan and West Germany, added to the rising uncertainty across the full spectrum of business enterprise; new technology made traditional regulatory barriers (price, product, and geographic) to competition obsolete and ineffective and allowed innovators inside and outside the industry to create and exploit a variety of new competitive advantages; social and demographic changes such as the "aging of America" and the multiple income family challenged conventional attitudes regarding the identification and satisfaction of consumer needs as well as employee motivation; the movement of younger and retired people from the rural heartland to the coastal and Sun Belt areas destabilized many local and regional economies; discontinuities in major industries such as energy and agriculture (not an aberration when viewed in a historical context) adversely affected those whose lack of appreciation for cyclical and structural economic realities caused them to ignore fundamental principles regarding concentration of risk; the shift to an information and service economy and the increased emphasis on technology as the primary basis of competitive advantage created the need for constant adaptation, ongoing education and training, and innovative strategic thinking and planning; legislative, political, and regulatory developments, which are almost always the *result* of other changes rather than their *cause*, created unparalleled opportunities for those whose vision and influence allowed them not only to anticipate emerging developments, but to play a role in their creation; and consumers and businesses, as a variety of alternative product offerings was introduced, become far more demanding and discriminating.

As we enter the last decade of not only the century—but of the millennium—there is one thing of which I am certain: *only those leaders who have the courage, vision, and power to master the six step process of strategic and cultural change will survive and prosper.*

First, traditional mind-sets must be replaced with a mentality that questions everything that is known, challenges the status quo, and eradicates groupthink from the process of strategic decision making. Everyone in the organization must be encouraged to make frequent use of the question "Why?"—and the penalty for answering "because that is the way we've always done it" should be immediate dismissal! People must be made to understand the life and death struggle taking place within the financial services industry; that failure to adapt strategically and culturally guarantees eventual extinction.

Second, the organization must benefit from truly enlightened leadership which succeeds in conceptualizing, articulating, and giving meaning to a Strategic Vision; a tangible manifestation of how the organization of the future will differ from today's reality in order to be compatible with emerging realities.

Third, consensus must be reached regarding those business(es) in which the organization will compete and how capital will be allocated and managed.

Fourth, Strategic Management and Planning, which balances sound conceptual thinking with implementation and accountability for results, must replace traditional strategic planning.

Fifth, a powerful sense of strategic focus must be achieved among directors, senior and middle managers, and staff.

Finally, the existing corporate culture must undergo an in-depth analysis to identify those strengths on which strategy can be crafted and implemented, as well as those weaknesses that inhibit successful adaptation and impede the implementation process. The culture must then be subjected to continuous modification in order to make it stronger, more positive, and increasingly adaptive and supportive of the Strategic Vision.

Once these initiatives have been undertaken successfully, key opportunities can be identified and prioritized in the areas of financial performance and shareholder value optimization, leadership and corporate culture, and market positioning and competitive advantage. These three areas will represent the focus of Section II.

SECTION II

REALIZING THE STRATEGIC VISION

The constant temptation of every organization is safe mediocrity.

—Peter Drucker

Anybody who knows anything about organizations knows how hard it is to get things done let alone to introduce new ways of doing things, no matter how promising they seem. A powerful new idea can kick around unused in a company for years, not because its merits are not recognized, but because nobody has assumed the responsibility for converting it from words into action. What is lacking is not creativity in the idea-creating sense but innovation in the action-producing sense. The ideas are not being put to work. There is no center of entrepreneurial energy.

—Ted Leavitt

As discussed in Chapter 2, an integral element in mastering the change process is the creation of a Strategic Vision: the conceptualization of what the organization must look like at the end of a specific time frame, typically three to five years.

All bank strategies, therefore, must be designed to convert the bank from today's reality to tomorrow's Strategic Vision. These strategies will typically fall into three categories: (1) strategies specifically designed to enhance financial performance, thereby leading to increased shareholder value, (2) strategies to make the organization's corporate culture (including leadership styles and priorities), stronger, more positive, and more strategically adaptive and supportive, and (3) marketing and sales strategies designed to create, enhance and/or sustain competitive advantage, thereby positioning the bank more powerfully and strategically in its target markets vis-à-vis its competitors.

These strategies are all interdependent. For example, as we will see in Chapter 3, financial strategies to increase interest income are meaningless and impotent without supportive and compatible strategies in the areas of corporate culture, human resource management and development (HRMD), and marketing. As will be discussed in Chapter 4, without the direction provided by clearly articulated financial and marketing strategies, initiatives in the area of corporate culture will be confused, fragmented, and without focus. Marketing and sales strategies, as we will observe in Chapter 5, unless driven by profitability and shareholder value enhancement, and supported by a sales and marketing-oriented culture, will be misdirected, counterproductive, and wasteful of scarce resources.

In each of the three areas, the process will be essentially the same. First, specific opportunities, offensive as well as defensive, will be identified, prioritized and, wherever possible, quantified. Second, strategies will be created to exploit these opportunities. Third, strategic action plans will be established for all strategies that (*a*) detail the timetable for implementation, (*b*) fix accountability for results, and (*c*) establish the basis by which results will be measured and monitored. Fourth, results must be diligently measured and monitored and appropriate consequences (positive and negative reinforcement) must take place in a consistent and relevant manner.

Strategic Management and Planning (see Chapter 6) refers to the ongoing process by which all this is accomplished, thereby mobilizing and focusing the entire organization on the Strategic Vision while allowing maximum adaptability and responsiveness to new opportunities.

CHAPTER 3

━━━━

FINANCIAL PERFORMANCE AND SHAREHOLDER VALUE OPTIMIZATION

━━

> If ever it was easy to be a banker, it isn't any longer. Deregulation in every major market combined with world-scale, world-class competition, have seen to that. The United States, Japan and Europe, all seriously overbanked, are entering a period of consolidation. And their stock markets are swift to punish banks that aren't adapting.
>
> —*Institutional Investor*
> September 1989

> Business strategies should be judged by the economic returns they generate for shareholders, as measured by dividends plus the increase in the company's share price.
>
> —*Alfred Rappaport*
> *Creating Shareholder Value*

CREATING SHAREHOLDER VALUE

The overriding objective, in any for-profit business, must be the creation of economic value for the shareholders. Shareholder satisfaction, quite simply, is the key to the ongoing viability of any corporate business enterprise. The fastest way to destroy a business is to lose sight of this fundamental economic reality.

The overriding strategy by which this objective is achieved is to maximize customer satisfaction, which will be a focus of Chapter 5.

69

GENERIC GROWTH AND PROFITABILITY STRATEGIES

In crafting the strategy which will optimize the creation of shareholder value for the individual firm, there are essentially four generic strategies from which to choose: (1) a pure growth strategy, (2) a pure profitability enhancement strategy, (3) a combination growth and profitability enhancement strategy, and (4) a "sell the bank" strategy.

The "pure growth" strategy makes sense when a window of opportunity presents itself to exploit a unique and temporary situation such as: (*a*) a competitor weakness, (*b*) a legislative change, (*c*) the introduction of a new and unique product, (*d*) a technological breakthrough, (*e*) overcapitalization and resulting inadequate ROE, (*f*) the need to leverage fixed assets more effectively through increased market share and/or volume, (*g*) inward focus by competitors to deal with issues such as problem loans, or (*h*) competitor distraction caused by issues such as real or perceived threats associated with mergers or acquisitions. The pure growth strategy may actually subordinate profitability considerations in the short run.

The "pure profitability" strategy, which ignores growth and may actually result in downsizing, can make sense when capital is weak, during a period of economic adversity, or even during a boom if management feels the risks are excessive. This strategy too must be viewed as temporary.

The "sell the bank" strategy is, in many instances, the best way to optimize shareholder return, especially when the franchise, for whatever reason, has greater value to a purchaser than it does to the existing owners. If the present value of earnings streams associated with the sale exceeds the present value of expected earnings streams from continued ownership, the best economic decision may be to sell, especially if the current owners believe that the existing financial performance, for whatever reason, is not sustainable.

As an ongoing strategy, the only one that makes sense in most cases is the "growth plus enhanced profitability" strategy. Therefore, management must determine which combination of earnings, financial leverage, dividends, internal growth, external growth, and risk will best meet the needs of the share-holders.

The Growth Component: Internal and External Growth Strategies

The growth portion of the strategic equation represents a com-bination of internal and external expansion. Internal growth is primarily a function of retained earnings, market opportunities, and marketing strategy. External growth includes mergers, ac-quisitions (including diversification), and joint ventures.

The strategic value of a growth strategy is well supported by research conducted by the Strategic Planning Institute. Based on research concerning the performance of more than 3,000 strategic business units worldwide, in a variety of indus-tries, those having market shares in excess of 50 percent had re-turns more than three times greater than those having a mar-ket share of 10 percent or less.[1] Market share was calculated based on the specific market being targeted, not on the market as a whole. For example, while Mercedes-Benz has a small share of the automobile market, it has a significant share of the luxury car market, the niche it has traditionally targeted.[2]

The research stressed, however, that any strategies de-signed to increase market share are unlikely to succeed unless a clear, competitive advantage has been created, communi-cated, and delivered successfully.[3] This may help to explain the results of a study conducted by Jeffrey D. Maddox and reported in *The Bankers Magazine*. According to Maddox: "Over the last five years, banks have demonstrated a negative correlation be-tween asset size and value creation. Larger institutions have generally achieved scale at the expense of value. At the margin, these companies invested in internal and external growth op-portunities that provided ROEs that were far short of share-holder's required returns."[4] Clearly, many bankers have con-fused strategy (growth) with objectives (increasing shareholder value). Capital invested in activities where the firm cannot cre-ate and/or sustain competitive advantage will not produce an acceptable return.

Because external growth strategies are a primary consideration in the strategic planning efforts of most banks, the results of a study by Michael Porter, as reported in the *Harvard Business Review*, are extremely relevant. Porter studied the diversification strategies of 33 prominent U.S. corporations, including firms such as Proctor & Gamble, IBM, ITT, Xerox, Exxon, and 3M. Based on his analysis of the results of those strategies for the period 1950 to 1986, Porter concluded: "The corporate strategies of most companies have dissipated instead of created shareholder value."[5]

Porter subsequently determined that three conditions must be met in order for diversification to succeed in creating shareholder value. First, the transaction must pass "the attractiveness test," that is, the industry into which the firm is diversifying must be structurally attractive or have the potential for being made attractive. Second, "the cost of entry test" must be met. In other words, all the future profits associated with the acquisition, including whatever value can be added by the acquiror, must not be capitalized by the cost of entry. Finally, a synergy must result from the marriage which will provide sustainable competitive advantage to one or both entities. Porter calls this the "better-off test."

Because it is so difficult for a potential transaction to pass all three tests, and because potential acquirors often tend to be strongly influenced by perceived benefits in one area, while disregarding the other two, diversification rarely succeeds.

Because banks can transfer skills, and gain considerable benefits from consolidation of activities such as data processing, marketing, human resource management, and so forth, bank acquisitions of like businesses typically have a greater likelihood of success than do acquisitions of less closely related businesses, for which skills transfer and consolidation opportunities may not exist.

As banks pursue external growth strategies, they must not lose sight of their strategic focus, and any acquisition must be driven by shareholder value considerations, rather than by a strategy (e.g., growth) masquerading as an objective, or by what Bob Walters, a leading bank merger-acquisition specialist, refers to as the "pin in the map" syndrome.

Industry Specialist's Perspective

Bob Walters is President of The Bank Advisory Group Inc., Austin, Texas. Formally, he was Senior Vice President of Sheshunoff and Company, Inc., in charge of all investment banking and merger/acquisition activities.

Question:

Bob, significant consolidation has occurred within the U.S. financial services industry over the past several years. Why does consolidation within the banking industry continue at an unabated pace given that so many mergers/acquisitions have had a minimal or even detrimental impact on shareholder value? What are the criteria for assuring that an acquisition/merger has a lasting favorable impact on shareholder value?

Answer:

Most observers, of which I am one, agree that consolidation within the financial services industry will continue to occur at a fairly brisk pace for at least several years. Countless forces are undeniably driving consolidation, including rapidly changing technology, aggressive marketing tactics, increased consumer sophistication, as well as liberalization of interstate banking laws. Despite the trend, the industry is littered with numerous acquisitions/mergers that were ill-conceived, badly timed, poorly structured, and improperly executed. There are a number of basic causes for such financially disastrous acquisitions/mergers.

Ego and empire-building surely rank as two significant propelling forces. The inflated ego of a "grow-at-any-cost" CEO won out over pure common sense on more than one occasion. So, the first criteria for a successful acquisition/merger is to assure that the transaction is based on sound, strategic vision rather than unbridled ego.

Second, a lack of planning is often a culprit. All too frequently, buyers fail to evaluate and prioritize acquisition candidates, opting instead to assess each acquisition opportunity independently of all other potential opportunities. Additionally, poor tax, legal, and regulatory planning have on more than just a few occasions provided cause for regretting an acquisition. Most importantly, however, is the role of planning in connection with preacquisition or "due diligence" investigations. Poorly planned or superficial due diligence investigations are certainly a leading cause of financially ruinous acquisitions/mergers.

Third, it seems to me that the most successful mergers/acquisitions are those that are either well envisioned or those that present extraordinary price opportunities. These appear in stark contrast to what I call "follow the leader" transactions. A herd mentality approach to mergers and acquisitions all too often results in buyers paying excessive prices for banks typically operating at peak performance in markets with economies that are frequently overheated. Transactions during the past decade in southwestern and northeastern regions of the United States clearly indicate that the riskiest time to acquire banking organizations is when the financial sector and the local economy are operating at stellar performance levels.

Fourth, most successful acquistions/mergers are products of organizational and operational integration plans that are uniquely suited for the specific dynamics of the acquired bank. I would term this the "sensitive" approach to integration planning. In other words, a successful integration plan must be designed to reflect the strengths and weaknesses of the acquired organization. I am convinced that a "cookie-cutter" approach for integrating staff and operations is not the mark of an acquiror with a successful record of acquisitions. If the seller has a record of poor performance, the buyer may need to take a somewhat heavy-handed approach to integrating operations. Alternatively, if the seller's management is strong and capable, the sensible buyer may choose to integrate operations with a deliberate yet more facilitative approach.

The Earnings Component: Economic Value, Cash Flow, and Earnings

According to commonly accepted financial theory, "value" is equivalent to the present value resulting from the capitalization of expected future cash flows.[6] For the shareholder, those cash flows include dividends and the proceeds of sale at some future date, consisting of the return of the original investment plus a capital gain (or minus a capital loss).

The implications inherent in this definition are numerous.

For example, because accounting conventions will almost always produce earnings results that are not consistent with actual cash flowing in and out of the business, earnings measures can be less reliable than cash flow as an indicator or determinant of value. In addition, expectations regarding future cash flows will be influenced by assumptions regarding the sustainability or enhancement of current performance. Therefore, the discount rate chosen to derive the net present value of expected cash flows will include not only a risk-free component (approximated by the rate on long-term government securities), but also a risk premium, which will include both financial risk (leverage) and operating risk (resulting from issues such as the five forces in the Porter model). The more uncertain or volatile the expected cash flows, the higher the risk premium must be.

The discount rate represents what the shareholders could expect to receive on an investment of similar risk, and as such, is an opportunity cost. Because investors have the alternative of investing elsewhere, they have no reason to tolerate returns below this rate in the long run. Therefore, any firm consistently earning less may ultimately go out of business.

When the net present value of expected cash flows is positive, thereby exceeding the cost of capital, value is created. When the return does not exceed the cost of capital (negative net present value of expected cash flows), shareholder value is reduced.

What is true for the individual shareholder is true for the individual bank as well in that the bank's value is equal to discounted future cash flows or—as is more common in bank valuation—discounted future earnings. Cash or earnings, in turn, originate from the bank's various operating units or businesses.

As noted earlier, because earnings measures of performance (such as net income, ROA, ROE, and earnings per share) are all subject to distortions inherent in GAAP accrual accounting conventions, and may not fully reflect operating and financial risks, they are theoretically less reliable than are cash flow performance measures. However, cash flow measures have limitations as well, and their ultimate validity also depends on a multitude of assumptions about the future. Projections regarding the future sales price of a stock, for example, needed to calculate expected future cash flows are based on many of the same fundamental assumptions as projections regarding future ROA and/or ROE.

Cash flow, too, can be manipulated in ways which may not be in the shareholder's long-term best interests. Patricia Dreyfus, writing in the *Institutional Investor*, says: "Even people who believe that cash flow is a better yardstick of value than earnings admit that it has its problems. For one thing, they disagree about what cash flow is. Arguments flare about whether to use post- or pretax income; how much, if anything, to subtract for capital spending; and whether debt repayment and dividends are discretionary expenses. One of the few points of agreement is that you must look at cash flow over long sweeps of time—at least five years—to avoid aberrations caused by unusually high capital outlays one year or by the sale of an asset in another."[7]

The truth of the matter is that no single measure is perfect; each has its faults. Therefore, the competent analyst will want to look at a variety of traditional measures, as well as factoring in the effects of any new developments.[8]

Regardless of the measure used, the key is to focus the organization on the creation of shareholder value as the bank's overriding objective. In this way ROE enhancement, for example, is not viewed as an objective, but as a strategy. Like every strategy, it must be evaluated, rejected, or defended based on the extent to which it contributes to the overriding objective. The same would be true of cash flow enhancement strategies.

Viewed in this manner, decisions to increase financial leverage, or to increase portfolio risk in search of higher returns, either of which could increase ROE, would actually be evaluated on the extent to which they might increase shareholder value, not on whether ROE might be enhanced. In other words, any additional operating and/or financial risks, and their potential impact on shareholder value, would be factored into the analysis. Such an approach would also tend to focus managers away from short-term considerations toward a longer-term perspective.

In addition, because most bankers continue to rely heavily

EXHIBIT 3–1
Shareholder Value

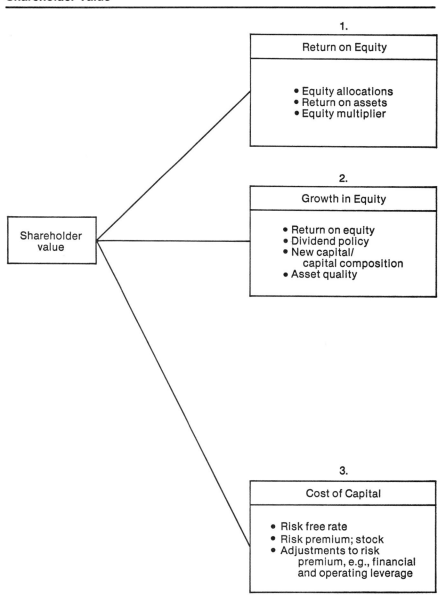

on ROE (and to a diminishing degree on ROA) in their planning and performance measurement activities, any financial performance optimization model, to be of any practical value to the vast majority of bankers, must be oriented to some degree around these concepts. However, it is my expectation that within the decade of the 1990s many banks, especially those with significant nonasset based earnings, will gravitate to cash flow-based performance modeling and analysis, while continuing to find benefits from more traditional concepts. The implementation of FASB 95, which requires reporting of cash flows from operations, investing activities, and financing activities is certainly a step in that direction. While FASB 104 amends FASB 95 for banks and certain other financial institutions, the increasing emphasis on cash flow analysis and reporting is obvious.

As shown in Exhibit 3–1, I recommend an approach which relates shareholder value creation with three key dynamic variables: return on equity, equity growth, and cost of capital (which also reflects "sustainability" considerations as part of the operating risk component).

THE PROFITABILITY DYNAMICS OF RETURN ON EQUITY

Step 1: Consensus on the ROE Target

Using this approach, management will want to begin the process of financial performance optimization by determining the actual cost of capital, developing a capital plan, and quantifying the desired ROE; that performance level that will be perceived by the shareholders and financial markets as contributing to shareholder value, thereby having a positive impact on the bank's stock price. Whereas the discount rate discussed earlier is a rate at which shareholder value will neither be created nor reduced, the target ROE, the level at which value will definitely be created, must be higher. After all, management's job is not to deliver a return that meets alternative risk-adjusted investment opportunities, but one which surpasses them (which may well be accepting an offer to purchase the bank). It seems to me that the greatest tribute a management team could possibly have would be a stock price so high, and performance expectations so strong, that no outside parties could conceive of achieving a higher value by doing a better job at managing those assets. This may be the ultimate test of shareholder value maximization.

One banker who has succeeded brilliantly in this regard is John Adam Kanas, president of the highly successful North Fork Bancorp in Mattituck, New York. In a *New York Times* interview, Kanas remarked: "Having said that, let me tell you the party line around here: the ultimate golden parachute and the ultimate poison pill against an unfriendly takeover is superior performance. If you rack up a string of successful performances year after year that's unparalleled by anyone else, then you can clearly look your stockholders in the eye and say we can do better for you in the future than anyone else. If our performance level slips, we'll get what we deserve."[9]

Such performance is extremely rare, and because buyers may have competitive and/or economy of scale advantages enabling the payment of an irresistible purchase price premium, in many cases the best that can be hoped for is to create so much value that a determined buyer will be forced to pay a price in excess of anything the shareholders might otherwise have expected. As the events of recent years have clearly established, there has not been a shortage of "irrational" buyers, although transactions being consummated today are generally more commercially sound, and less driven by ego, than those that dominated the 1980s.

Step 2: Desired Capital Ratio and Allocation

Once the target ROE has been agreed upon, and has become an integral part of the organization's strategic focus, the next step is to determine the desired (or required) capital ratio and capital composition over the planning horizon, not only for the bank and/or holding company, but for each individual operating unit or "business." Obviously, regulatory considerations, especially risk-adjusted capital guidelines, will play a major role in this determination. However, the philosophy of shareholders, directors, and senior managers will also influence the capital composition and ratio chosen. Again, consensus must be reached and the organization strategically focused on a clearly defined capital management strategy.

Step 3: Required ROA and Incremental Earnings

Step 3 is to determine the required ROA, incremental ROA, and incremental pretax earnings needed to reach the target ROE, given the required capital ratio.

An actual example demonstrating those steps is shown in Exhibit 3–2 below:

EXHIBIT 3–2

Subject Bank

• Asset size	$1 Billion
• Planning horizon	3 Years
• ROE target year 3	17.5%
• Capital ratio and equity multiplier	8%/12.5
• Desired capital ratio and equity multiplier	8%/12.5
• Current ROA	.83
• Required ROA year 3 (17.5 ÷ 12.5 = 1.40)	1.40
• Required incremental ROA by year 3 (1.40 − .83 = .57)	.57

Required Incremental Pretax Earnings ($000)

Year	Ave. Assets	Ave. Capital	ROA	EM	ROE	Incremental ROA	Incremental Pre-Tax Earnings*
1	$1,000,000	$80,000	1.05	12.5	13.1	.22	$2,948
2	1,100,000	87,875	1.25	12.5	15.5	.20	2,944
3	1,226,125	98,090	1.40	12.5	17.5	.15	2,465
					Total	.57	8,357

*Assumes 34% tax rate and 25% dividend payout.

In this specific case, management believed that the shareholders would be patient enough to allow three years to reach the 17.5 percent target ROE. In actuality, management strategies, in many cases, may have to be more dramatic, producing results more quickly. The longer the management team waits before taking action, and the more impatient the shareholders become as a result, the more true this will be.

Projected Value Creation
In this particular scenario, total value to be created over the planning horizon, and over a five-year period, is shown below:

EXHIBIT 3–3
Shareholder Value Creation* ($000)

Year	Ave. Book Value	Asset Size	ROA	EM	ROE	PAT	RE
1	$80,000	$1,000,000	1.05	12.5	13.1	$10,500	$ 7,875
2	87,875	1,100,000	1.25	12.5	15.5	13,620	10,215
3	98,090	1,226,123	1.40	12.5	17.5	17,166	12,875
4	110,965	1,387,063	1.40	12.5	17.5	19,419	14,564
5	125,529	1,569,113	1.40	12.5	17.5	21,968	16,476

EM = Equity multiplier
PAT = Profit after taxes
RE = Retained earnings
      (assumes 25% dividend payout)

*Additional assumption: Retained earnings are fully leveraged 12.5 times.

These results reflect the three dynamic variables of shareholder value creation previously mentioned: ROE, equity growth, and cost of capital (used in computing the net present value of earnings or cash flows)

The steps to this point, which involve establishing the overall financial performance goals, are the easy ones, and are primarily dependent on sound financial analysis, which, as discussed in Chapter 2, is essentially a left-hemisphere activity.

From this point forward, the required steps will become more and more dependent on input from the right hemisphere. Innovation will be required to confront existing paradigms, and to become more innovative in finding new solutions to the challenges created by change. After all, it is one thing to agree that $8.4 million in incremental pretax income is needed over the next three years, yet quite another to figure out from where it is going to come. It certainly will not result from doing the same old things in the same old ways—from digging the same hole deeper.

Many brilliantly analytical bankers have accomplished the first step, the quantification of earnings objectives, but have failed miserably with the second, creating the strategies to achieve those objectives. That should come as no surprise since even the most astute financial analyst may be trapped by the constraints and rules of a traditional paradigm, while the strategic solutions he or she seeks lie elsewhere. The left-hemisphere input to any strategic plan may succeed in asking all the right questions, but the answers that really matter will almost invariably come from the creative, irreverent, and insatiably curious right hemisphere. According to Donovan and Wonder: "Problems of communication, listening, memory, management, organization, stress—these are the dilemmas facing American businesses. Increasingly, business is recognizing that they cannot be solved by logic, discipline, and attention to detail alone. They require not only these traditionally valued skills, but also intuition, free-spirited invention and comprehension of the overall picture."[10] In the 1990s, the senior management skills of greatest value will be conceptual, in contrast to the emphasis on technical skills inherent in the old paradigm. Furthermore, it is rare indeed to find an exceptional financial specialist who also has an in-depth understanding of corporate culture, human resource management, and strategic marketing, and the critical role they play in translating financial objectives into bottom-line results.

The importance of this point cannot be overstated. The strategies that must be developed and implemented through the process of Strategic Management and Planning must not be the exclusive domain of the bank's financial gurus. The broader the cross section of those consolidating their creative energies to break new ground strategically, the greater the likelihood of success. Furthermore, when those whose responsibility it will be to implement the strategies play a meaningful role in their creation, the overall level of enthusiasm and commitment will be infinitely higher.

Step 4: Opportunity Identification, Prioritization, and Quantification

First, consensus and focus must be reached with respect to:

1. Target ROE.
2. Capital ratio.
3. Required ROA.
4. Required incremental ROA.
5. Required incremental pretax and after-tax earnings.

Then, the next step is to determine from *where* those incremental earnings will be generated.

THE PROFITABILITY DYNAMICS OF ROE

ROE, of course, is a function of but two dynamic variables:

1. The equity multiplier (the reciprocal of the equity/assets ratio).
2. Return on assets.

Therefore, once the appropriate capitalization has been determined, including its cost, for the bank as a whole, or for a strategic business unit, functional area, or line of business, *ROE becomes totally dependent on ROA*. Therefore, in many instances, ROA analysis is every bit as relevant, if not more so, than ever before. The exception, of course, relates to revenue streams that are not asset-based. However, such revenue streams may also be viewed as the ultimate ROA enhancement strategy since they increase earnings without increasing average assets.

Capital Allocation by Business Unit
Bankers have traditionally viewed capital as a shared cost, with one capital pool supporting a variety of divergent functions. This resulted in profitable activities subsidizing unprofitable activities, and compensation and advancement decisions

based on other than performance-based criteria. Now, as a result of the increased demands from shareholders and financial markets for vastly improved value creation, over-capacity and the resultant need to reallocate capital, and the new risk-adjusted capital guidelines, enlightened bankers are attempting to develop better ways to determine the cost of capital and where it has actually been allocated and to measure and evaluate individual operating units based on ROE criteria. Once unit managers know precisely the amount of capital for which they have stewardship and its cost, they become far more accountable. Future capital allocations, in turn, will be based less on politics and comfortable but outdated conceptions of business definition and purpose, and more on shareholder value creation. *Within the individual bank, as within the industry as a whole, capital in the 1990s will increasingly come under the control of those who demonstrate the greatest ability to create shareholder value, and will be taken from those who can only talk about it—or write about it in their annual reports.* Business lines and operating units—as well as managers who cannot create value—will, of necessity, be discarded. There will simply be no other choice.

Because the stock market value of a bank or bank holding company is a reflection of the perceived aggregate value of its various business units, the extent to which an individual unit contributes value is of the utmost importance. The greater the earnings contribution vis-à-vis required capital, the more significant is the contribution of that unit. Because traditional commercial banking delivers a relatively poor return on equity, the stock market has clearly discounted the value of commercially oriented banks.[11] Therefore, enlightened bankers are seeking to reallocate capital in order to more effectively create value for their shareholders. In so doing they have attempted to emulate the successful strategies used by top companies in other industries. Such strategies, referred to collectively as "strategic restructuring," include downsizing, consolidation, securitization, diversification, spin-offs and spin-outs, mergers, acquisitions, divestiture, stock repurchase, and sale-leasebacks. It is expected that this trend will gain tremendous momentum in the next few years as more and more banks attempt to allocate capital in ways which maximize shareholder value creation, and to exit those businesses whose returns fail to do so.

An editorial in *Euromoney* on the restructuring revolution sweeping Europe and the United States comments: "The unanswered question is this: Will this wave of restructuring wash over the banking industry as well? Certainly it should: despite a rise to 11 percent return on equity by the banks in the *Euromoney* 500, legions of major banks plainly do not make as much money as they should. The stock market knows this, which is why P/E values of, for example, major U.S. banks are languishing in the 6 to 7 range."[12] In point of fact, many leading U.S. and European banks have already begun the process, with impressive results.

THE PROFITABILITY DYNAMICS OF
RETURN ON ASSETS

Once capital allocations have been determined, based on decisions regarding business definition and focus, achieving ROE goals, as stated earlier, becomes in large measure a function of ROA.

Because there are only six ways to improve ROA, the banker must determine, by analyzing the bank's performance in these specific areas, where earnings improvement opportunities exist. In the case previously used, for example, the subject bank's projected incremental pretax earnings for each year of the planning period, in order to achieve its objectives, are as follows:

Year	Ave. Asset Size (000)	Incremental ROA	Incremental Pretax Earnings ($000)
1	$1,000,000	.22	$2,948,000
2	1,100,000	.20	2,944,000
3	1,226,125	.15	2,465,000
Total		.57	$8,357,000

These incremental earnings must come from one or more of the following sources, as a percentage of average assets:

1) Interest income.
2) Interest expense.
3) Noninterest income.
4) Noninterest expense.
5) Asset gains (losses).
6) Taxes paid.

If a bank cannot find earnings enhancement opportunities in one or more of these areas, they are not to be found, since there is simply no place else to look. Were that to be the case, management would have to go back and rethink issues such as business definition, lines of business, capital allocation, and restructuring alternatives (including new ownership and/or management).

Peer Group Analysis

An excellent way to identify and quantify earnings opportunities at this point involves comparing the bank to several carefully selected peer groups. The Sheshunoff Information Services, Inc. "High Performance Planning Report," for example, allows management to relate the bank's performance in each ROA component, and its subcomponents, with (a) a national peer group, (b) a national *high performance* peer group (the top 25 percent of the national peer group), and (c) a state peer group. The Sheshunoff "Competitive Analysis Report" permits the bank to create its own peer groups, which, for example, might be (a) a group of competitors, (b) banks in the same holding company, (c) top performers in the same state or region, or (d) banks which are in the same businesses.

In Exhibit 3–4, a subject bank's most recent one year performance is compared to 12 other banks in its holding company. All of these banks are operating in the same state and, with the exception of banks 5, 12, and 13, are in similar competitive environments. While this analysis only presents comparisons for

EXHIBIT 3-4
Peer Group Analysis

Bank	Total Assets (000)	ROA	EM	ROE	as a percentage of average assets*						
					Int. Income	Int. Exp.	Net Int. Margin	Non-Int. Income	Non-Int. Exp.	Asset Losses	Taxes
1	$430,000	1.51	16.00	24.69	8.94	3.86	5.08	.80	2.78	.31	1.07
2	320,000	1.32	15.85	21.86	9.05	3.58	5.47	1.06	2.96	1.12	1.01
3	253,000	1.24	18.02	22.73	8.22	3.57	4.65	1.04	3.02	.36	.83
4	247,000	1.12	16.34	18.57	8.76	3.89	4.87	.86	3.53	.12	.77
5	228,000	1.03	14.12	14.47	9.56	4.06	5.50	.55	3.94	.31	.44
6	79,000	.93	12.69	12.00	9.75	4.26	5.49	.66	3.88	.64	.60
7	685,000	.86	17.64	15.13	9.39	4.52	4.87	.76	3.74	.32	.54
8	605,000	.79	16.37	13.03	8.28	3.94	4.34	1.04	3.54	.39	.45
Subject Bank	981,000	.75	15.46	11.63	8.48	4.27	4.21	1.13	3.72	.33	.38
10	208,000	.75	17.33	14.09	8.77	4.16	4.60	1.18	4.01	.41	.46
11	616,000	.74	15.72	11.71	8.99	4.41	4.58	1.51	3.87	.85	.30
12	155,000	.68	13.99	9.33	9.47	4.31	5.16	1.10	4.81	.26	.34
13	135,000	.13	11.03	(1.48)	9.11	4.73	4.38	.38	3.66	1.34	(.24)
Subject bank ranking		10	9	11	11	9	13	3	7	6	4
Average	—	.91	15.43	14.44	8.98	4.12	4.86	.93	3.65	.52	.53
Subject bank	—	.75	15.46	11.63	8.49	4.27	4.21	1.13	3.72	.33	.38
Difference	—	.16	.03	2.81	(.50)	.15	(.65)	.20	.07	(.19)	(.15)

*In this example the provision plus securities gains and losses is used as a surrogate for asset losses. As with each of the six areas, supporting information must be thoroughly analyzed before any conclusions are reached. Also, taxes reported by a bank can be very misleading due to holding company consolidation, and further research is always needed in this area as well.

one year, a five year analysis, focusing on the same issues, was also performed, as were analyses comparing each bank with a variety of carefully selected peer groups.

As the subject bank's performance is analyzed vis-à-vis its holding company peers in an effort to identify specific sources of earnings enhancement, certain facts immediately attract the analyst's attention. First, only 5 of 13 banks are providing ROEs which the market might consider acceptable (in excess of 15 percent). Second, the subject bank's target of 17.5 percent would not quite place it within the top quartile, and, therefore, management may want to consider rethinking the target, if not now, perhaps in 12 to 18 months.

Third, in terms of earnings enhancement opportunities, the subject bank ranks 11th in interest income, 9th in interest expense, and last in net interest margin. Compared to the peer group average, the subject bank's interest income/average assets ratio is *50 basis points lower*, while its interest expense/ average assets ratio is *15 basis points higher*. Since the total target ROA improvement by year three is 57 basis points, that goal could be met and surpassed simply by achieving "average" performance in net interest margin vis-à-vis its holding company peers.

Fourth, looking at the overhead expense/average assets ratio, the analyst will quickly note that the subject bank, the largest in the group, is not benefiting from potential economy of scale advantages, and ranks 7th among the 13 banks.* Reaching the average in this case would contribute an additional 0.07 to ROA. Naturally, since being "average" in any area should hardly be an acceptable goal, management's planning should reflect the expectation of doing considerably better.

Fifth, noninterest income is excellent, and asset quality and tax management do not appear to be areas where signifi-

---

*As many analysts point out, bank performance data do not support the existence of economies of scale in banking. I am convinced, however, that this is invariably a result of poor strategic focus and resource allocation decisions which are not driven by shareholder value considerations. Many banks may not be realizing economies of scale, but others are; it's a function of management quality and focus.

cant opportunities exist. This does not mean, however, that efforts will not be made to seek improvements in these areas.

From this initial effort in seeking specific opportunities through peer group analysis, and assuming average assets over the 3 year period of $1,100,000, we might reach the following preliminary conclusions:

Opportunity Ranking	Area	Additional ROA Potential	Annual $ Equivalent
1	Interest income	at least .50	$5.5 million
2	Interest expense	at least .15	$1.7 million
3	Overhead expense	at least .07	$ .8 million
Total			$8.0 million
		.72	(after tax)

This is fairly consistent with research conducted by the author comparing financial performance of national peer groups to that of the top 25 percent of banks within each peer group. With banks larger than $500 million in assets (see Exhibit 3–5), the biggest differences are in the areas of (1) interest income, (2) overhead expense, (3) noninterest income, (4) interest expense, and (5) charge-offs. For banks under $500 million in assets, noninterest income has been far less significant as a discriminating factor.

Further analysis on the subject bank, using additional peer group comparisons, five year comparisons, and internal studies, confirmed the opportunities cited above. In addition, opportunities to improve the bank's performance in each of the other three areas were identified (non-interest income, asset gains or losses, and taxes).

The next step in the financial performance optimization process, the identification and prioritization of specific earnings enhancement opportunities, is accomplished by conducting in-depth analyses of the profitability dynamics, and related strate-

EXHIBIT 3–5
Dynamics of High Performance (banks $500–$999 million for the year ended 12.31.88)*

Average Asset Analysis	National Peer Group 50th Percentile	High Performance Peer Group (top 25%) 50th Percentile	Difference
ROA	.98	1.49	.51
Interest income	9.06	9.43	.37
Interest expense	4.90	4.80	(.10)
Net int. margin	4.20	4.52	.32
Nonint. income	.91	1.07	.16
Overhead expense	3.35	3.09	(.26)
Salaries and benefits	1.44	1.43	(.01)
Net charge-offs	.31	.22	(.09)
Provision	.31	.22	(.09)
Earning Assets/ Total assets	90.18	91.28	1.10
Loans and leases/ Ave. total assets	64.12	65.58	1.46

*Source: Sheshunoff Information Services, Inc.

gic alternatives, in each of the six areas previously mentioned, starting with interest income.

As a result of this type of analysis, specific strategies can be developed enabling the individual bank to exploit the opportunities having been prioritized.

For each strategy, one or more *strategic action plans* will be created that (*a*) fix accountability for results *with one person*, regardless of how many other individuals and/or departments will make a contribution, (*b*) establish a timetable for implementation, showing each step in the process and by when it is to be completed, (*c*) quantify the financial contribution expected from the strategy, and (*d*) identify all anticipated impediments, and set forth specific tactics for overcoming them.

EXHIBIT 3–6
Mastering the Profitability Dynamics of High Performance

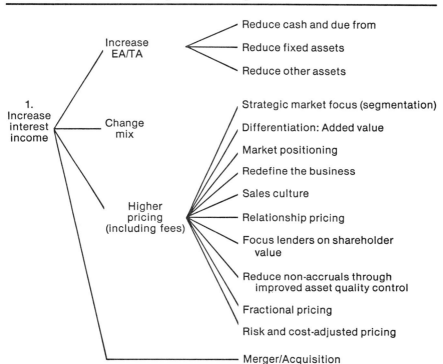

The Profitability Dynamics of Interest Income

As shown in Exhibit 3–6, there are three primary profitability dynamics which influence the interest income/average assets ratio: (1) earning assets/total assets ratio, (2) earning asset mix, and (3) pricing, including fees, as well as an external dynamic, merger/acquisition, which can also be used to enhance interest income/average assets.

Earning versus Nonearning Assets

Attention should first be directed at the possibility of converting nonearning assets to earning assets, especially given the unique leveraging opportunities available to commercial banks. The three categories of nonearning assets, (1) cash and due-from, (2) fixed assets, and (3) "other" assets, must be subjected to an in-depth analysis to identify specific opportunities.

Continuing with the same subject bank and peer group, an analysis of nonearning assets indicates the following (Exhibit 3–7):

EXHIBIT 3–7
Nonearning Asset Analysis (as a percent of total assets)

Bank	Cash and Due-from	Fixed Assets	Other Assets	Total Nonearning Assets	Total Earning Assets
1	8.5	.9	1.3	10.7	89.3
2	7.1	1.0	1.2	9.2	90.8
3	8.3	.6	2.9	11.8	88.2
4	6.0	1.3	1.3	8.6	91.4
5	5.4	.6	1.1	7.1	92.9
6	4.7	1.0	1.4	7.1	92.9
7	5.8	.8	1.4	8.0	92.0
8	7.8	1.4	1.5	10.6	89.4
9*	6.9	1.5	1.7	10.1	89.9
10	7.2	1.1	1.9	10.1	89.9
11	6.5	1.6	1.2	9.2	90.8
12	6.3	1.1	2.0	9.5	90.5
13	6.3	.7	1.5	8.5	91.5
Subject bank ranking	8	12	11	9	9
Average	6.7	1.1	1.6	9.3	90.7
Subject bank less average	.2	.4	.1	.8	.8

*Subject bank.

Clearly, the type of businesses in which a bank elects to compete will have an impact on the level of nonearning assets, as will factors such as the bank's location, number of facilities, and growth rate. However, by comparing a bank to banks of similar size, in similar markets, and in similar lines of business, opportunities for improvement can generally be found.

Because most bankers have not benefited from exposure to

the back room operations of a broad cross section of banks, and or find it impossible to keep up with the proliferation of new technology available to commercial banks, significant operating improvement frequently requires outside intervention from specialists who can share their broad experience and expertise. For those banks which have been unsuccessful in finding solutions to the problems of excessive nonearning assets and/or operating expenses, outside assistance may be extremely beneficial.

As an illustration of the importance of the earning asset/average asset ratio, a $500 million bank that can reduce nonearning assets from 10 percent to 9 percent by converting $5 million to earning assets (assuming an interest income/average assets rate of 10 percent), could theoretically increase interest income by approximately $500,000 per annum.

Recall that the subject bank's interest income/average assets ratio was 0.50 below its peer group *average*. Since the bank's average assets for the year reviewed were $981 million, the interest income shortfall vis-à-vis the peer group was $4.9 million ($981 million × .50 percent). How much of this was attributable to the fact that the bank's earning assets/total assets ratio is lower by 0.80 (90.7 percent to 89.9 percent)? Obviously, not much. The excess nonearning assets totaled $7,848,000 (0.80 percent × $981 million). If we apply the subject bank's interest income/average assets rate of 8.48 percent, we have a shortfall (lost opportunity) of $665,510 ($7,848,000 × 0.0848), which represents but 14 percent of the total shortfall of $4.9 million. This means, of course, that the bulk of the problem, approximately $4.2 million, is a result of mix and/or pricing weaknesses. (Recall that we have already discounted market differences as a significant factor in this particular instance.)

Earning Power Enhancement via Sale-Leaseback

Even though the analysis to this point indicates that only 14 percent of the "problem" is due to high nonearning assets, the possibility of generating upwards of $665,510 in additional interest income is not insignificant. Furthermore, it fails to take into account the ongoing asset expansion made possible by the conversion as earnings are capitalized and leveraged. There-fore, all options should be explored to reduce cash and due-from, fixed assets, and/or other assets, thereby improving the bank's earning power. For example, the subject bank in this case rec-ognized an opportunity to convert specific nonearning assets to earning assets through real estate and equipment sale-lease-backs, an increasingly popular strategic restructuring tool. Be-cause the market value of the bank's real property exceeded book value by almost $4 million, its reported ROA was actually

EXHIBIT 3–8
Sale-Leaseback Summary

Background Information
1. Bank assets $950 million
2. Sale-leaseback (RE)
    A. Fair market value (net) $8,002,500
    B. Book value (including land) $4,237,287
    C. Land value $ 593,323
    D. Gross profit $3,765,213
    E. Tax basis $4,237,287
    F. Taxable gain $3,765,213
3. Capital/assets—7.77% (equity multiplier 12.87)
4. ROA prior to sale-leaseback .80%
5. Tax rate 38.87%
6. Lease term 15 years
7. Capitalization/discount rate 10%

Sale-Leaseback Impact (total over 15-year term)
1. Conversion spread* $3,877,515
2. Gross profit differential* $3,765,213
3. Depreciation stretch* $3,312,695
4. Expansion profit* $52,724,382
5. Total incremental $55,924,775
    pretax income
6. Tax expense   ($21,737,960)
7. Total incremental $34,186,815
    aftertax income
8. ROA (sale-leaseback
    transaction only)

Year	1	2	3	4	5	6	7	8
ROA	6.95	4.25	3.25	2.82	2.57	2.41	2.27	2.20

Year	9	10	11	12	13	14	15
ROA	2.16	2.12	2.10	2.09	2.08	2.08	2.08

*Industry technical terms with reference to sale-leasebacks.

overstated. By releasing the total earnings power (includes asset expansion) represented by its real property nonearning assets ($8,002,500) the bank, as shown in Exhibit 3–8, could actually generate over $34 million in incremental aftertax income over the 15 year term of the sale-leaseback, thereby significantly improving ROA, ROE, and shareholder value.

Whereas sale-leasebacks were once viewed as a desperation move to provide liquidity, their ability to enhance capital and increase earnings, utilizing proper structuring techniques, were virtually ignored. Properly structured sale-leasebacks of both real and personal property, especially in light of new tax laws, accounting conventions, and analysis techniques, are now recognized as one of the most viable restructuring alternatives available to a financial institution.[13] Unlike many restructuring techniques, which are essentially defensive in nature, sale-leasebacks are designed to enhance an organization's earnings power and as such represent an offensive strategy.

Analyzing Earning Asset Mix

Once opportunities to improve the earning assets/total assets ratio have been identified and prioritized, the next step is to conduct a thorough analysis of earning asset mix, including loan mix, investment mix, and the impact of nonaccruals.

At this point the analyst will want to reassess past decisions regarding the various earning asset "businesses" in which the bank operates. While volume, yield, and risk for each category must be evaluated, so too must the capital requirements, funding costs, overhead expenses, noninterest income contribution, tax considerations, and asset/liability management considerations. In this way ROA can be evaluated for each earning asset "business," as can the relative interest rate risk. This will often prompt some degree of strategic restructuring as the earning asset mix is realigned to improve return on capital and shareholder value. Furthermore, much of the tax planning in financial institutions relates to managing the mix of earning assets.

Referring again to the peer group example used above, the subject bank had the highest loan/deposit ratio among the 13 banks, and a loan mix that differed but slightly from the more profitable banks in the group. While the subject bank had somewhat higher percentages of commercial and real estate loans, and a slightly lower percentage of consumer loans, the differences in mix could explain but a small portion of the remaining $4.2 million shortfall in interest income. Therefore, the primary problem was determined to be pricing. Had opportunities been identified relating to changing earning asset mix, the reader will note from Exhibit 3–6 that the strategic alternatives are primarily marketing related.

For example, increased penetration in a specific area, such as mortgage lending, requires the development of exploitable and sustainable competitive advantage, a sales culture, and an intelligent promotion plan, all of which are marketing oriented.

Pricing

Referring to Exhibit 3–6, the reader will observe that the key strategic issues dealing with increased pricing are, for the most part, not financial but rather a function of the organization's corporate culture and marketing strategies. (These issues will be covered in more detail in Chapters 4 and 5.)

The primary cultural issue deals with the extent to which the bank's lending officers (a) realize they are working for the shareholders—not the borrowers (are strategically focused), (b) perceive a direct relationship between performance reviews, compensation, and shareholder value creation, (c) understand the profitability dynamics of the bank as a whole, and their "businesses" specifically, (d) are committed to bringing added value *personally* to the relationship that will justify premium pricing, (e) have the skills, confidence, and product benefits to become aggressive and successful salespeople, and (f) have assimilated the bank's philosophy and core values.

The marketing issues relate primarily to the concept of added value or competitive advantage. If all a bank offers is a generic product, which is perceived by the market as such, its lending officers have good reason to believe that they have nothing other than price with which to compete. In essence, they simply have nothing to sell. The single biggest difference between high performing banks and their less successful counterparts is that the high performers have created added value on the earning asset side, primarily in the form of exceptional personnel and superior technological support which allows a premium pricing strategy and a sales-oriented culture. They also tend to be cost-effective operators.

Fractional Pricing

One highly effective pricing strategy (which was shared with me by Mike Morrow at Alex Sheshunoff & Co.) is known as "fractional pricing" (referred to in Exhibit 3–6). Instead of pricing at the quarter (10 percent, 10.25 percent, 10.50 percent, 10.75 percent, etc.) many successful banks will add a fraction and price the loan at, say 10.19 percent, 10.44 percent, 10.69 percent, and so forth.

Pricing at the quarter encourages price negotiation. When the borrower says "What, 10.50 percent? I was expecting 10 percent!" the lender, all too often, will "compromise" at 10.25 percent. Fractional pricing makes negotiation, and lender concession, less likely, and has proved to work well for many banks throughout the country.

While there is no shortage of pricing models available, the important considerations, in my view, are to (a) begin with shareholder value and return on equity targets, (b) factor in the relevant capital requirement(s), (c) factor in all the ROA criteria (cost of funds, overhead expense, asset loss or risk factor, fee-income potential, and a tax factor), and (d) establish the pricing matrix. However, it is important to bear in mind that it is not the pricing model used which creates the added value, commitment, and earnings needed to be a high performer; it is the bank's overall strategic focus, marketing and sales competence, and corporate culture from which that is derived. Therefore, when banks create financial strategies, no matter how sound, and fail to modify the culture and develop appropriate supportive marketing strategies, performance rarely improves.

As seen in Exhibit 3–6, a fourth dynamic variable, merger/acquisition, can also be used to enhance overall interest income/average assets. Quite often, in fact, a major consideration in a merger or acquisition is the extent to which the resulting entity will contribute to greater interest earning power.

To summarize, interest income/average assets can be enhanced in four primary ways: (1) increasing earning assets/total assets, (2) changing earning asset mix, (3) higher pricing, including fees, and (4) merger/acquisition. For strategies in these areas to succeed, cultural impediments must be identified and overcome, and added value-oriented marketing strategies created, implemented, and managed.

In the case of the subject bank, real and personal property sale-leasebacks were structured to convert nonearning assets to earning assets, minor changes were made in earning asset mix, and an aggressive new pricing strategy was implemented (including fractional pricing) supported by (a) changes in leadership style, (b) greater strategic focus (including performance standards and targets, performance review, and performance-based compensation), (c) measurement of yields on all portfolios by officer, (d) accelerated training for all lenders, including sales training, and (e) added value marketing strategies.

The overall impact of these changes was projected to be a 50 basis point improvement in interest income/average assets by year 3 of the three-year planning horizon. In addition, an intense training program was initiated to convert lending officers to "financing" officers, to make them customer and market needs driven rather than product driven.

The Profitability Dynamics of Interest Expense

As shown in Exhibit 3–9, there are only two dynamic variables affecting interest expense: (1) mix and (2) pricing, with merger/acquisition also representing a viable external strategy, as it does for interest income.

There are several reasons why interest expense is not nearly as discriminating a factor in differentiating high performing banks as is interest income. Deposit products are perceived as a commodity to a greater extent than are loan products and, as such, are less easily differentiated. In addition, deposit advertising tends to be almost entirely oriented around price. Also, many banks, especially high performers, tend to be asset driven, that is, they are successful in generating quality loans, price aggressively, and are willing to be competitive in deposit pricing in order to fund their earning assets. Their in-

EXHIBIT 3-9
Mastering the Profitability Dynamics of High Performance

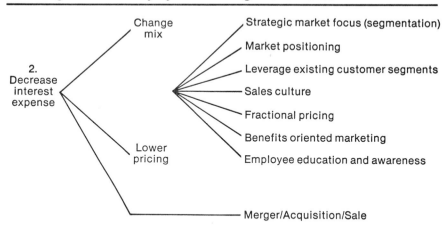

2.
Decrease
interest
expense

Change
mix

Lower
pricing

Strategic market focus (segmentation)

Market positioning

Leverage existing customer segments

Sales culture

Fractional pricing

Benefits oriented marketing

Employee education and awareness

Merger/Acquisition/Sale

terest expense ratio may be high, but they more than offset that disadvantage with higher interest income.

In managing interest expense for high performance, therefore, it is important to bear in mind that a bank's ability to keep the controllable interest expense component of funding costs as low as possible, through mix and/or pricing, is primarily a function of creating added value that transcends price.[14] Realistically, however, it must be recognized that it is easier to create added value on the asset side, that interest expense is only one component of total funding cost, and that the spread is more important than interest expense alone.

Interest Expense, Corporate Culture, and Strategic Focus

Cultural issues also play an important role in managing interest expense for high performance. In my experience, too few customer contact people in most banks are focused strategically. More specifically, a large percentage of the work force believes that (*a*) the bank is already as profitable as it needs to be (even when it is losing money!), (*b*) the bank's overriding objective, and theirs, is to make customers happy, (c) the bank's prices are not competitive, and are therefore unfair, (d) management preaches "customer satisfaction" but, based on pricing decisions and policies, clearly doesn't mean it, and (e) the bank is immortal and will be there forever (therefore, they will always have a job).

Because, in many cases, employees have been told so often that the bank's overriding objective is to satisfy the customer, they quite naturally perceive as irrational any pricing decisions, whether relating to deposits, service charges, or loans, which are not the most competitive in town. After all, if the objective is truly to make the customer happy, the proper strategies are clear: (1) pay the highest rates on deposits, (2) eliminate service charges, (or at least keep them lower than everyone elses), (3) charge the lowest rates in town on loans, and (4) implement a "just say yes" lending policy. It should come as no surprise that in many banks the majority of the employees, through no conscious fault of their own, are part of the problem rather than part of the solution. Because they have not been focused strategically, they are confusing strategies (satisfy the customer) with objectives (profitability and shareholder value creation).[15]

To implement and manage successfully a high performance pricing strategy requires strategic focus *at all levels*. Customer contact personnel, who more than anyone else need to understand and support the rationale underlying pricing strategy, are typically the least informed. Creating strategic focus at the customer contact level is therefore one of the key imperatives in managing interest expense. The preconception held by many bankers is that customer contact employees don't want to know about goals and objectives, especially those involving ROA and ROE, and couldn't understand them anyway. My experience, in banks all over America, indicates just the opposite; bank employees not only want to know where the bank is going and what their role is, but are fully capable of understanding the financial goals and why they are important.

In the case of the subject bank, strategies were designed and implemented to reduce interest expense by 15 basis points.

The cornerstone of this strategy included: (1) a major program to educate and focus strategically all customer contact employees, (2) a greater emphasis on market research (focus groups) and value-added product development, (3) an incentive plan to support a sales strategy designed to change mix, (4) sales and product knowledge training, (5) sales tracking, (6) a sales manager, and (7) a benefits-oriented (as opposed to price-oriented) marketing strategy using TV, radio, outdoor, and print media, along with direct marketing.

The Profitability Dynamics of Noninterest Income

Noninterest income has become increasingly important in recent years. Whereas noninterest income accounted for only 9.6 percent of gross revenue for U.S. commercial banks in 1984, it contributed 14.3 percent in 1988. However, improvement is becoming harder to achieve and growth in noninterest income relative to gross revenue is clearly slowing.[16]

Exhibit 3–5 indicates that for banks in the $500 million to $1 billion peer group, noninterest income is a fairly significant discriminating factor for high performers, contributing 16 basis points of the total 51 basis point superiority. Because many noninterest earning streams are not asset based and can have a powerful impact on overall bank ROA, they will become increasingly important in the 1990s for banks of all sizes. As illustrated in Exhibit 3–10, there are essentially four dynamic variables associated with noninterest income: (1) pricing, (2) waiver management, (3) diversification (new sources of fee income either generated internally or through strategic alliances), and (4) deposit-mix management.

Every bank, in my opinion, should have a pricing committee, comprised of representatives from all levels and functional areas of the bank. On a regular basis (quarterly, for example), all services provided by the bank (even those given away free), as well as the current price structure, should be reviewed and compared to the competition and to the value provided. Costs for each service should also be quantified as precisely as possi-

EXHIBIT 3–10
Mastering the Profitability Dynamics of High Performance

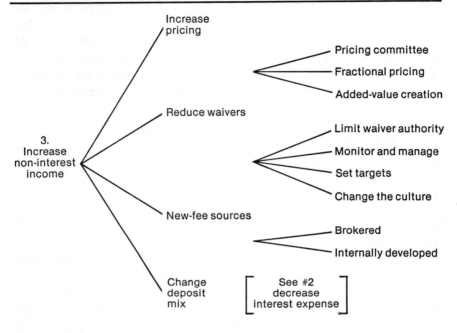

ble, and an attempt should be made to estimate the extent to which volume might be affected by a pricing change (elasticity of demand). Ways to add value should be considered when the incremental cost will be more than offset by incremental pricing opportunities. Naturally, decisions to add value should not be made based on assumptions regarding customer reaction and interest, but should emanate from market research, including focus groups, whenever possible.

Fractional pricing strategies can also be used effectively when pricing services. When raising the charge for an overdraft from $10.00, for example, it is not necessary to wait until $12.50 can be defended, although it is surprising to observe the number of bankers who impose such a constraint on their thinking. It is quite possible to go to $10.85, or $11.15—less noticeable changes which might be implemented sooner.

Managing Waivers Effectively

With respect to waivers, most banks in recent years have managed to improve dramatically their control in this area. Five key steps are needed to maintain an effective waiver control program:

1. Ongoing education and awareness sessions for all employees (strategic focus).
2. Limiting of waiver authority to a few key people.
3. A system that (*a*) makes it harder to waive than not waive, (*b*) monitors total waivers by officer, and as a percentage of total potential service charges, (*c*) sets specific targets (such as waivers not to exceed 5 percent of total potential service charges), and (*d*) outlines clearly the conditions under which waiving a charge is acceptable.
4. Consequences for those who violate or abuse the system and rewards for those who refuse to "give the bank away."
5. The proper example set by senior management (especially the CEO, who is often the person waiving the most charges in many smaller banks).

Diversification and New Sources of Fee Income

As increased pressure on spreads makes intermediation alone less capable of generating adequate earnings streams, bankers are quite naturally seeking new sources of fee income. This makes good strategic sense to the extent that the existing customer base and delivery system can be leveraged more effectively. Just as McDonald's has added breakfast, chicken and fish products, salads, and sundaes to its original burger options, so might a bank, in theory at least, provide additional services, either generated internally or brokered from third parties, to its existing customer base through its in-place delivery system and existing capital base. This will be discussed in greater depth in Chapter 5.

The delivery of insurance and brokerage services, often via strategic alliances with third parties specializing in such relationships, represents perhaps the most logical application of this concept. In addition, the leveraging of existing technology and expertise to provide specialized services to specific market segments, including other financial institutions, can make sense strategically for those banks innovative enough to have established a competitive advantage. The key is to motivate bank officers to think and act as entrepreneurs; to be sensitive to opportunities which they are currently not seeing because they are blinded by the traditional paradigm. This, in turn, will require a change in leadership style and focus from the top.

Important fee income opportunities also lie hidden in the commercial borrowing base of most banks. As mentioned earlier, leasing, including vendor finance programs and sale-leasebacks, has become a rapidly growing $120 billion per year business. Many leasing companies borrow from commercial banks to fund leases made to the banks' own customers, and are generating a higher return on equity than the banks themselves!

By positioning themselves to meet the total financing needs of their corporate customers, perhaps through strategic fee sharing alliances with outside financing specialists, banks can improve earnings while at the same time bringing added value to their corporate relationships.

In the case of the subject bank, a 15-basis point improvement in noninterest income was projected. Major strategies included (a) sales training and incentives for all lending officers on Trust-oriented products, (b) an incentive plan for the Trust department itself, (c) a Trust pricing committee, (d) tighter waiver control in the bank's 24 branches, (e) fractional pricing on business account charges, (f) elimination of the "volume discount" on NSF and OD charges, (g) consideration of "space and fee sharing" with a leading mutual fund company, and (h) the delivery of marketing services, including research (where the bank has a competitive advantage), to other holding company banks for a fee.

The Profitability Dynamics of Overhead (Noninterest) Expense

Like each of the other five dynamic variables of ROA, overhead expense must not be analyzed in a vacuum. All expenses are, in theory at least, related somehow to earnings. Because a bank's ability to conduct earnings-generating activities is granted by regulatory entities, even expenses to meet the broad array of compliance requirements can be allocated to profit centers.

Essentially, the primary expense control challenge banks face is to lower the expense of intermediation by reducing per-unit costs relating to (*a*) the creation and management of earning assets and (*b*) funding, while at the same time delivering fee-based services as cost effectively as possible.

Based on research conducted by First Manhattan Consulting Group, and reported in *ABA Bankers Weekly:* "Superior expense control can increase return on equity more than 3 percent

EXHIBIT 3–11
Mastering the Profitability Dynamics of High Performance

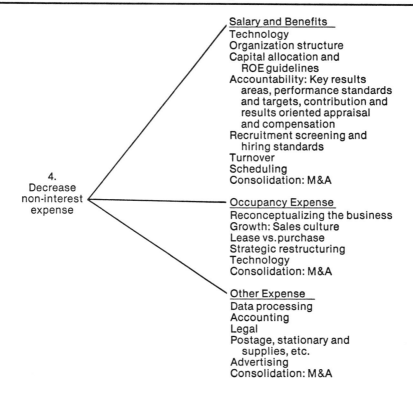

and stock price more than 40 percent."[17] Clearly, the financial markets, in placing a value on bank stocks, seem to be influenced strongly by the extent to which management is perceived as controlling overhead costs. Inefficiencies in this area tend to make a bank more vulnerable to an unwanted takeover attempt and, one way or another, shortchange the shareholder.

As can be seen in Exhibit 3–11, and as discussed below, there are three broad categories of noninterest expense: (1) salary and benefits, (2) occupancy expense, and (3) "other" expense.

1. Salary and Benefits

Because salary and benefit expense represents approximately 50 percent of total overhead expense, and because it is often perceived as being less fixed and more amenable to intervention, much of the emphasis in expense control is on reducing salary and benefit costs. In this regard, one of the best solutions relates to organization structure redesign.

Changes in the Organization Structure

Because most bank organization structures have evolved over time, rather than having been designed as a strategic tool, they often impede rather than support the realization of the bank's Strategic Vision. Organization redesign, therefore, represents one of the most important areas of opportunity for those bankers seeking more efficient operations, and a reduction in salary and benefit expense.

Organization structure refers to issues such as (*a*) how jobs are defined, (*b*) how jobs are combined or grouped, (*c*) the appropriate size of each work group, (*d*) management span of control, (*e*) reporting relationships, (*f*) how people and technology will be integrated, (*g*) how the organization will be exposed to the "outside" world, and (*h*) how authority will be distributed.

There is no such thing as a perfect "one size fits all" organization structure. Attempting to copy someone else makes no sense because organization structure, to be effective, must be customized to meet the strategic needs of the individual institution, and will undergo modification as strategy changes.

Key Issues in Organization Structure Redesign

In my view, as a bank attempts to redesign its organization structure to make it more compatible with, and supportive of, the bank's Strategic Vision, several relevant issues should be considered:

The structure should be designed around the bank's business definition, Strategic Vision, and master strategy. Capital should then be allocated to the various operating or business units as they are reflected in the organization structure. Only then can management eliminate with confidence those which are inefficient and incapable of generating returns which exceed the cost of capital, while reallocating that capital to those that can. In other words, the banker must make sure there is compatibility between the lines of business the organization chooses to be in, the organization structure, and the allocation and management of capital. This will contribute greatly to more cost-effective operations.

Bankers must not allow preconceived notions regarding structure to constrain their ability to become more efficient. Most banks have no choice but to reduce salary and benefits expense in order to reduce per-unit costs and deliver more acceptable shareholder returns. The savings needed will not come from eliminating lower paid people but will result from having fewer highly paid people, with broader spans of control, greater management skills and accountability, *and supervisory responsibility which may cross existing functional boundaries.* In other words, banks must not let "turf" considerations and the artificial barriers created by functions or divisions constrain their ability to achieve larger spans of control and greater operating efficiency.

Two of the key developments supporting broader spans of control are new information technology and more creative use of that already in place. According to an article in *Fortune,* "With the help of information technology, managers can increase by several magnitudes the number of people reporting to them."[18]

Writing in *Harvard Business Review,* Drucker agrees: "The second area that is affected when a company focuses its data processing capacity on producing information is its organization structure. Almost immediately, it becomes clear that both the number of management levels and the number of managers can be sharply cut."[19]

The stratification of a bank's human assets by salary typically reveals a ratio of lower paid to higher paid workers approximating 3.5:1. I believe that banks seeking high performance can, and must, increase that ratio to somewhere in the neighborhood of 6:1 within the next few years. This will generally improve ROA by at least 10 basis points. The only constraints are (a) paradigm paralysis, (b) poor strategic focus, or (c) a lack of commitment to the change process itself.

In redesigning the organization structure, every effort should be taken to make it as flexible and adaptable as possible and to accommodate future needs rather than those of the past.

Structure must be viewed as an integral component of the organization's corporate and competitive strategies and, as such, must reflect the needs and priorities of the organization *going forward*, not those which no longer exist. An adaptive, dynamic strategy and a rigid, static structure are simply not compatible. This is not to say that structure must be modified every time strategies are changed. However, the appropriateness of the existing structure must constantly be challenged when new strategic initiatives are considered, developed, and implemented. An inappropriate organization structure can doom a new strategy before it ever has a chance to get off the ground.

Bank organization structures in the 1990s must be designed with the bank's sales and marketing goals in mind. They must put the bank's key people closer to the customers, especially the most profitable 20 percent, and must be designed to allow the bank to receive continuous, immediate input from its markets, and to respond immediately to customer needs and changing market conditions, including competitor initiatives. Senior managers especially, under traditional structures, have been too far removed from the front lines by an excessive number of management layers. As a result, too many key strategic decisions have been made with no feel whatsoever for the marketplace. That has got to change. In addition, because suc-

---

Organization Structure Redesign

Make sure that the organization structure:

1. Reflects the business in which the bank has chosen to compete, as well as the manner in which capital has been allocated;
2. Supports the overriding objective of increasing shareholder value, and does not mask inefficiences and incompetence;
3. Is compatible with, and supportive of, the bank's strategic vision;
4. Is not limited by self-imposed constraints based on imaginary boundaries between functional areas;
5. Uses information technology, accountability-based reporting systems, and higher standards of management performance to increase spans of control, reduce layers of management, increase the ratio of lower paid to higher paid people, and provide instant feedback on organizational performance;
6. Supports sales and marketing goals by accelerating the flow of information between the bank's personnel and its customers and potential customers;
7. Creates competitive advantage; adds value for the customer;
8. Makes the organization more flexible and adaptable to change;
9. Replaces rigid hierarchies with informal, open systems, and makes everyone feel important, valuable, needed, appreciated, and "part of the team"; adds to feelings of achievement and self-actualization; and
10. Improves the quality and openness of all communication; upward, downward, and horizontal.

---

cessful product development and design must result from a cooperative effort between data processing, operations, legal, marketing, and finance, as well as line functions such as Trust, Retail, and Commercial, bank structural change in the 1990s must enhance dramatically the teamwork and strategically focused interaction between these functional areas.

To the extent possible, organization structures should be designed with an eye to how they might facilitate the creation and delivery of competitive advantage, that is, add value to the relationships with funds providers, funds users, and fee-based service customers. Inherent in such an analysis is the identification of ways in which the existing structure may be doing precisely the opposite.

Organization structure should be used to enhance the ability of people at all levels to (a) comprehend the Strategic Vision, (b) provide creative input to strategy design, (c) work together as a team toward its attainment (rather than at cross-purposes as is so often the case), (d) monitor and reward contribution, and (e) identify and correct behavior or performance which is dysfunctional. Rigid hierarchies must be discarded in favor of more informal systems so that all communication, upward, downward, and horizontal, can be facilitated and enhanced.

Structure should be designed to make *everyone* feel important, so that the individual roles they play are vital and appreciated. All too often, organization structures, especially those that fail to recognize social change and the needs of today's worker, create a rigid class system which one banker, in a corporate culture survey, defined as "an arrogant and detached aristocracy enjoying all the benefits and status of power—while presiding over us 'grunts' who are not considered bright enough, loyal enough, or important enough to be told what's going on." While this clearly represents an extreme example, bank managers must have the courage to take a good, hard, objective look at their existing structures in order to make sure this is not how they are perceived by the majority of the work force. The inflexible class hierarchies of the past are simply not compatible with the needs of today's employees, especially high achievers.

Better Expense Control through Accountability for Results at All Levels

The importance of establishing accountability for results at all levels was discussed in Chapter 2 as being indispensable to mastering the change process, and will be discussed further in Chapter 4. Accountability in banks has traditionally been shared by so many individuals, departments, and committees that no single business unit or person has had "ownership" for specific expense categories. Even when allocations are made, they result as much from political as from economic issues. Often all they really achieve is distributing the excessive costs so broadly that meaningful analysis cannot take place, and no one person can be called to account.

A major factor, therefore, in reducing overhead expense is to design and implement systems at all levels that (*a*) fix accountability for all expense categories by assigning them to operating or business units based on fair economic analysis, and, ultimately, to specific individuals within those units, (*b*) monitor and measure results, and (*c*) provide the appropriate intrinsic and extrinsic consequences.

Technology

Companies such as American Airlines[20] and Fiat[21] have gained significant competitive advantage in highly competitive industries through the strategic use of new technology and many banks throughout the world are doing the same. According to a city of London analyst, for example, European banks will spend $20 billion on new hardware, software, and other technology during the first half of the 1990s, $8 billion more than they are expected to spend on strategic acquisitions related to the new European Community being formed in 1992.[22] Clearly, the strategic use of new technology to create, enhance and/or sustain competitive advantage is an important cornerstone of their competitive strategies. Many major U.S. financial institutions such as Citicorp, Banc One, Bankers Trust, First Wachovia, and CoreStates Financial, have done an excellent job of managing technology strategically and are well positioned to exploit their technological superiority in the 1990s.

Unquestionably, many new technology applications, such as image processing, EDI (electronic data interchange), and networking, all have the potential for improving financial performance in the coming decade, through reduced per-unit costs and/or greater added value, and could provide the basis for sustainable competitive advantage. This is especially true for those banks who are targeting large corporate customers. Security Pacific Automation Company, for example, which has been using imaging in one form or another since 1982, estimates

Industry Specialist's Perspective

Harold Brewer, a former banker and senior officer with Florida Software and Sheshunoff and Company, is a banking consultant living in New Smyrna Beach, Florida.

Question:

Harold, you help banks in adapting strategically to the realities of the new environment—and are a leading specialist in the application of technology to that process. What do you see as the two or three most important technology applications for banks as we enter the 1990s?

Answer:

A common misconception is that the typical bank represents a reasonably good example of how to use advanced technology. In most banks, especially small and medium sized, and all but a few large institutions, this is simply not the case. Generally speaking, banks use very basic technology that has been around for many years to process checks and to process and retrieve accounting information. Beyond that, only a relative few of the more than 14,000 banks could be termed sophisticated, innovative, or advanced. Another interesting situation exists in that the vast majority of bank technology applications deal with the past or at best with the present rather than with the future needs of either the institution or its customers. In other words, technology is used to record events as they occur rather than to shape them.

During the early- and mid-1990s this is certain to change. Less expensive and more capable methods of storing and communicating information will become widespread. Optical disk systems will proliferate and will largely replace physical documents and the attendant inefficiencies in overhead that they entail. This will lead even small banks into a true paperless environment in which computer printouts, loan files, and paper copies of documents of every description will be eliminated completely. Customers will continue to use checks but banks will deal with images.

Improved communication systems involving variations of cellular and microwave technology, as well as improvements in more conventional fibre optic and wire-based fax systems, will allow information and reports that now move via paper to be instantly assessible in virtually any location, fixed or mobile. This technology alone will provide the support medium for a greatly restructured system of branches, credit approval, liability acquisition, and skills allocation in the delivery of financial services.

The 1990s will also see widespread use of so called "expert systems" in all but the smallest banks and even these will be using shared systems. This forward looking technology will become widely used to reduce overhead by optimizing staffing levels to provide "just in time staffing" for customer contact and transaction processing functions such as teller, customer service, and item processing. Additional uses will include asset and liability management and pricing decisions and, of critical importance, the direction and management of sales and marketing efforts at specific customer segments. Expert systems offer the opportunity to spread the skills of a few among many. This will be essential in the 1990s as the business becomes increasingly the domain of those institutions offering superior service at lower per-unit costs while remaining flexible enough to adapt quickly and strategically to initiatives of strong competitors which may not be constrained by geographic and/or product limitations.

that imaging applications could help eliminate two thirds of the 4.5 billion item passes it sends annually through check processing equipment. Payback is projected in 40 months with savings the first five years of $65 million.[23]

However, in many instances where sophisticated new technology is acquired the result will be deteriorating ROE and a reduction in shareholder value. Blake Stiller, writing in *Bankers Monthly*, relates the enormous increase in bank spending on technology to an industry study by Stephen Roach of Morgan Stanley which suggests an actual decline in industry productivity over the same period. Stiller concludes: "Although Roach is a firm believer in the value of technology, his analysis suggests that the continuous acquisition of technology without measuring the value of the benefits produced can easily result in diminishing returns—so diminishing that productivity can actually take a step backward."[24]

The key, once again, is not to confuse objectives with strategies and to make sure that management maintains its strategic focus on competitive advantage and shareholder value creation when making technology decisions. Quite often there are a multitude of good reasons for acquiring new technology, yet the most important questions are never asked: "Will this technology allow the bank to create, enhance, and/or sustain competitive advantage leading to increased shareholder value? If so, how, and by how much?" Based on information provided by the 1989 State of Automation Report (SOAR), few banks ever make an effort to measure technology's actual impact on the bottom line.[25]

Michael Violano makes the point convincingly with respect to platform automation: "The source of the problem lies in the pre-planning stages, because when it comes to branch automation, platform automation in particular, bankers have an amazing propensity for asking the wrong questions. As you dig down to the roots of decision process you find confused or unrealistic objectives, unfocused strategies, and botched banker-vendor communications."[26]

Perhaps the best starting point for most banks is to make sure that the benefits available from existing systems are being fully exploited, especially those that have recently been acquired. Generally speaking, the cultural bias against change limits tremendously the benefit enhancement potential inherent in newly acquired technology. In working with banks having recently gone through data processing conversions, I have almost invariably found that well over 50 percent of the potential benefits and enhanced capabilities associated with the new technology are never utilized. Instead of matching every feature and benefit of the new technology against the strategic priorities of the company (in a matrix, for example), and thereby developing tactics with which to make the resulting system as supportive of strategic change as possible (enhancing productivity or creating competitive advantage, for example), an unconscious conspiracy develops between data processing and the users to make the new system perform as much like the old system as possible, thereby minimizing stress, conflict, and inconvenience. Those whose status results largely from their expertise with the old system will generally be the most resistant to change yet they are often the very ones entrusted with managing the conversion. Until these individuals are focused strategically and reconceptualize their missions, they will be part of the problem rather than part of the solution.

This is just one manifestation of an organization's obsession with preserving the status quo, and just one example of why strategic change must be accompanied by cultural change, the focus of Chapter 4.

In the 1990s the mission of every bank data processing and/ or technology manager (regardless of what they perceive their role to be) must include: (a) helping create shareholder value; (b) reducing per-unit costs related to funding, and the creation, promotion, delivery, and servicing of earning assets and fee-based services; (c) delivering more strategically relevant management information in a more timely fashion and in more appropriate formats; (d) creating targeted added value and superior customer satisfaction which provides a sustainable competitive edge; (e) maximizing sales and marketing effectiveness; (f) contributing to enriched job content and design that increasingly meets the needs of today's workers for achievement and self-actualization; and (g) ensuring that adequate audit and security safeguards are in place to mitigate the risks associated with new technology. Obviously, the fulfillment of such a mission will require a much closer and more focused working relationship on the part of DP with virtually every functional area of the bank, the active participation of the DP manager in the process of strategic management and planning, and new approaches to goal setting, performance review, and compensation.

In my opinion, every bank DP department must have a mission statement, as well as specific, measurable goals in each of the above seven areas against which performance can be evaluated on a regular basis. In other words, bank data processing managers must play a far more proactive role in strategy development and implementation.

2. Occupancy Expense

Referring again to Exhibit 3–11, key strategy areas are listed relating to reducing occupancy expense/average assets.

The first, "reconceptualizing the business," involves rethinking business purpose, mission, and definition, particularly as it relates to the bank's earning assets, fee-based services, and funding.

A classic example is the bank branch; most bank branches exist essentially as funding sources, generating deposits to fund earning assets. However, when the underlying overhead expenses, including occupancy, are converted to a "noninterest funding rate" (through dividing them by total deposits generated), and added to the interest cost, the *total funding cost* is often so high that those funds cannot be invested at a return that exceeds the cost of capital.

If a branch is to be a funding source, an analysis must be performed to determine what levels of deposit volume, interest rate funding cost, noninterest rate funding cost, and fee-based income are needed to deliver funds at an acceptable total funding cost. The market must then be analyzed as to potential, and the branch team strategically focused as to their goals. This almost never happens in the real world. Inefficient branches are a major cause of excessive occupancy expense. A Booz-Allen and Hamilton study in 1988 for the ABA, for example, estimated that nearly 50 percent of all bank branches are unprofitable.[27]

The Branch as a "Retail Store"

One example of attempted reconceptualization is the conversion of the bank branch to a "retail store." The idea, of course, is to leverage the delivery system and customer base by cross-selling more traditional products, as well as new and existing fee-based services, often brokered through or by third parties. "Space and fee sharing" schemes are one example of this overall plan and, quite often, can result in occupancy expenses being fully amortized. A related strategy is to convert an existing branch to a "loan production center," with loans securitized and sold to investors.

A word of caution in branch reconceptualization is in order at this point. Again, the key word is focus. If converting the branch to a "retail store" is the strategy, what is the objective? Higher sales? Not necessarily, because sales in and of themselves don't automatically translate into profits. Hopefully, the objective in most cases will be seen as reducing total funding costs from that source to an acceptable level by offsetting an increasing percentage of those costs with income. Studies supporting the notion that a bank branch/retail store can be economically viable strictly as an outlet for nondeposit related fee-based services. Given the fairly high costs of converting a bank to a "retail store," the underlying analysis should be able to quantify the reduction in funding costs before such a conversion receives serious consideration. In other words, retail bankers must make sure that the objective is clearly understood, that it is indeed an objective, and that the strategy under review makes sense when viewed against that objective.

The second strategy area, "growth and sales culture" is, for most banks with high occupancy expense, the only salvation. Growth may be internal, supported by aggressive sales and marketing strategies and a more supportive culture, or external, via merger or acquisition. The latter can often be an excellent way to leverage excessive fixed costs quickly, thereby justifying a reasonable premium.

The third strategy mentioned in Exhibit 3–11, "lease versus purchase," is an important occupancy expense control issue. The decision to lease or purchase is all too often made on the basis of emotional rather than economic considerations. Owning a nonearning asset, given a bank's ability to leverage capital 12.5 times (at an 8 percent capital ratio), may not make good economic sense. Furthermore, having capital allocated to funding activities, which represent costs rather than earnings, may likewise represent a poor allocation of resources.

Bankers, in order to maximize a bank's earning power, should be able to make sound lease versus purchase decisions regarding all fixed assets. If those skills are currently weak or nonexistent they should be developed or acquired.[28] Increased competency in this area represents a significant opportunity in most banks today.

The fourth strategy, "strategic restructuring," involves a whole series of tactics to reduce occupancy expense. A bank may decide to "spin-off" (sell controlling interest), or "spin-out" (sell less than 50 percent) a subsidiary or line of business. Consolidation, perhaps in conjunction with a merger or acquisition, may represent an appropriate strategy to reduce occupancy and other costs. In other cases, a properly structured sale-leaseback can result in far more effective leveraging of fixed assets, and enhanced earnings power.

Securitization, based on the notion that higher returns on equity can result from packaging and selling, rather than retaining, pools of earning assets, is very much an expense control strategy, as well as a funding and capital management strategy. It will become increasingly important to larger banks in the coming decade.

3. "Other" Noninterest Expense

The third and final component of noninterest expense, "other," contains a major expense category, data processing, as well as less significant but important areas such as advertising, legal, accounting, postage, and so forth. As mentioned earlier, outside intervention may well be needed to realize operating efficiencies fully in these areas.

Referring again to the subject bank in our example, 12 strategic action plans were developed to reduce overhead expense/average assets by at least 15 basis points. Key strategies included: (a) organization structure redesign (consolidation of like departments in different divisions, reduction of several middle management positions, and the ratio of lower paid to higher paid employees increasing from 3.81 percent to 5.50 percent over the planning horizon), (b) the use of new information, analysis, and documentation technology in lending areas to increase productivity, (c) consolidation of investment functions at the holding company, (d) new trust management software and staff reaction, (e) greater use of part-timers and improved scheduling throughout the branch system, (f) an incentive plan for all senior officers with expense reduction as a key component, (g) the reorientation of all branches toward more strategically appropriate objectives with supportive training and compensation programs, and (h) the closing of two branches that could not realistically provide funding at an acceptable cost.

The Profitability Dynamics of Asset Quality

While asset losses are not the most powerful discriminating factor in differentiating high performing banks from the national average, they are certainly a dominant, if not predominant, factor in bank failure. The OCC Failure Report, not surprisingly, shows that 98 percent of failed banks suffered from asset quality problems.[29]

Reducing asset losses in the individual bank represents a journey, not a destination; it is a never ending challenge with one of the greatest dangers being complacency and satisfaction with past performance. Virtually every aspect of the asset management function must be subjected to in depth review on a regular basis. It may also be advisable to commission an outside assessment from time to time.

EXHIBIT 3–12
Mastering the Profitability Dynamics of High Performance

As seen in Exhibit 3–12, 12 key dynamic variables relating to asset quality are listed, each of which has a significant impact on asset quality.

Loan and Investment Policies

Because their purpose is to facilitate the bank's ability to operate successfully and to meet objectives, policies and procedures must be viewed as strategic. As such, they must be reevaluated on a regular basis to ensure that they support, rather than impede, the realization of goals. With the pervasive changes taking place in areas such as (a) the financial and capital markets, (e.g., LBOs), (b) the global macroeconomic environment (globalization), (c) technology (e.g., image processing), (d) the legislative environment (e.g., environmental issues), (e) the legal environment (e.g., lender liability), and (f) accounting conventions (e.g., FASB 95), to list but a few, regular policy reassessment is critical.

Because the bank's overriding objective is the creation of shareholder value, not the minimization of risk, policies and procedures should be directed to the same end.

To be effective, a bank's policies (a) must be understood by everyone whose performance they affect, which requires ongoing training and periodic testing and (b) must be followed, which requires regular monitoring for compliance and the prompt imposition of consequences for failure to comply.

Marketing Focus and Quality

Marketing is every bit as much a profession and a discipline as is commercial lending, trust administration, or investment banking. Credit quality begins with professional marketing, which includes: (a) determining which market segments and specific prospects are most desirable strategically (and which are not), (b) identifying the needs (especially those that are being poorly satisfied) of target market segments, (c) assessing competitor strengths and weaknesses in order to determine which competitor weaknesses can be most effectively exploited, (d) creating added value benefits packages which create competitive advantage, (e) designing a promotion strategy to facilitate the sales effort, and (*f*) creating and supporting a sales culture.[30]

Banks that lack a professional marketing discipline will increasingly be forced to take those credits that no one else wants.

Strategic Focus, Accountability, and the Lending Officer

In my experience, one of the many significant causes of problem loans is the lending officer who (*a*) believes he or she is working for the customer, not the shareholders, (*b*) does not understand the profitability dynamics of the business he or she is in, and (*c*) lacks clearly defined accountability for specific results.

Every lender must first of all understand the bank's financial goals and how his or her job relates to those goals.[31] Key results areas, those that have the greatest impact on the organization's performance, must be identified and prioritized for each job. Examples might include: (*a*) volume (by total dollars and/or by relationship), (*b*) yield, (*c*) trust and other referrals, (*d*) charge-offs and delinquency, (*e*) documentation quality, (*f*) new business, (*g*) account retention, and (*h*) skills upgrading. Performance standards (the minimal acceptable level of performance) and performance targets or goals must then be quantified for each key results area. Individual performance must then be carefully and regularly measured and monitored relative to those goals and extrinsic and intrinsic consequences distributed accordingly.

Training

Because the professional lender must be an expert in many fields, training must be perceived as never ending. Lenders should always be upgrading their skills and knowledge in areas such as accounting, tax law and regulation, macroeconomics, finance, financial analysis, competitive alternatives available to their clients (e.g., leasing), sales, securities underwriting, leveraged buyouts, industry trends, and so forth. In today's increasingly demanding environment, as soon as the lender's learning curve begins to flatten, the lender's value and professionalism begin to decline.

Micro and Macro Analyses

"Micro" analysis deals with properly interpreting all the information revealed in the financial statements, including that which is noticeable by its absence and that which may only be found by reading between the lines. In addition, cash flow analysis has become an integral element in any comprehensive credit analysis package.

"Macro" analysis, on the other hand, involves the "big picture" and deals with issues affecting the borrower's health such as (a) the actual cause of the need to borrow (which is only partially revealed in the financial statements, and even then may only appear well after the request for credit is made), (b) the vulnerability of the business and its industry to economic cycles, (c) vulnerability to rapid technological change, (d) management experience, depth, succession, and breadth, (e) risk management (all insurance coverages), (f) competitive structure and stability of the industry, (g) reliability, concentration, and relative bargaining power of suppliers, (h) diversity, quality, demographics, and relative power of customer base, (i) legal and regulatory vulnerability (IRS, EPA, OSHA, etc.), (j) culture and values, philosophy, and manager/owner "lifestyle," (k) product-line quality, stage of life cycle, breadth, and so forth, (l) quality control, (m) marketing and distribution strength, (n) vulnerability resulting from existing or future unionization, and (o) noncredit risks such as sovereign risk, cross-currency risk, and so forth.

When the negative impact of these issues finally surfaces in the financial statements, it is generally too late to take constructive action. Macroanalysis, therefore, is in many ways more important and valuable than microanalysis, even though they must be used in tandem.[32]

Loan Review: Quality Control

No bank in the environment of the 1990s can afford not to have professional loan review. In smaller banks, where the necessary skills may not be available in-house, they should be contracted from a competent third party, such as a CPA, retired banker or examiner, or a firm specializing in providing that service. Loan review is the bank's early warning system and, if credit policies are up to date and strategically relevant, can be the single best defense against a catastrophic breakdown in asset quality. In those banks for which loan review is "old hat," periodic third party assessment may be advisable to make sure that bad habits have not become normalized, a problem common to troubled banks.

Portfolio Mix: Concentration of Risk

This is, of course, an issue which should be covered in the bank's loan and investment policies. All too often loan portfolios reflect the bank's traditional competencies, the background and "comfort zone" of the CEO, or prior economic and/or market conditions and are not the result of strategic decisions regarding today's realities. As such, the existing portfolio mix may not reflect market opportunities, the highest yield potential, niches where the bank might exploit a competitive advantage, or up-to-date risk considerations.

As has been proven over and over again, concentration of risk, whether in energy, agriculture, real estate, international, or any other area, is a time bomb waiting to go off. In a *Forbes* article extolling the superior performance of Louisiana's Hibernia Corp., the point was emphasized that: "In the early 1980s, when other banks were making as much as 50 percent of their loans in oil and gas, Hibernia never had more than 10 percent of its portfolio in energy."[33] Hibernia is an organization with a powerful sense of strategic focus and refuses to let the herd instinct distract it from its mission. According to Vice Chairman O. C. Russell, Jr., as quoted in *Bankers Monthly*: "Our first obligation is to maximize the return for our shareholders through satisfying our customers. Our philosophy and our mission are always uppermost in our minds and provide us with direction for running our business."[34]

Banks which tolerate excessive concentrations of risk are truly "betting the bank," while those which resist the "herd instinct" generally benefit from their restraint.

Recruitment, Screening, and Hiring Standards

The old ways of recruiting, screening, and hiring those whose decisions have the potential to make or break the bank are no longer good enough. Consolidation in the 1990s will result in many qualified and experienced bankers suddenly finding themselves in the job market, along with an equal number who probably should have been fired long ago. In addition, many highly competent bankers will find the philosophies, corporate cultures, and leadership styles of their new owners not to their liking and will look elsewhere. In other words, the 1990s will be a decade of opportunity with respect to upgrading key positions. Furthermore, a far more competitive and unforgiving environment will make upgrading a necessity. New recruitment techniques, more sophisticated screening and hiring practices, and more strategically sensible compensation policies will all be mandatory.

Approval Process
The loan approval process (including decisions regarding credit limits) and the guidelines and controls underlying investment buying and selling play a vital role in asset quality. There is no "right" system which will fit every bank. The bank's unique circumstances will determine which approach is best. The important thing is to structure an approval process which does not allow anyone, for any reason, to dominate the decision-making process, intimidate other committee members, or violate sound banking practice and bank policy, yet which responds responsibly to borrower needs. Designing systems appropriate to the intensified demands of the 1990s will become a critical success factor for most banks.

The Sixth Dynamic Variable of ROA: Taxes

The decade of the 1980s saw major changes in tax regulations affecting the banking industry. Under the guise of tax "simplification," the management of taxes has become more complicated than ever and the outlook for the 1990s is more of the same. Despite the political commitment to "no new taxes," the burgeoning federal deficit, the S&L bailout, and the need to fund social programs, including the war on drugs, will likely result in additional "simplification," meaning more tightening of perceived loopholes and the creation of new forms of "hidden" taxes. The Alternative Minimum Tax (AMT) is a perfect example.

EXHIBIT 3–13
High Performance Strategy

Financial Strategies	Cultural Change Required?	Marketing Strategy Change Required?
Increase Interest Income		
1. Increase earning assets/total assets	No	No
2. Change earning asset mix	Yes	Yes
3. Change pricing strategies	Yes	Yes
4. Merger or acquisition	Yes	Yes
Decrease Interest Expense		
5. Change funding (deposit) mix	Yes	Yes
6. Change pricing strategies	Yes	Yes
7. Merger or acquisition	Yes	Yes
Increase Noninterest Income		
8. Change pricing	Yes	Yes
9. Reduce waivers	Yes	Yes
10. Find new sources	Yes	Yes
11. Change customer base	Yes	Yes
Decrease Noninterest Expense		
12. Reduce salary/benefits costs	Yes	No
13. Reduce occupancy expense	Yes	Yes
14. Reduce "other" expense	Yes	No
Reduce Asset Losses		
15. Upgrade loan and investment policies	Yes	Yes
16. Sharpen marketing focus and sales skills	Yes	Yes
17. Better strategic focus and accountability for results	Yes	No
18. Enhance training effectiveness	Yes	No
19. Better microanalysis	Yes	No
20. Better macroanalysis	Yes	Yes
21. Better loan review, quality control	Yes	No
22. Lessen portfolio risk	Yes	Yes
23. Higher recruiting, screening, and hiring standards	Yes	Yes
24. More objective approval process	Yes	No
25. Better A/L management	Yes	No
26. Greater responsiveness to problems	Yes	No

SUMMARY

The ongoing viability of any for-profit company is a function of the economic value created for the shareholders. Shareholder value, a function of return on equity, the cost of equity, and the growth of equity, is created when the present value of expected future cash flows or earnings is increasing.

Return on equity, which to a large extent has replaced return on assets as the single most commonly used measure of bank performance, is a function of return on assets and the equity multiplier. Therefore, once the capital ratio has been established for a business entity, ROE is exclusively a function of ROA.

Once a bank has determined the target ROE and capital ratio, and has determined how capital will be allocated, incremental ROA and pretax earnings objectives can be quantified. The next step is to determine from where those incremental earnings will be generated. Because there are only six sources of ROA enhancement, high performing banks will be those who best understand the profitability dynamics of ROA (including the generation of fee income from nonasset-based sources, the most powerful way to enhance noninterest income/average assets for the bank as a whole) and are adept at managing each of the six profitability dynamics strategically.

High performance banks, generally speaking, achieve the bulk of their performance superiority from higher interest income/average assets and lower overhead expense/average assets. Noninterest income is also a significant factor for banks with over $500 million in assets and can be the major source of performance excellence when the bank has a particular specialty where it enjoys a significant competitive advantage.

To be successful, financial performance and shareholder value optimization, as shown in Exhibit 3–13, must be accompanied by supporting and compatible strategies in two other areas, leadership and corporate culture and market positioning, the focus of Chapters 4 and 5.

CHAPTER 4

HIGH PERFORMANCE
LEADERSHIP AND CULTURE

Smart executives are becoming as concerned about their organization's culture as they are about next quarter's earnings. The reason is simple; they realize it affects the bottom line.

—John K. Clemens
Fortune

The only way to influence behavior is to change the culture.

—William G. Ouchi
Theory Z

Once the process of strategic change has begun, initiated by a leader whose commitment is unequivocal, supported by enlightened and enthusiastic followers who have been made accountable for results, and focused firmly on a Strategic Vision driven by competitive advantage and shareholder value considerations, a supportive corporate culture becomes increasingly essential for success. When those attitudes and behaviors which create value for the shareholders also create value for the work force and for the customer, superior performance is all but assured. Therefore, in conjunction with the process described in Chapter 3 to master the profitability dynamics of the business, thereby optimizing financial performance and shareholder

---

CEO's Perspective

Robert Zullinger is President and CEO of Franklin Financial Services Corporation in Chambersburg, Pennsylvania.

> **Question:**
>
> **Bob, you have made corporate culture analysis and modification an important part of your strategy to continue your excellent performance in the 1990s. Why do you feel it is so important?**
>
> **Answer:**
>
> The Corporate Culture Analysis has been very important in strategic planning at F & M Trust. Used as an annual "physical examination" or "check-up," we were better able to establish a strategic plan that focused upon our existing strengths and improved upon areas where weaknesses were identified and where possible problems could arise in the future.
>
> Our organization is not only more in tune with the attitudes of our people, but we feel better equipped as a total team to achieve superior performance as a result of this endeavor. Our people know that their input is valued because we have been quick to respond to the weaknesses which the analysis brought to our attention. As a result, they are far more receptive to management's Strategic Vision of our company going forward and are anxious to make a positive contribution. Our culture is becoming far more adaptive and proactive, our strategic focus as a company is much sharper, communication has improved dramatically, and the overall sense of esprit de corps and teamwork has never been better. Because strategies are developed within a broad company framework, the quality of implementation has improved dramatically.
>
> To continue our superior performance in the 1990s will require a much different culture than the one we had in the past and we are confident we are in control of the process by which that culture will be created.

value, a simultaneous process of corporate culture assessment and modification must be undertaken.

WHAT IS CORPORATE CULTURE?

Corporate culture represents the sum total of beliefs, values, attitudes, ideologies, and behavior patterns and norms which are shared and adhered to by a group. To better understand what culture means, consider the related word *cult*. Commonly held beliefs and values typically bind the members of a cult together and strongly influence individual and group behavior. Also, within a company individual and group behaviors are determined to a considerable degree by its corporate culture, and by the subcultures that dominate individual groups throughout the organization. As might be expected, the weaker the overall culture, the greater the likelihood of strong and potentially conflicting subcultures, each with its own set of values and priorities.

Because culture has such a profound impact on the daily behavior of organization members, it is more than something an organization has; in a very real sense, culture defines what the organization *is!* A high performing organization will be characterized by a strong, positive, performance-oriented culture while cultures in poorly performing companies will tend to be weak and fragmented, with little or no emphasis on performance-oriented values. Research provides incontrovertible evidence of the link between corporate culture and organizational performance.

Hofstede, in *Culture's Consequences*, writes: "In general we find that outstandingly successful organizations usually have strong and unique cultures: the successes themselves contribute to the company mythology which reinforces the subculture. Unsuccessful organizations have weak, indifferent subcultures or old subcultures that become sclerosed and can actually prevent the organization's adaptation to changed circumstances."[1]

Schwartz and Davis, writing in *Organizational Dynamics*, go even further: "Apparently, the well-run corporations of the world have distinctive cultures that are somehow responsible for their ability to create, implement, and maintain their world leadership positions."[2]

Within each organization, it seems, are powerful, unwritten behavioral norms or rules which affect virtually every aspect of individual and organizational functioning. The sum total of these rules represents, in essence, a behavioral paradigm: "the way we do things around here." Once these norms are internalized, they are reinforced in a variety of ways, perhaps the most powerful of which is the selection for employment and advancement of those who best reflect and embody those norms, and the rejection and banishment of those who do not. In this way the "purity" of the culture is reinforced and perpetuated.

LEADERSHIP AND CULTURAL CHANGE

Cultural change begins when someone with sufficient power and influence recognizes that the prevailing values, attitudes, behavior patterns, shared conception of "how we do things around here," and notions of what constitutes acceptable performance no longer support the strategic initiatives necessary for survival and superior performance. Traditional bank cultures, for example, because they were created for a world which no longer exists, inhibit the bank's ability to adapt, and must be modified—in many cases dramatically—to support the key strategies on which realization of the Strategic Vision depends. There simply is no other choice.

Even when the need for change is undeniable, however, the initiator of cultural change often acts at considerable personal risk. The first person to expose a culture's weaknesses and flaws vis-à-vis emerging new realities, and to sponsor change initiatives which challenge or violate traditional norms, will generally be perceived as a heretic and, all too often, will suffer a heretic's fate. This is especially true when the initiatives threaten the sources of power of those with considerable influence and authority, whether it be formal or informal. Machiavelli's insights are worth keeping in mind: "The innovator makes enemies of all those who prospered under the old order, and only lukewarm support is forthcoming from those who would prosper under the new."[3]

Therefore, prior to attempting cultural change, the CEO must build an informal coalition of support, a cadre of informed, influential, and dedicated people at all levels who understand the consequences of failure to adapt, are willing to challenge the status quo and commit themselves to the change process, and who will put everything on the line to make positive change happen. Naturally, it is particularly important at this stage to make sure that the board is truly committed to cultural and strategic change. On more than one occasion I have seen a board pull the rug out from under a CEO simply because they didn't have the vision or the courage to see the process through. Once the CEO has the proper support, however, the process of changing the culture can be initiated with a greater degree of confidence.

Employee Reaction to Cultural Change Initiatives

An organization's culture can be its single greatest attribute when that culture is strong, positive, strategically supportive, and in tune with the demands imposed by economic and competitive realities. Conversely, an entrenched culture, dominated by fear of the unknown and preservation of the status quo, can prove extraordinarily impervious to change initiatives regardless of their value, thereby ensuring the company's ultimate demise if radical steps are not taken. According to Ralph H. Killman, writing in *Psychology Today:* "Normal human fear, insecurity, oversensitivity, dependency, and paranoia seem to take over unless there is a concerted effort to establish an adaptive culture. People cope with uncertainty and perceived threats by protecting themselves, by being cautious, by minimizing their risks, by going along with a culture that builds protective barriers around work units and around the whole organization. An adaptive culture, alternatively, requires risk and trust; employees must actively support one another's efforts to identify problems and adapt to solutions. The latter can be accomplished only by a very conscious, well-planned effort at managing culture."[4]

Because the process of crafting and implementing a high performance corporate strategy cannot succeed without an adaptive corporate culture, which will invariably require some degree of culture modification, it is important that the organization's leaders understand what to expect when the process of cultural change is undertaken.

As change initiatives threaten the framework on which an individual's comfort and security have been based, the first reaction is typically *denial*. Stories have been told of people actually reporting to work after being fired, seemingly unable to accept that they no longer have a job. Denial is destructive because it prevents the healing process and keeps one's focus on the past—thereby impeding the individual's ability to come to grips with the changing and uncertain realities which represent the future.

Once an employee finally begins to acknowledge that things are truly different, and that his or her comfort level has been altered permanently, a common reaction is resentment, anger, depression, and *resistance*. Negative aspects of the new reality are often taken personally, and the employee attempts to get even by sabotaging, consciously, and subconsciously, the process of cultural adaptation and strategic change. Absenteeism and tardiness tend to increase, while work quality and productivity decline. Work group cohesiveness, interdepartmental teamwork, and commitment to the customer all suffer as certain individuals and groups attempt to prove that "the whole thing was a dumb idea in the first place."

While many employees will leave the organization during the resistance phase, and others will simply go underground and become perpetual troublemakers, most, at some point, will enter what is known as the *exploration* phase.

As individuals begin to accept that things will never again be the same, recognize that new coalitions of influence are emerging, and realize that they must either buy into the change process or be excluded from the mainstream, a willingness develops, based largely on self-preservation, to explore the new values, assumptions, standards, and realities upon which the new culture is being erected. This phase is critical in that it represents the shift from living in the past to an orientation toward the future. The exploration phase is typically characterized by considerable experimentation as the organization, and almost everyone in it, attempt to create a new order which is compatible with the Strategic Vision and with heightened leadership expectations. Therefore, this phase will be highly stimulating to some, and unbearably stressful to others.

As employees move through the exploration phase, and *if the organization's leadership remains steadfast in its resolve,* more and more people will buy in and reach the *commitment* phase, thereby assimilating the values and behavioral expectations imposed by the new culture.

Because the adaptive company will be characterized as dynamic rather than static, exploration and commitment will become cultural norms and a cornerstone of the new paradigm. A major leadership priority, therefore, must be to devise ways to limit the time spent in the denial and resistance phases, while accelerating the shift to exploration and commitment. One of the best ways to do this, of course, is to communicate clearly (a) the rationale, nature, and direction of the desired changes; (b) leadership's commitment to the change process; (c) the benefits accruing to those who are willing to adapt; and (d) the fate of those who persist in subverting the process. Clear, honest, and rational two-way communication is essential, and must become a characteristic of the new culture.

THE CULTURAL CHANGE PROCESS

To reiterate from Chapter 2, mastery of the process of strategic and cultural change requires the following six components:

1. A new change-oriented state of mind which reflects the absolute and unwavering commitment of the organization's top leadership, and which pervades the entire organization.
2. A Strategic Vision of the organization's future which is different in positive and fundamental ways from today's reality.
3. A clear conception of what business(es) the company is actually in.
4. A shift from annual strategic planning to ongoing Strategic Management and Planning.
5. Strategic focus and accountability for results at all levels.
6. Assessment and modification of the corporate culture in order to create and sustain a culture which is adaptive and strategically supportive.

Whereas the process of cultural change will begin unofficially the moment that someone realizes the old culture is inappropriate and must be changed and will continue with steps one through five above, it begins formally when the decision is made to evaluate the existing culture, the first step in a four-step process.

This process by which culture is made more adaptive and strategically supportive involves four major steps:

1. *Comprehensive Analysis of the Existing Culture.* The existing culture must be analyzed comprehensively to identify, quantify, and rank all cultural strengths and weaknesses. This is generally accomplished through surveys and personal interviews. The results of the analysis must then be shared with the work force. Cultural strengths and weaknesses should be reviewed in a positive and constructive manner in order to get all key issues out in the open.

2. *Definition of the Characteristics of the Desired Culture.* The characteristics of the desired culture must be clearly defined, based on the Strategic Vision, key objectives, and financial performance and market positioning strategies. In my experience, this step is best accomplished using employee work groups. When employees at all levels play a meaningful role in defining the culture that is needed, based on the organization's strategic focus and Strategic Vision, they are more likely to experience a sense of ownership in the cultural change process, thereby minimizing resistance. This also tends to reinforce and clarify the organization's focus, as well as management commitment to the change process itself.

3. *Prioritization of the Specific Areas Requiring Cultural Change.* The major areas where cultural change is required (the "cultural gap") must be prioritized and specific cultural modification strategies developed. This, too, is best accomplished as a group activity. Strict accountability for results must be established at this point, along with an implementation timetable for each culture modification strategy. Because some resistance is inevitable, the major obstacles anticipated by the group should be identified as should the means by which those obstacles will be overcome.

4. *Ongoing Management of the Cultural Change Process.* A system must be put in place to monitor the implementation process, to reassess the culture at regular intervals in order to measure the extent to which tangible and meaningful change is taking place, and to take corrective action when necessary. A detailed discussion of each step follows.

EXHIBIT 4–1
Anatomy of Corporate Culture

Key Culture Components	Specific Cultural Issues
I. Strategic focus	1. Strategic focus. 2. Attitude toward change; adaptability. 3. Accountability for results. 4. Morale. 5. Existence of subversive groups.
II. Leadership	6. Leadership style. 7. Quality of supervision. 8. Organization structure. 9. Conflict resolution. 10. Teamwork. 11. Work group cohesiveness. 12. Favoritism; office politics. 13. Management sensitivity.
III. Rewards and punishments	14. Rewards and punishments; recognition. 15. Rituals. 16. Training. 17. Discrimination. 18. Performance appraisal and employee involvement. 19. Pay for performance. 20. Achievement and self-actualization.
IV. Marketing and customer orientation; sales	21. Commitment to customer satisfaction. 22. Sales culture. 23. Pricing strategy. 24. Policy strategy.
V. Standards and values	25. Value cohesiveness. 26. Personal commitment to excellence. 27. Corporate commitment to excellence. 28. Satisfaction and complacency. 29. Tolerance of mediocrity. 30. Excitement, pride, esprit de corps. 31. Honesty and integrity. 32. Myths and heroes.
VI. Communication	33. Communication.
VII. Systems and policies	34. Systems and policies.

Changing the Corporate Culture: Step 1, Comprehensive Analysis of the Existing Culture

Efforts to assess the culture of a company may range from highly informal (management by wandering around) to extremely formal (elaborate surveys and intervention by change management specialists).

The most effective approach combines the use of a comprehensive survey, completed anonymously by all officers and employees; informal, unannounced visits; and a series of personal interviews. The focus of the interviews, as well as the number of people to be interviewed, will be determined to some extent by the results of the survey and by impressions gathered during the visits.

The survey instrument developed by the author over the past decade includes 66 questions covering 34 important cultural issues in seven major component areas, as shown in Exhibit 4–1. In addition, trends in each of the seven areas are evaluated. Each of the seven areas, including example questions in most cases, will be discussed below, using actual survey results from two U.S. banks, one a high performer (23 percent ROE) with a positive culture (Bank A), and the other a poorly performing bank (6.35 percent ROE) with an extremely weak culture (Bank B).

Methodology

The questionnaire itself presents a series of statements, such as "My own personal philosophy and value systems are very compatible with the philosophy and value system of this organization." The respondent is asked to select the most appropriate response from the following scale:

Response	Points
Strongly agree	6
Agree	4
Weakly agree	2
Neutral	0
Weakly disagree	(2)
Disagree	(4)
Strongly disagree	(6)

The respondent may also select "not relevant to my job."

For each question and component area, the average response score, as well as the percentage selecting each of the eight responses, are then tabulated. These results are presented for each of the following: (a) officers, (b) nonofficers, (c) functional and/or geographical areas, and (d) total. This allows for an analysis of the culture of the organization as a whole as well as for subgroups.

Exhibit 4–2 shows the interpretation scale used to evaluate average responses by individual question, cultural issue, and major component area.

Corporate culture analysis, it should be noted, is considerably more comprehensive and meaningful than employee opinion or attitude surveys. The latter are primarily designed to determine employee's satisfaction levels relative to a variety of issues. Often, in a culture which stresses "warm and fuzzy" relationships rather than high performance, employees are quite satisfied—simply because they are never held accountable for results. *Satisfied employees are not necessarily focused, moti-*

EXHIBIT 4–2
Corporate Culture Assessment Interpreting the Data

4.00 or above	Strong positive Will support corporate strategy; a major corporate strength; nurture and reinforce.
2.00–3.99	Positive Will support strategy but will need ongoing reinforcement to strengthen, especially at lower end.
0–1.99	Weak positive Potential problem area; positive but requires attention; significant negative undercurrent.
(1.99)–0	Weak negative Inadequate organizational support for strategy in this area; will hold the organization back; requires corrective action and monitoring.
(3.99)–(2.00)	Negative A serious impediment to strategy implementation; immediate corrective action and quarterly monitoring required.
(4.00) or below	Strong negative Extremely serious problem; potentially destructive to the organization; demands immediate corrective action and monitoring, perhaps monthly.

vated, or productive. Culture, on the other hand, is highly complex and many dimensions, including employee satisfaction, must be assessed. When it comes to consistently superior financial performance nothing is more important than a strong, positive, adaptive, and strategically supportive culture.

The seven key components of corporate culture follow.

Component 1: Strategic Focus

At this point, it should come as no surprise to the reader that the author considers strategic focus to be a major component of corporate culture. Whether the endeavor be sports, war, politics, or business, one of the primary factors in how well an organization functions is the extent to which the group's energies are integrated toward the attainment of a common goal.

Two important statements related to this issue, and the responses from Banks A and B, are shown below.

STATEMENT 6

"I am confident that I understand the company's financial objectives, be they ROA (return on assets), ROE (return on equity), EPS (earnings per share), or some other measure of performance."

	Bank A			Bank B		
	Officers	Nonofficers	Total	Officers	Nonofficers	Total
Strongly agree	19	6	10	9	0	3
Agree	24	21	22	18	9	12
Weakly agree	24	20	21	18	10	13
Neutral	7	2	4	3	2	2
Weakly disagree	11	12	12	17	19	18
Disagree	10	12	12	18	23	21
Strongly disagree	0	8	5	9	19	16
Not relevant to my job	5	19	14	8	18	15
Average response	2.06	.49	1.01	.02	(2.29)	(1.52)

As the responses indicate, strategic focus in Bank B is extremely weak; approximately one third of the work force has no

STATEMENT 56

"It appears to me that this company has a sound and well-thought-out strategic plan which keeps everyone clearly focused on where we are going and how we intend to get there."

	Bank A			Bank B		
	Officers	Nonofficers	Total	Officers	Nonofficers	Total
Strongly agree	34	36	35	0	0	0
Agree	34	35	35	0	3	2
Weakly agree	20	20	20	0	3	2
Neutral	1	3	2	10	2	5
Weakly disagree	8	3	5	30	35	33
Disagree	2	3	3	43	40	41
Strongly disagree	1	0	0	9	13	11
Not relevant to my job	0	0	0	8	4	6
Average response	3.50	3.78	3.68	(2.86)	(2.90)	(2.88)

idea what the organization's financial objectives might be, and only 4 percent agree that a strategic plan is in place which keeps everyone focused. Another 15 percent consider the issue of financial objectives to be irrelevant to their jobs while 6 percent fail to see the relevance of whether or not a strategic plan exists. Obviously, serious cultural weaknesses exist in this area.

In Bank A, 57 percent of the work force agrees to having an understanding of specific financial goals, and 90 percent believes that a strategic plan is in place which directs the company's efforts. Clearly, Bank A is far more focused strategically. However, since 31 percent of the work force disagrees with Statement 6, while another 14 percent does not feel the existence of a strategic plan is relevant to their jobs, significant room for improvement exists.

One of the primary components of strategic focus is *attitude toward change*, and responses from the two banks relative to this issue are revealing:

STATEMENT 25

"As change increasingly affects our industry, the focus of this organization is on the opportunities, rather than on the threats, which change creates."

	Bank A			Bank B		
	Officers	Nonofficers	Total	Officers	Nonofficers	Total
Strongly agree	25	11	16	0	1	1
Agree	42	42	42	20	19	20
Weakly agree	25	23	24	24	22	25
Neutral	3	8	6	5	3	4
Weakly disagree	3	2	2	21	21	21
Disagree	2	1	2	14	18	16
Strongly disagree	0	0	0	0	6	4
Not relevant to my job	0	13	8	8	10	9
Average response	3.54	3.13	3.26	.54	(.27)	.00

Clearly, Bank A is perceived as having a far more adaptive and proactive attitude toward change. Note that only 3 percent of the officers were neutral while everyone considered the issue to be relevant. In Bank B, 8 percent of the officers felt the issue was irrelevant while another 5 percent were neutral. Imagine how effective these officers must be in directing and motivating their employees to meet the challenges of the new environment.

Exhibits 4–3 and 4–4 show the analysis of the strategic focus component for Bank A and Bank B, respectively.

Component 2: Leadership
According to Edgar H. Schein in *Organizational Culture and Leadership*: "Organizational cultures are created by leaders, and one of the most decisive functions of leadership may well be the creation, the management, and—if and when that may become necessary—the destruction of culture. Culture and leadership, when one examines them closely, are two sides of the same coin, and neither can really be understood by itself. In fact, there is a possibility—underemphasized in leadership re-

EXHIBIT 4–3
Corporate Culture Component Analysis—Bank A
Component 1: Strategic Focus

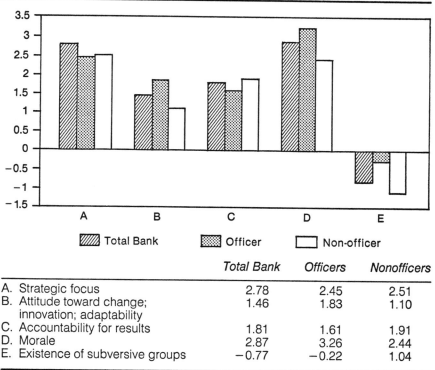

	Total Bank	Officers	Nonofficers
A. Strategic focus	2.78	2.45	2.51
B. Attitude toward change; innovation; adaptability	1.46	1.83	1.10
C. Accountability for results	1.81	1.61	1.91
D. Morale	2.87	3.26	2.44
E. Existence of subversive groups	−0.77	−0.22	1.04

search—that the *only thing of real importance that leaders do is to create and manage culture* and that the unique talent of leaders is their ability to work with culture."[5]

Nothing has a more profound and visible impact on a culture, for good or for ill, than the style, values, and priorities of the organization's leaders. Every strong culture bank has at least one dynamic, focused, and visible leader whose vision and commitment have helped shape the culture to conform to the requirements of the Strategic Vision.

Survey statements dealing with this critically important component include the following:

STATEMENT 49

"The style of leadership in this organization is effective in motivating me to do the best job possible."

	Bank A			Bank B		
	Officers	*Nonofficers*	*Total*	*Officers*	*Nonofficers*	*Total*
Strongly agree	35	18	23	0	0	0
Agree	33	36	35	16	8	11
Weakly agree	16	26	23	20	5	10
Neutral	1	4	3	2	2	2
Weakly disagree	12	9	10	20	30	26
Disagree	2	5	4	26	20	22
Strongly disagree	1	2	2	9	31	24
Not relevant to my job	0	0	0	7	4	5
Average response	3.36	2.54	2.81	(1.01)	(2.96)	(2.31)

   In this comparison, the strong culture in Bank A is epito-
mized by the impact that the leader's style has on motivation
and productivity. Despite the bank's size (over $1 billion in as-
sets) the bank's president makes every effort to talk to individual employees on his frequent visits throughout the branch system. Addressing them by name, he takes the time to inquire
about their children, educational pursuits, hobbies, special projects, and so forth. He has a clear vision of where he wants the
bank to be in the 1990s, knows he can't do it alone, and has
enlisted the enthusiastic support of the vast majority of the
work force to make that shared vision a reality. He understands
that being a leader doesn't necessarily *make* him one and he
works hard at being effective.
   Bank B, on the other hand, is characterized by a leadership
style reminiscent of a bygone era. Paralyzed with fear regarding the future, management rarely communicates with employees (and only then by memo), demonstrates a total lack of
concern for their needs, and makes no effort to solicit their cre-

EXHIBIT 4-4
Corporate Culture Component Analysis—Bank B
Component 1: Strategic Focus

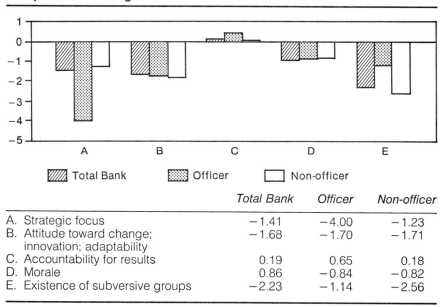

	Total Bank	Officer	Non-officer
A. Strategic focus	−1.41	−4.00	−1.23
B. Attitude toward change; innovation; adaptability	−1.68	−1.70	−1.71
C. Accountability for results	0.19	0.65	0.18
D. Morale	0.86	−0.84	−0.82
E. Existence of subversive groups	−2.23	−1.14	−2.56

ative input. Three out of four workers in this organization do not feel that the prevailing leadership style motivates them to perform to their potential. The organization's consistently substandard performance should come as no surprise.

Quality of Supervision. Leadership style at the top has a significant impact on the quality of supervision throughout the entire organization. When the culture is strong and positive, managers generally seek to emulate the leadership style of the organization's senior officers, especially the CEO. Because superior performance results are expected, the leader's example sets the standard for everyone.

One of the more general statements dealing with quality of supervision is the following:

STATEMENT 19

"Most employees here trust and respect their supervisors."

	Bank A			Bank B		
	Officers	Nonofficers	Total	Officers	Nonofficers	Total
Strongly agree	11	5	7	0	0	0
Agree	32	22	25	13	9	11
Weakly agree	29	21	24	14	10	11
Neutral	4	12	9	0	4	2
Weakly disagree	11	17	15	32	32	32
Disagree	11	20	17	32	34	32
Strongly disagree	2	3	3	9	12	11
Not relevant to my job	0	0	0	0	0	0
Average response	1.72	.28	.76	(1.66)	(2.13)	(1.97)

Bank B continues to demonstrate a strongly negative culture, as might be expected. Trust is practically nonexistent. As is customary in highly negative cultures, the nonofficer response to this question is far more negative than the officer response.

Analyzing Bank A, the 1.72 response from the officers is reasonably high, to some extent a function of the relationship with the organization's charismatic leader. The nonofficer response, however, at 0.28, is quite weak and a cause for concern. *Even in strong culture companies weaknesses exist, and specific opportunities for improvement can always be identified.* In this case, senior management was shocked, and set out immediately to define and correct the problem, which had resulted from extremely fast growth, including the purchase of two branches of another financial institution, and the need to hire a number of managers from the outside who were not products of the bank's culture. A comprehensive orientation program to acquaint all new employees with the bank's cultural values had not previously been needed. Given the bank's geographic expansion, however, and based on the insights provided by the cultural analysis, the need became abundantly clear, as did the advisability of ongoing management and supervisory training.

Organization Structure.   Organization structure, which was discussed in Chapter 3, influences, and is influenced by, the prevailing corporate culture and is related closely to leadership style. Traditional organization structures are a reflection of the old paradigm, designed to exert control over the activities of people and to maintain conformity in a regulated and relatively unchanging world. Bank leaders in the 1990s, however, must be more sales and marketing oriented, more creative and adaptive, more involved in energizing and focusing the culture, and more adept at reconfiguring organizational resources quickly to meet emerging threats and opportunities. As discussed in Chapter 3, modern organization structures must be designed to facilitate these efforts.

Conflict Resolution.   The manner in which conflicts are resolved is another important indicator of how leadership style affects the corporate culture. According to Warren Bennis: "As a former organizational consultant, and now as one who presides over a large institution, I am convinced that how an organization deals with conflict is probably the best clue to its proper functioning."[6]

Organizational conflict is inevitable. The objective, therefore, is not to eliminate conflict, but to manage it in such a way that it becomes healthy and productive, rather than dysfunctional. Management pioneer Mary Parker Follett was one of the first researchers to deal effectively with the notion of "constructive conflict." She observed that conflicts are generally dealt with in one of three ways: (*a*) domination, where one party imposes his or her will or power, (*b*) compromise, where each party gives up something, and (*c*) integration, where a solution is created that accommodates all parties. Naturally, the latter approach is recommended.[7] More recently, several researchers have suggested that conflicts may be approached in one of five ways: (1) *withdrawing or avoiding*—hoping it will simply go away, (2) *smoothing*, which involves covering the conflict up, placating the parties, and pretending conflict doesn't really exist, (3) *bargaining* or compromising, which attempts a solution representing a middle ground, (4) *forcing*, which forces a resolution with the stronger party winning and the weaker party losing, and (5) *constructive confrontation*, or "win-win" problem solving, which attempts to pit the conflicting parties against the problem, rather than against each other.[8] Numerous studies support the notion that high performing companies have, in fact, made win-win problem solving a cultural norm to a greater degree than have their less successful counterparts.[9]

A primary factor in how well an organization resolves conflict internally is the maturity and professionalism of its managers. When managers have a strong sense of self-esteem, are focused strategically, and have clearly defined performance standards and targets for their subordinates with which to evaluate individual contribution, conflicts can be confronted and resolved with a minimum of subjectivity and emotion, thereby facilitating a win-win outcome. On the other hand, when a manager is insecure, goals poorly defined, priorities confused, and no quantifiable standards exist with which to evaluate performance, the almost inevitable outcome is conflict and a "win-lose" situation. A solution is forced, thereby polarizing individuals and work groups within the company.

In traditional bank cultures, conflict was generally dealt with by avoidance, or, when that didn't work, through win-lose outcomes. The emphasis was on control and compliance, not on team building and preserving the self-worth of the individual.

The potential for internal conflict will increase dramatically in the 1990s, and the manner in which conflict is resolved will become an even more important cultural issue. There are several reasons for this: (*a*) organization structures will become flatter, more responsive to the environment, and more flexible, thereby putting greater pressure on individual managers to provide tangible results through their subordinates; (*b*) functional barriers will break down, and ad hoc task forces will be used more extensively to solve problems and develop strategies; (*c*) increasingly, efforts will be made to bring together right-hemisphere and left-hemisphere thinkers in order to develop innovative and analytically sound strategic solutions to emerging competitive challenges; (*d*) the input of workers at all levels, many of whom will have markedly different values and priorities, will be solicited in order to develop new solutions to competitive pressures; (*e*) standards of performance will be quantified even more, thereby making substandard or dysfunctional results more immediately visible, which, in turn, will demand more frequent supervisory intervention; (*f*) increasingly, nonbankers, with different cultural orientations, will be hired as banks redefine their business(es) and seek fresh ideas; (*g*) because banks must become highly adaptive entities, continuous evolution and development will become the norm, thereby causing disruptions with ever increasing frequency; and (*h*) entry-level positions will be filled with increasing numbers of ethnic minorities representing diverse cultural and social backgrounds, thereby creating additional challenges for supervisors and managers.

Avoidance and win-lose conflict resolution styles are totally incompatible with the types of corporate cultures required by banks in the 1990s. Therefore, it is important that bankers gain a clear understanding of how conflicts are currently being dealt with throughout their organizations. Because a particular conflict resolution style tends to become deeply imbedded in an organization's culture, change will not be easy, and will generally require a significant commitment to ongoing training, monitoring, testing, intervention, and reinforcement.

Teamwork.   When the organization's leadership is strong and properly focused, there tends to be a far greater sense of teamwork at every level. Because everyone knows where the organization is going and how it intends to get there, the role of each functional area becomes more clear, as does the need for cooperation and interdependence.

One of the great turnarounds in American corporate history is that of Ford Motor Company. Ford, which most analysts agree was in serious trouble in the 1970s, largely as the result of dramatic changes in government regulation, technology, and competition, became one of the true success stories of the 1980s, due primarily to the visionary guidance of its chief executive,

Donald Petersen. A *Forbes* article provides interesting insights into Petersen's perceptions regarding the importance of culture, teamwork, and his leadership role:

> He could be remembered for the array of pleasing products— Taurus, Probe, Continental—that flowed under his direction, or the record profits, $5.5 billion, expected this year. Or the thirteenfold increase in the stock price the past eight years when the Dow industrials tripled.
>
> But he prefers to dwell on people, attitudes, participation, and teamwork. After all, its no secret that Ford was a clique-ridden company just a few years ago. It was his leadership that turned it into one of the best run companies in the world. How did he work the enormous improvement in teamwork? 'By talking,' he says, 'by listening, by seeing that the shy guy in the corner is encouraged to speak up with his ideas for doing things better.' He says that at Ford today ideas flow from the bottom up, not solely the other way.
>
> 'Changing how people work together is the be-all and end-all of my time with the Ford Motor Co., my contribution.'[10]

By changing the culture at Ford, with a major focus on "changing how people work together," Petersen met the challenge of change head on, created a new paradigm that was compatible with the highly competitive and technologically advanced world of the 1980s, enhanced shareholder value tremendously, and positioned his company to survive and prosper in the 1990s. The challenges many banks face today are remarkably similar to those facing Petersen a decade ago, including the need for cultural modification.

Reinforcing the importance of teamwork as a culture component is the conclusion reached by Levering, Moskowitz and Katz in *The 100 Best Companies to Work for in America*. They report that the number one factor on their list of what makes companies successful is that the excellent firms "make people feel part of a team."[11]

Work Group Cohesiveness. Directly related to teamwork is work group cohesiveness. When organizational teamwork is strong, the cohesiveness and focus of individual work groups generally tend to be strong as well. Occasionally, however, weaknesses may be found in specific work groups even though teamwork overall is perceived positively. In such cases, the interview process can be used to isolate individual problem areas so that corrective measures can be designed and implemented.

Favoritism and Office Politics. According to Mintzberg, "politics" generally includes three types of behavior:

1. Behavior outside of the legitimate systems of influence (or at least outside their legitimate uses), and often in opposition to them; in other words, behavior that is technically illegitimate, and often clandestine.
2. Behavior designed to benefit the individual or group, ostensibly at the expense of the organization at large.
3. As a result of points 1 and 2, behavior typically divisive or conflictive in nature, pitting individuals or groups against the organization at large or against each other.[12]

When favoritism and office politics dominate an organization's functioning, it becomes clear that upward mobility and influence are less a matter of talent and contribution and more a function of "playing politics." Therefore, top performers are encouraged to leave, and organizational priorities are subjugated to ego gratification. Consequently, the extent to which favoritism and office politics are perceived as being an integral part of a culture is an important clue to organizational effectiveness.

A powerfully revealing statement in this regard is the following:

STATEMENT 62

"In this company we do not have any subversive groups (2 or more members) which disrupt effective functioning and/or threaten the stability and integrity of the organization."

	Bank A			Bank B		
	Officers	Nonofficers	Total	Officers	Nonofficers	Total
Strongly agree	11	11	11	0	0	0
Agree	32	30	30	13	9	11

STATEMENT 62 (*continued*)

	Bank A			Bank B		
	Officers	Nonofficers	Total	Officers	Nonofficers	Total
Weakly agree	32	20	24	14	10	11
Neutral	4	10	8	0	4	2
Weakly disagree	11	13	13	32	32	32
Disagree	10	13	13	32	34	33
Strongly disagree	0	3	2	9	12	11
Not relevant to my job	0	0	0	0	0	0
Average response	1.96	1.30	1.52	(1.66)	(2.13)	(1.97)

While the average response for Bank A is in the weak positive range, it appears that 29 percent of the nonofficers believe that at least one subversive group may be disrupting organizational effectiveness. Further inquiry is warranted.

In Bank B the overall negative response of (1.97) indicates a serious problem. Over two thirds of the work force believe that disruptive groups exist.

This particular statement can help bring serious problems to management's attention, thereby presenting an opportunity for positive intervention. On the other hand, failure to identify these types of problems can threaten seriously the organization's ability to bring about necessary strategic and cultural change.

Concern for People: Management Sensitivity. In any organization, employees will have definite feelings regarding the extent to which management is concerned about their needs, opinions, and feelings. Many companies claim "people are our most important asset" yet the rhetoric is often inconsistent with management actions and/or with employee's perceptions. Ironically, the more concerned a company claims to be about its employees, the greater are the expectations, and the more visible the shortcomings. Officer and employee percep-

EXHIBIT 4–5
Corporate Culture Component Analysis—Bank A
Component 2: Leadership

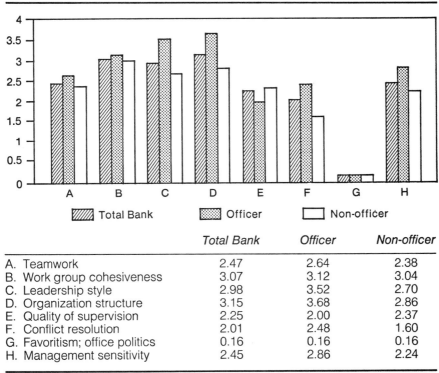

	Total Bank	Officer	Non-officer
A. Teamwork	2.47	2.64	2.38
B. Work group cohesiveness	3.07	3.12	3.04
C. Leadership style	2.98	3.52	2.70
D. Organization structure	3.15	3.68	2.86
E. Quality of supervision	2.25	2.00	2.37
F. Conflict resolution	2.01	2.48	1.60
G. Favoritism; office politics	0.16	0.16	0.16
H. Management sensitivity	2.45	2.86	2.24

tions in this area are extremely important, and, in my experience, are almost always a revelation to top management.

Exhibits 4–5 and 4–6 show the analysis of the leadership component for Bank A and Bank B, respectively.

Component 3: Rewards and Punishments

How an organization elects to reward and punish its members has a profound impact on virtually every aspect of culture. Rewards represent a visible and highly personal manifestation of leadership and management priorities and values, and communicate more powerfully than written and oral pronouncements what behaviors are most highly valued. According to Lawler:

EXHIBIT 4–6
Corporate Culture Component Analysis—Bank B
Component 2: Leadership

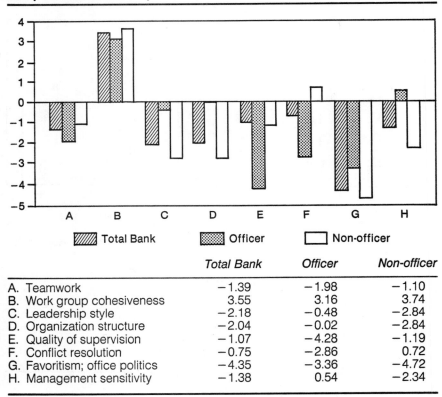

	Total Bank	Officer	Non-officer
A. Teamwork	−1.39	−1.98	−1.10
B. Work group cohesiveness	3.55	3.16	3.74
C. Leadership style	−2.18	−0.48	−2.84
D. Organization structure	−2.04	−0.02	−2.84
E. Quality of supervision	−1.07	−4.28	−1.19
F. Conflict resolution	−0.75	−2.86	0.72
G. Favoritism; office politics	−4.35	−3.36	−4.72
H. Management sensitivity	−1.38	0.54	−2.34

"Reward systems are one feature of organizations that contribute to their overall culture or climate. Depending on how reward systems are developed, administered, and managed, they can cause the culture of an organization to vary quite widely."[13]

Because an organization undergoing strategic change requires unusually strong commitment from its members, they will expect something tangible in return, and the extent to which their expectations are met has a profound influence on the culture that emerges.

One of several revealing statements dealing with this issue is the following:

STATEMENT 55

"Monetary rewards in this company are based on performance and contribution to goals and objectives, not on subjective and nonperformance-based criteria."

	Bank A			Bank B		
	Officers	Nonofficers	Total	Officers	Nonofficers	Total
Strongly agree	13	12	12	0	0	0
Agree	40	40	40	5	6	6
Weakly agree	23	20	21	4	7	6
Neutral	2	3	3	18	13	15
Weakly disagree	7	15	12	36	28	31
Disagree	10	10	10	28	33	31
Strongly disagree	0	0	0	9	13	11
Not relevant to my job	5	0	2	0	0	0
Average response	2.42	2.02	2.15	(2.10)	(2.28)	(2.22)

This statement has proved to have significant discriminating power in that the average response is almost invariably high in strong culture companies, and low in companies with weak and/or negative cultures. Whereas 73 percent of Bank A's employees agree with the statement, only 12 percent of the work force in Bank B feel that monetary rewards reflect performance and contribution. Given the relative financial performance of the two entities, the responses to this question are extremely enlightening.

Rituals to Support Values. Deal and Kennedy write: "Without expressive events, any culture will die. In the absence of ceremony or ritual, important values have no impact."[14]

Rituals are designed to reinforce, in a powerful and incontrovertible way, what the organization's values really are. If new business development is an important value underlying the organization's competitive strategy, then when someone makes a home run—or perhaps even a single—the best way to reaffirm the value's significance to that individual, and, more importantly, to everyone else in the organization, is to do something which reinforces its importance. It may be nonmonetary, such as special recognition in a meeting or an article in the company newspaper. In team sports there are "player of the game" awards, stars on the player's helmets, "golden glove" awards, presentation of the game ball, "all-star" recognition, and even the "high five," all of which are rituals to reinforce desired performance—performance which helps the organization achieve its goals and objectives. Of course, a variety of monetary rewards can also be used to reinforce effectively high performance values.

Many strong culture companies not only have powerful value systems, but also rituals and ceremonies to reinforce those values. Nordstrom, for example, is a top-performing company known for its strong, positive culture and emphasis on rituals. As related in a *Wall Street Journal* article: "The executives also hand out monthly cash prizes to stores that provide the best service. The choice is made on the basis of scrapbooks bulging with letters from customers, copies of thank-you notes salespeople write to their customers, and notes called 'heroics' that salespeople write about each other.

> Salespeople who do especially well are honored monthly as All-Stars. Nordstrom shakes their hand and gives them $100, and the right to big discounts in the store. The most productive are inducted annually into the Pacesetters Club, which also entitles them to big discounts. And the best managers get their names engraved on a plaque in the executive suite."[15]

Rituals seem to be an important priority in high performing companies, especially those that are sales and marketing driven.

Training. In strong culture companies, the commitment to customers and employees is reinforced by an obsession with training as a never ending activity. Furthermore, training is not limited to technical issues, nor is the curriculum designed in a vacuum. Employees have a voice in prioritizing training needs and in developing and evaluating the programs.

In weak culture companies, one of the most frequently reported frustrations concerns a lack of adequate training opportunities, and/or training programs which are perceived as inappropriate. Clearly, training is viewed by most workers as an extremely important issue, especially by high achievers.

How the work force perceives (*a*) the quantity and quality of training opportunities and (*b*) management commitment to providing the support needed to allow people to grow and develop, is an integral part of the organization's culture. At the same time, the quality and strategic relevance of a firm's training efforts have direct relationship to overall financial performance, especially in an era of dramatic change and intense competition.

For those organizations committed to providing training which meets the needs of both the organization and the work force, the results of a joint two year study by the U.S. Department of Labor and the American Society for Training and Development may be of interest. Based on the results, the 13 skills most wanted by employers and most needed by workers are the following:

1. Learning to learn—the ability to acquire the knowledge and skills needed to learn effectively, no matter what the learning situation.
2. Listening—the ability to heed the key points of customers', suppliers', and co-workers' concerns.
3. Oral communication—the ability to convey an adequate response to those concerns.
4. Problem solving—the ability to think on one's feet.
5. Creative thinking—the ability to come up with innovative solutions.
6. Self-esteem—the ability to have pride in one's self and believe in one's potential to be successful.
7. Goal-setting/motivation—the ability to know how to get things done.
8. Personal and career development skills—the awareness of the skills needed to perform well in the workplace.
9. Interpersonal skills—the ability to get along with customers, suppliers, and co-workers.
10. Teamwork—the ability to work with others to achieve a goal.

11. Negotiation—the ability to build consensus through give and take.
12. Organizational effectiveness—the understanding of where the organization is headed, and how one can make a contribution.
13. Leadership—the ability to assume responsibility and motivate co-workers when necessary.[16]

Most bank training tends to be technical and the issues listed above are clearly outside the traditional bank training paradigm. Therefore, as banks design training programs for the 1990s, consideration should probably be given to each of these issues.

Discrimination. Discrimination based on sex, age, and race continues to be a serious problem in the American workplace. The more orthodox the culture, and the less responsive it is to changing realities, the greater will be the likelihood that discrimination, in one form or another, is present in the organization's culture.

Banking has traditionally been an industry where management positions have been the almost exclusive reserve of Caucasian males, even though the majority of the work force has been female. Naturally, there is a common tendency among managers, regardless of the industry, to hire in their own image, which has resulted in systematic, and often unintentional, discrimination against women and minorities.[17] In the liberalized environment of the 1980s, this led to charges of discrimination from those individuals and groups who felt they had not been treated fairly, despite affirmative action requirements and sincere efforts to comply with those requirements. Such feelings continue to pose a challenge for bank management.

When discrimination exists in a company (even when it is not the result of deliberate and conscious management attitudes or decisions) or when it is perceived to be a cultural norm, it is extremely difficult to generate a strong sense of commitment, teamwork, and esprit de corps. Trust becomes weak or nonexistent. Therefore, a key issue in the cultural revolution is the extent to which organizations are successful in purging themselves of discriminatory tendencies.

EXHIBIT 4–7
Corporate Culture Component Analysis—Bank A
Component 3: Rewards and Punishments

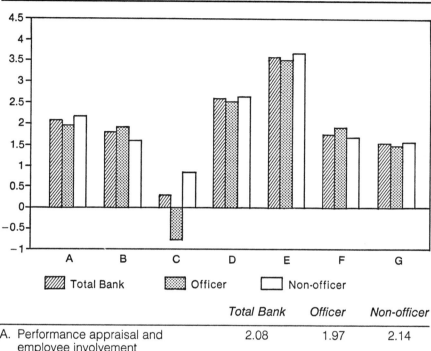

	Total Bank	Officer	Non-officer
A. Performance appraisal and employee involvement	2.08	1.97	2.14
B. Rewards and punishments; recognition	1.71	1.90	1.61
C. Rituals	0.31	−0.72	0.82
D. Training	2.62	2.51	2.67
E. Discrimination	3.53	3.50	3.54
F. Pay for performance	1.77	1.92	1.70
G. Achievement and self-actualization	1.55	1.52	1.56

The analysis of the Rewards and Punishments component for Bank A and Bank B can be seen in Exhibits 4–7 and 4–8.

Component 4: Marketing and Sales
The degree to which a bank has shifted successfully from a product driven and control-oriented organization to one which is marketing driven and customer-needs oriented represents

EXHIBIT 4–8
Corporate Culture Component Analysis—Bank B
Component 3: Rewards and Punishments

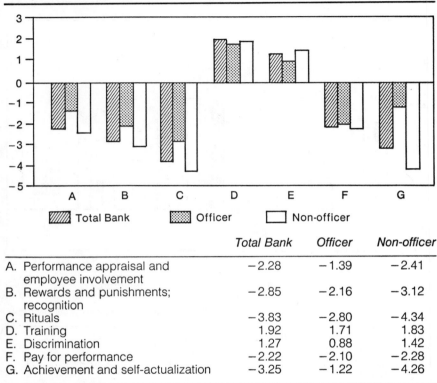

	Total Bank	Officer	Non-officer
A. Performance appraisal and employee involvement	−2.28	−1.39	−2.41
B. Rewards and punishments; recognition	−2.85	−2.16	−3.12
C. Rituals	−3.83	−2.80	−4.34
D. Training	1.92	1.71	1.83
E. Discrimination	1.27	0.88	1.42
F. Pay for performance	−2.22	−2.10	−2.28
G. Achievement and self-actualization	−3.25	−1.22	−4.26

one of the most critical elements of cultural transformation. Seventeen of the 66 statements in the survey deal specifically with various aspects of the marketing and sales culture issue. As such, they are designed to identify specific cultural impediments to the successful implementation of marketing, sales, and customer satisfaction strategies.

Two important marketing and sales culture statements and the responses from banks A and B are shown:

STATEMENT 14

"In my opinion, there is a general perception in our market area that this company, and its products and services, are unique and/or different in positive ways."

	Bank A			Bank B		
	Officers	Nonofficers	Total	Officers	Nonofficers	Total
Strongly agree	3	3	3	0	0	0
Agree	0	18	12	18	10	13
Weakly agree	17	18	18	18	15	16
Neutral	17	8	11	2	0	1
Weakly disagree	18	26	23	16	30	25
Disagree	20	26	24	21	33	29
Strongly disagree	25	1	9	18	6	10
Not relevant to my job	0	0	0	7	7	6
Average response	(.38)	(.36)	(.36)	(1.25)	(1.68)	(1.45)

As expected, Bank B shows serious weakness in this area, as do most banks as they attempt to adjust to a deregulated environment. Only in recent years have banks begun to fully accept that they must differentiate themselves, and their product offerings, if they expect to gain new customers, keep the ones they now have, and compete successfully with a host of highly focused competitors.

Even Bank A shows considerable weakness, with 63 percent of the officers, and 53 percent of the nonofficers, expressing their opinion that the market does not view the bank and its products as unique. Even if they are wrong, which is possible, their attitudes and perceptions clearly inhibit their sales effectiveness.

Another critically important issue relating to marketing and sales culture is the perceived relationship between product knowledge and sales success on the one hand, and performance and salary reviews on the other.

This is a core sales culture issue. Many banks give lip service to the importance of becoming sales driven yet never upgrade performance review and compensation strategies to sup-

STATEMENT 43

"My performance and salary reviews are based in part on how well I understand and sell bank products and services and/or support someone who does."

	Bank A			Bank B		
	Officers	Nonofficers	Total	Officers	Nonofficers	Total
Strongly agree	8	7	7	0	0	0
Agree	37	25	29	5	0	2
Weakly agree	20	14	16	4	0	1
Neutral	3	6	5	3	6	5
Weakly disagree	10	15	13	34	30	31
Disagree	7	10	9	30	38	35
Strongly disagree	4	3	4	9	6	8
Not relevant to my job	11	20	17	15	20	18
Average response	1.84	1.03	1.30	(2.52)	(3.10)	(2.91)

port the new corporate priorities. As a result, everyone concludes properly that management isn't serious, and nothing changes.

Again, the negative response in Bank B comes as no surprise. Only 3 percent of the work force perceives a relationship between sales and/or sales support and performance and salary review. In Bank A we continue to see signs of weakness which were evident with Statement 14, especially among the nonofficer group. Overall, 17 percent of the work force does not consider the issue to be relevant to their jobs. Just over half of the work force responded positively.

As Bank A identifies its cultural weaknesses, those that must be corrected in order to compete effectively in the 1990s, the issue of market and customer orientation, especially as it relates to sales culture, must become a major priority, and a vital component of the bank's strategic plan. It may very well be the single greatest issue affecting the bank's ability to compete successfully.

Exhibits 4–9 and 4–10 present the analysis of the marketing and sales component for Bank A and Bank B, respectively.

EXHIBIT 4–9
Corporate Culture Component Analysis—Bank A
Component 4: Marketing and Sales

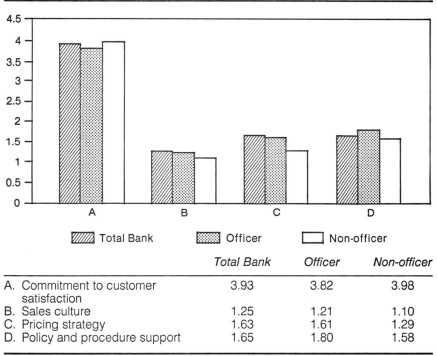

	Total Bank	Officer	Non-officer
A. Commitment to customer satisfaction	3.93	3.82	3.98
B. Sales culture	1.25	1.21	1.10
C. Pricing strategy	1.63	1.61	1.29
D. Policy and procedure support	1.65	1.80	1.58

Component 5: Standards and Values

Peters and Waterman write: "Every excellent company we studied is clear on what it stands for, and takes the process of value shaping seriously. In fact, we wonder whether it is possible to be an excellent company without clarity on values and without having the right sorts of values."[18] Their observation would have been impressive had they simply said "most companies." That they found a strong system of shared values to be characteristic of "every" excellent company they studied is difficult to ignore and is consistent with experience.

In assessing the strengths and weaknesses of a culture, it is extremely important to focus on the types of values which influence employee behavior, the appropriateness of those values,

EXHIBIT 4–10
Corporate Culture Component Analysis—Bank B
Component 4: Marketing and Sales

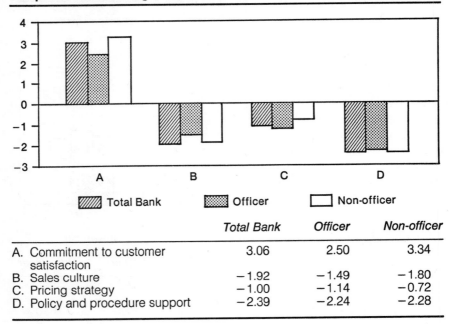

	Total Bank	Officer	Non-officer
A. Commitment to customer satisfaction	3.06	2.50	3.34
B. Sales culture	−1.92	−1.49	−1.80
C. Pricing strategy	−1.00	−1.14	−0.72
D. Policy and procedure support	−2.39	−2.24	−2.28

and the extent to which they have been assimilated into the
culture. The following represents one of the 14 statements dealing with this key culture component:

STATEMENT 20

"I have a personal commitment to making and/or keeping this company a 'high
performer' (top 25% of its peer group in terms of profitability)."

	Bank A			Bank B		
	Officers	Nonofficers	Total	Officers	Nonofficers	Total
Strongly agree	50	26	33	18	31	27
Agree	26	39	35	50	30	37
Weakly agree	20	20	20	32	33	32
Neutral	3	3	3	0	0	0

STATEMENT 20 (*continued*)

	Bank A			Bank B		
	Officers	Nonofficers	Total	Officers	Nonofficers	Total
Weakly disagree	1	2	2	0	3	2
Disagree	0	1	1	0	3	2
Strongly disagree	0	1	1	0	0	0
Not relevant to my job	0	8	5	0	0	0
Average response	4.42	3.67	3.92	3.72	3.54	3.60

It may come as a surprise that the average response in Bank B was nearly as strong as that in Bank A, with 96 percent of the work force agreeing with the statement. In spite of the extremely negative culture in Bank B, the employees, *like employees everywhere,* want to feel a sense of meaningfulness and purpose; they want to feel like winners. This is consistent with findings in banks of all sizes and in all parts of the country;

STATEMENT 50

"This organization fosters a climate which encourages the top performers to stay and the worst to leave, rather than the other way around."

	Bank A			Bank B		
	Officers	Nonofficers	Total	Officers	Nonofficers	Total
Strongly agree	38	30	34	0	0	0
Agree	34	33	33	3	2	2
Weakly agree	20	20	20	3	3	4
Neutral	1	9	6	3	6	5
Weakly disagree	4	7	6	30	17	21
Disagree	2	1	1	32	20	24
Strongly disagree	1	0	0	19	50	39
Not relevant to my job	0	0	0	10	2	5
Average response	3.82	3.34	3.50	(2.56)	(4.12)	(3.60)

people are desperate for dynamic, inspirational, and focused leadership that will give their work lives purpose and meaning. For any bank the opportunities for improvement in this area are virtually limitless.

Employee perceptions in this area have a powerful impact on the quality of personnel in key positions throughout any company. An interesting example is provided by Gary Hector in *Breaking the Bank:* "Low pay sent good lenders to other jobs. Less competent officers tended to stay, especially since Bank America rarely fired anyone."[19] Unfortunately, many banks foster similar cultures, which practically guarantees mediocrity and substandard performance in a highly competitive environment.

In the current example we see clearly the implications of this cultural weakness; while the work force in Bank B is eager to play a positive role in achieving superior performance, the culture drives out excellence—and provides a haven for mediocrity. Only 6 percent of the work force, and the reader can speculate as to who they are, believe that the climate encourages top performers to stay. In Bank A we see precisely the opposite. Fully 87 percent of the work force believes that the prevailing climate encourages excellence. However, before assuming that tolerance of mediocrity is not a problem in Bank A, we need to review the response to Statement 41.

The negative average response in Bank B is not unexpected, and is consistent with the response to Statement 50. The weak average response in Bank A, however, especially among the officers, may come as a surprise, as it did to Bank A's president.

Further analysis revealed that two key officers in the organization were perceived by many of their co-workers as lazy, marginally competent, dictatorial and repressive in their management styles, and not representative of the core values which the president was attempting to nourish and reinforce. In both instances the officers had been with the bank for several years, had built impressive bases of power, and, most importantly, were perceived as favorites of the president and "untouchable." The behaviors and attitudes that the president himself was seeing were not at all consistent with the manner in which these

STATEMENT 41

"Those employees who cannot or will not perform are not allowed to subvert the goals of the organization and create extra work for others."

	Bank A			Bank B		
	Officers	Nonofficers	Total	Officers	Nonofficers	Total
Strongly agree	5	11	9	0	0	0
Agree	32	30	30	15	10	12
Weakly agree	20	20	20	16	9	11
Neutral	12	10	11	0	4	3
Weakly disagree	15	13	14	20	21	20
Disagree	15	13	14	30	25	27
Strongly disagree	1	3	2	19	24	22
Not relevant to my job	0	0	0	0	7	5
Average response	1.02	1.30	1.21	(1.82)	(2.45)	(2.24)

officers were perceived by their subordinates, yet no one felt comfortable taking action given the perception that they were "protected."

Once the issue surfaced in the survey, and subsequent interviews brought the underlying problems to light, the president was in a position to initiate constructive action designed to encourage those individuals to become positive contributors to cultural renewal, rather than impediments. One of the officers, once the dysfunctional nature of his management style was out in the open, was able to make a positive transition, supported by outside intervention. The second officer went immediately to the denial phase, became highly resistant, and was ultimately asked to leave. Through this process, powerful messages were sent to everyone in the bank, and important cultural values were reinforced, as was the president's commitment to cultural change.

Another extremely important issue under standards and values, especially in an industry such as banking, concerns the degree to which the work force believes that integrity and honesty underlie corporate decision making.

STATEMENT 15

"Honesty and integrity are important considerations in the decisions that are made in this organization."

	Bank A			Bank B		
	Officers	*Nonofficers*	*Total*	*Officers*	*Nonofficers*	*Total*
Strongly agree	17	24	22	18	0	0
Agree	50	39	43	40	20	27
Weakly agree	25	25	25	33	32	26
Neutral	7	9	8	0	0	0
Weakly disagree	1	2	1	5	22	16
Disagree	0	1	1	4	22	16
Strongly disagree	0	0	0	0	13	9
Not relevant to my job	0	0	0	0	0	0
Average response	3.50	3.42	3.45	3.08	(.84)	.47

As can be seen in Statement 15, the response from Bank A is very strong, with only 2 percent of the work force in disagreement. The response in Bank B is interesting; while 91 percent of the officers agree, 57 percent of the nonofficers disagree, with not a single person remaining neutral. Clearly, incidents have occurred that have caused a majority of the nonofficer work force to question the integrity of top management. This is the type of issue requiring intensive analysis through personal interviews when, as in this case, significant negativism is observed.

"Honesty and integrity" is one of the truly core culture issues. While most cultural weaknesses can be corrected quite readily, this is one of several which typically requires radical change intervention.

Another core issue relative to standards and values is treated in Statement 4. The strong congruence between organizational and personal philosophy and values is evident in Bank A, and undoubtedly is an important factor in the bank's consistently superior financial performance. In Bank B, however, over 50 percent of both officers and nonofficers admit to being

STATEMENT 4

"My own personal philosophy and value system are very compatible with the philosophy and value system of this organization."

	Bank A			Bank B		
	Officers	Nonofficers	Total	Officers	Nonofficers	Total
Strongly agree	22	14	16	9	0	3
Agree	37	32	34	13	21	18
Weakly agree	30	31	31	14	21	19
Neutral	7	5	6	7	3	4
Weakly disagree	2	5	4	19	15	16
Disagree	1	5	4	18	16	17
Strongly disagree	1	0	0	18	19	19
Not relevant to my job	0	8	5	2	5	4
Average response	3.26	2.65	2.85	(.86)	(.86)	(.86)

philosophically incompatible with what the bank stands for. This bank will never become a high performer, and, in fact, has a slim chance of even surviving, as long as this philosophical and value gap exists.

One of the most important values any organization can have is a strong and unifying sense of *excitement, pride, and esprit de corps*, another issue treated under standards and values. In a memorable *Harvard Business Review* interview, the irrepressible Red Auerbach of the Boston Celtics was asked: "How do you motivate the players?" His response was short and to the point: "Pride, that's all. Pride of excellence. Pride of winning."[20]

In strong culture organizations, an almost tangible spirit of excitement and pride exists which seems to have a profound influence on the majority of the organization's human resources. People enjoy what they are doing. They have fun. They take great pride in what the organization stands for, understand and support the strategic focus, and are excited about their role in making it all happen. Because they have assimilated the organization's values, they are innovative in seeking new and better ways to help the organization achieve its objectives. They work

EXHIBIT 4–11
Corporate Culture Component Analysis—Bank A
Component 5: Standards and Values

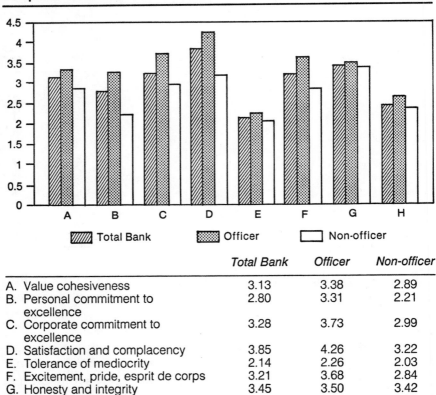

	Total Bank	Officer	Non-officer
A. Value cohesiveness	3.13	3.38	2.89
B. Personal commitment to excellence	2.80	3.31	2.21
C. Corporate commitment to excellence	3.28	3.73	2.99
D. Satisfaction and complacency	3.85	4.26	3.22
E. Tolerance of mediocrity	2.14	2.26	2.03
F. Excitement, pride, esprit de corps	3.21	3.68	2.84
G. Honesty and integrity	3.45	3.50	3.42
H. Myths and heroes	2.47	2.64	2.38

together as a team toward a common goal. They are alive. They care. And it shows in how they treat customers, how they treat each other, and in the quality and quantity of their work.

As one of the most revealing components of corporate culture, "excitement, pride, and esprit de corps" embodies all the other components, and has a powerful impact on each employee within the organization. In assessing the strengths and weaknesses of an organization's culture, it is helpful to pay particular attention to this component.

The analysis of the standards and values component for

EXHIBIT 4–12
Corporate Culture Component Analysis—Bank B
Component 5: Standards and Values

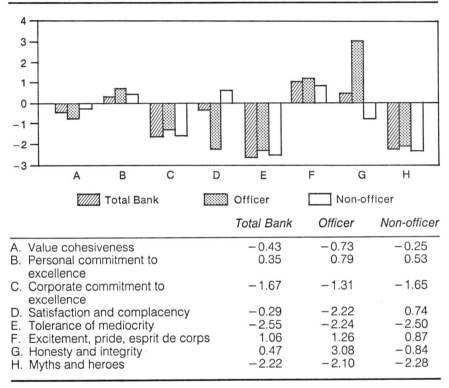

	Total Bank	Officer	Non-officer
A. Value cohesiveness	−0.43	−0.73	−0.25
B. Personal commitment to excellence	0.35	0.79	0.53
C. Corporate commitment to excellence	−1.67	−1.31	−1.65
D. Satisfaction and complacency	−0.29	−2.22	0.74
E. Tolerance of mediocrity	−2.55	−2.24	−2.50
F. Excitement, pride, esprit de corps	1.06	1.26	0.87
G. Honesty and integrity	0.47	3.08	−0.84
H. Myths and heroes	−2.22	−2.10	−2.28

Bank A and Bank B is presented as Exhibits 4–11 and 4–12, respectively.

Component 6: Openness and Quality of Communication

Few things are as important in any organization as good internal communications; upward, downward, and horizontal. In fact, all other components of corporate culture are highly dependent on effective communication patterns. Communication, external as well as internal, should be thought of as strategic in that its purpose is to help bring about the realization of corporate objectives. It is the means by which the firm's human assets are brought together in a common purpose, that is, are focused strategically. It provides the organization with everything it knows about its markets, their needs, and the attitudes and opinions of individual market participants relative to the company and its product offerings vis-à-vis competitors. At the same time, it is the means by which the organization influences its own image and standing within its various constituencies: customers, stockholders, customer prospects, employees, prospective employees, and government agencies. It affects the quality and appropriateness of decision making and the implementation of every aspect of the strategic plan. In weak culture companies, the emphasis is almost exclusively on formalized downward communication. In strong culture companies, communication (upward, downward, and horizontal), tends to be much more open, honest, spontaneous, and informal.

Consequently, in managing culture, it is vital that the communication process, like any other critical success factor, be managed. The CEO must first understand the prevailing communication style and patterns prevailing in his or her organization. Ineffective and/or dysfunctional patterns must then be identified and changed. Communication as strategy must be given the same degree of thought and attention as any other function affecting the ability of the organization to achieve its objectives. One of several communication statements deals with upward communication, where the key phrase is "nonthreatening."

Again, in Bank A the positive culture is reflected in the openness and quality of the communication process. In Bank B the officers respond positively while the nonofficers are extremely negative, further confirming the serious gulf which exists between these two groups. The response here is consistent with the response to Statement 19, dealing with the quality of supervision.

Because the communication component contains but one cultural issue, communication, no graphic exhibit is presented for this component.

Component 7: Systems, Policies, and Procedures

According to Silverzweig and Allen, "Organizational policies and procedures convey clear messages from the power structure

STATEMENT 22

"Upward communication in this organization occurs in an effective, open and nonthreatening manner."

	Bank A			Bank B		
	Officers	Nonofficers	Total	Officers	Nonofficers	Total
Strongly agree	16	12	13	0	0	0
Agree	39	36	37	30	15	20
Weakly agree	20	22	21	34	16	22
Neutral	9	10	10	0	0	0
Weakly disagree	8	9	9	16	10	12
Disagree	8	8	8	20	15	17
Strongly disagree	0	2	1	0	44	29
Not relevant to my job	0	1	1	0	0	0
Average response	2.44	2.01	2.15	.76	(2.52)	(1.43)

as to the organization's cultural priorities. Unfortunately, many of these policies, structures, budgets, and procedures support prior cultures and patterns of expected behavior that are no longer valued by either employees or management."[21] Therefore, the thoughtful reevaluation of all policies and procedures must become an integral part of the process of cultural change.

The systems, policies, and procedures of an organization say a great deal about (1) which values are important, (2) the extent to which the organization's human resources are valued and trusted, (3) management's attitude regarding positive versus negative reinforcement, (4) the internal versus external focus of the organization, and (5) the quality of the communication process within the company.

It is fascinating to observe the frequency with which employees in organizations express confusion relative to the prevailing policies and procedures affecting their jobs. Often they have never seen a policy manual; "policy" is communicated orally by co-workers and/or supervisors as specific incidents occur. In other cases they know that a manual exists but they aren't sure where to find it. Frequently, policy seemingly changes overnight with no explanation provided. If people fail to "get the word," it is their fault. Even lending officers are often in the dark regarding current lending policies, which often appear to change suddenly with seeming disregard for customer relationships and/or previous directives. Customer satisfaction and quality service are often preached as the organization's primary mission yet policies and procedures are perceived as impeding the employee's ability to deliver on the promise. Such are the complaints and frustrations commonly expressed by employees.

Clearly, the ways in which an organization (1) establishes and modifies policies and procedures, (2) involves the organization's human assets in the process, (3) communicates policies and policy changes, (4) reinforces policy, and (5) uses systems, policies, and procedures strategically, that is, in support of organizational values and objectives, all have a material bearing on the organization's corporate culture, and on the day-to-day performance of the organization's human assets.

An interesting statement which relates policies and procedures to marketing and sales culture is the following:

STATEMENT 60

"Policies and procedures in this company, while contributing to sound business practice, also support our sales, marketing, and customer satisfaction strategies."

	Bank A			Bank B		
	Officers	Nonofficers	Total	Officers	Nonofficers	Total
Strongly agree	10	12	11	0	0	0
Agree	30	30	30	10	10	10
Weakly agree	34	28	30	15	9	11
Neutral	4	3	3	4	6	5
Weakly disagree	11	12	12	23	26	25
Disagree	10	12	12	20	30	27
Strongly disagree	1	3	2	28	19	22
Not relevant to my job	0	0	0	0	0	0
Average response	1.80	1.58	1.65	(2.24)	(2.28)	(2.27)

Many banks attempting to become more marketing, sales, and customer satisfaction driven are seeing their efforts compromised by an "operations mentality" that refuses to reconsider policies and procedures which may impede the successful implementation of market and customer-oriented strategies. Clearly, in a low margin business such as banking, it is imperative that sound policies be implemented and enforced in order to protect the interests of customers and shareholders. However, policy should be viewed as strategic, that is it must be designed to support the organization's strategic priorities. As such, it should be subjected to rigorous analysis on a regular basis in order to ensure it is facilitating, rather than impeding, desired results. This is an issue which is receiving inadequate attention in most banks today.

In summary, as can be seen in Exhibits 4–13, and 4–15, Bank A has a positive culture which appears to play a significant role in its consistently superior performance. Even so, weaknesses have been identified, thereby permitting the thoughtful creation, implementation, and management of intervention strategies.

EXHIBIT 4–13
Corporate Culture Assessment—Bank A

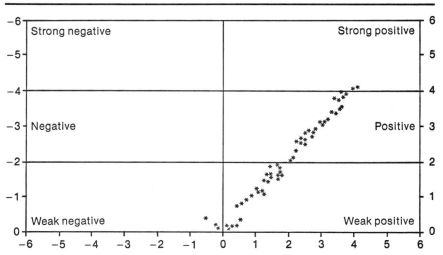

EXHIBIT 4–14
Corporate Culture Assessment—Bank B

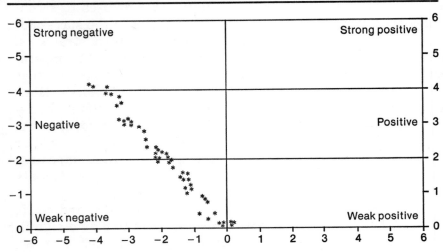

As shown in Exhibits 4–14 and 4–16, Bank B, a perennial poor performer, has an extremely weak corporate culture which is clearly an impediment to positive strategic change. It is the author's assessment, supported by a considerable body of research in numerous industries, that a leadership change in extreme cases such as this represents the only viable solution. With the right leadership, and a concerted effort to modify the culture positively, an organization can generally begin to see improved performance almost immediately.

Changing the Corporate Culture: Step 2, Definition of the Characteristics of the Desired Culture

Once the existing culture has been evaluated thoroughly, the prevailing cultural norms can be outlined, along with the areas where the greatest weaknesses are evident.

The next step is to define the cultural characteristics or norms, within the framework of the seven key corporate culture components discussed above, that will be required for the organization to realize its Strategic Vision, fulfill its mission, and meet or surpass its objectives. For example, under "standards

EXHIBIT 4–15
Corporate Culture Component Analysis—Bank A
Component Order Based on Total Bank Results

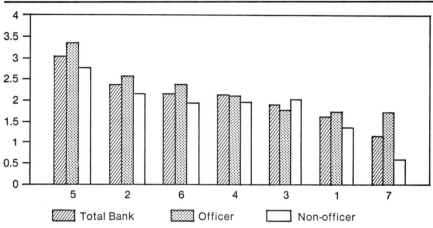

	Total Bank	*Officer*	*Non-officer*
1. Strategic focus	1.63	1.79	1.38
2. Leadership	2.32	2.56	2.17
3. Rewards and punishments	1.94	1.80	2.01
4. Marketing and sales	2.12	2.11	1.99
5. Standards and values	3.04	3.35	2.75
6. Communication	2.19	2.36	1.97
7. Systems, policies, procedures	1.13	1.78	0.58

and values," what specific core values and performance standards will be required in the 1990s?

The most effective method in defining the desired culture is through the use of employee and officer work groups. This will accomplish several related goals:

　a. The Strategic Vision itself will be better understood by all participants. In addition, any misconceptions can be cleared up in a safe, nonthreatening atmosphere.

　b. The strategic focus of the company will be reinforced.

　c. The dysfunctional consequences of old culture patterns will be discussed and understood, thereby making everyone much more aware of those behaviors or attitudes which are no longer appropriate.

　d. Because employees at all levels will be involved, the

process of breaking down communication and team-work barriers will be enhanced, and patterns of inter-departmental cooperation established.

e. The commitment of senior management to cultural change will be strongly reinforced, as will the fact that many influential individuals are also committed to positive involvement in creating a new order.

f. Numerous cultural issues which may not have surfaced previously will now be brought to the surface as it becomes clear that it is safe to do so.

g. Synergies of creativity will occur, thereby enhancing the quality of the overall vision.

h. A greater sense of personal ownership in the process of strategic and cultural change will develop.

As seen in Exhibit 4–17 on pages 178–80, major differences exist, in each of the seven key culture components, be-

EXHIBIT 4–16
Corporate Culture Component Analysis—Bank B
Component Order Based on Total Bank Results

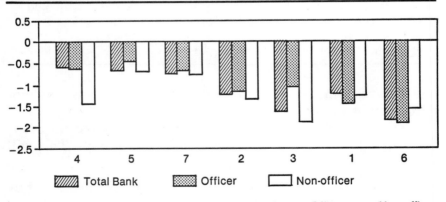

	Total Bank	Officer	Non-officer
1. Strategic focus	−1.20	−1.41	−1.23
2. Leadership	−1.20	−1.16	−1.32
3. Rewards and punishments	−1.61	−1.01	−1.88
4. Marketing and sales	−0.56	−0.59	−1.46
5. Standards and values	−0.66	−0.43	−0.67
6. Communication	−1.80	−1.89	−1.53
7. Systems, policies, procedures	−0.73	−0.66	−0.74

tween traditional bank cultures and the more modern cultures needed to survive and prosper in the 1990s. This exhibit is not intended as a comprehensive assessment of all the relevant issues, simply as an example of several significant cultural differences.

Changing the Corporate Culture: Step 3, Prioritization of the Specific Areas Requiring Cultural Change

Once the existing and desired cultural characteristics have been defined, the next step is to prioritize all changes that must take place (the cultural gap), and to develop the related strategic action plans. Each strategic action plan must include: (a) the objective of the change, (b) how the change will take place, (c) how outdated patterns will be exorcised, (d) all anticipated obstacles and how they will be overcome, (e) accountability for implementation, (f) implementation timetable, (g) how future success will be evaluated, and (h) how ongoing commitment will be maintained.

Again, I believe the most effective approach is to use employee work groups. Carl Carballada, the charismatic CEO of Central Trust Company, in Rochester, New York, presented the results of the culture assessment at an evening meeting to which all the bank's employees had been invited. In an inspirational address, Carl expressed his absolute commitment to cultural change and asked for volunteers to form groups dealing with specific cultural change issues. The response from all employee levels and locations was overwhelming, and the process of constant cultural renewal has now become an important characteristic and value of the Central Trust culture, and a process in which everyone can participate in a meaningful and tangible way.

Changing the Corporate Culture: Step 4, Ongoing Management of the Cultural Change Process

Several initiatives will facilitate the ongoing management of cultural change. First, an orientation program, established to indoctrinate all new employees in the company's culture, in-

EXHIBIT 4–17
Cultural Change

	Old	*New*
Stategic focus	Emphasis on control and risk minimization; little focus beyond the CEO on financial performance and shareholder value; no real accountability for performance results; employees and middle managers nonparticipants; no clear marketing plan or strategy; no strategic vision; change feared; pooled capital.	Full accountability for results at all levels; clear strategic focus on profitable performance creating shareholder value; everyone's job to contribute; capital allocated by business unit and ROE goals established and reinforced; positive attitude toward change; strong sense of interdependence and teamwork; clear marketing focus.
Leadership	"Theory x management"; "Do things right" orientation; tall, rigid hierarchies; win-lose conflict resolution; boss orders things done; highly centralized; leader's job to preserve the status quo; leaders selected based on technical skills or loyalty rather than performance.	"Theory Y management"; "do the right things" orientation; leader-managers at all levels; high visibility; visionary; people oriented; flat, open structure; win-win conflict resolution; agents for change; challengers of the status quo; small, ad-hoc task forces; flexible structure; fewer middle managers; decentralized, decisions made at lowest possible level; leaders picked for people and conceptual skills; high accountability for performance.
Rewards and punishments	Negative rather than positive reinforcement; minimal recognition; no rituals; low pay; no incentive plans; promotion based on conformity; one-shot technically oriented training; subjective nonperformance-based appraisal; tolerance of mediocrity; transfer of problems to other	Emphasis on positive reinforcement; constant recognition; rituals to reinforce desired behavior; competitive pay; liberal use of incentives; promotion based on results; continuous multi-disciplinary training; appraisal based on performance standards and targets in key results areas;

EXHIBIT 4–17—(*Continued*)

	Old	New
	departments; no performance standards or targets; little or no consideration of intrinsic rewards.	no tolerance for mediocrity; heavy emphasis on intrinsic rewards.
Marketing and sales	Product driven; no market research or focus groups; generic standardized products; "all things to all people"; nonresponsive to customer needs; bankers hours; minimal product knowledge and/or sales training; no sales goals or incentives; no sales manager; price-oriented advertising; little or no attempt to measure customer satisfaction.	Ongoing market research; focus on market segments; customer and noncustomer focus groups; value added to generic products to create competitive advantage; innovative product development; sales manager; rituals to support sales heroes; incentive compensation; ongoing product knowledge and sales training; customer satisfaction constantly monitored and measured.
Standards and values	No articulated and reinforced core values; informal values mostly control and conformity oriented; "doing things right" more important than "doing the right things"; values internal rather than oriented around customer or competitive superiority; values oriented more around "not doing certain things" than "doing certain things." No quantifiable standards of performance; emphasis on meeting norms, not on achieving excellence.	Clearly stated and reinforced core values; values oriented around customer and competitiveness; rituals to recognize those whose performance best personifies values. All job positions contain clear, quantifiable performance standards; high expectations.
Communication	Emphasis on formal downward communication; tall, rigid hierarchies; little upward communication; liberal use of memos to communicate; meetings oriented around one-way	Open, informal communication in all directions; flatter, more flexible structures; input solicited from all levels; group idea sharing and problem solving; fewer

EXHIBIT 4–17—(Continued)

	Old	New
	communication; no effort to communicate financial objectives and strategies, including pricing rationale; minimal integration between senior management and staff; communication through chain of command slow and cumbersome.	barriers; senior management more visible and accessible; open channels of communication to suggest new ideas, challenge existing strategies, etc.
Systems, policies, and procedures	Systems, policies, and procedures designed to maximize conformity; not viewed as strategic; emphasis on what people cannot do—not what they can; no input from lower levels.	Systems, policies, and procedures viewed as strategic; constant reassessment; oriented around core values; emphasis on customer satisfaction and efficiency.

cluding performance standards and core values, can be an extremely powerful and valuable tool. Second, CEOs, boards of directors, and senior management teams, as guardians of their bank's cultural values, must constantly challenge themselves to set a consistent example of desired behavior; *they too must make fundamental changes in style and priorities if they expect others to do so.* Third, rituals should be established to publicly recognize those whose performance reflects most powerfully and positively the values for which the company stands. Fourth, those whose behavior is inconsistent with cultural values must not be allowed to subvert the change process. However, because the culture itself will be more flexible and adaptive, care must be taken to distinguish between those who challenge positively and constructively the cultural norms, and those who are deliberately violating core values in a negative and dysfunctional manner. In fact, the organization's leadership may wish to play devil's advocate from time to time, challenging cultural norms and patterns in a positive way in order to reinforce both the need for ongoing adaptation, as well as the appropriateness of challenging existing habits in search of better ways to realize the vision. Fifth, areas where the greatest weaknesses are identified and/or where cultural change has been directed at core cultural issues (those having a particularly powerful impact on the bank's ability to be strategically focused and competitive), should be subjected to reassessment on a regular basis, perhaps quarterly or semiannually. In addition, the overall culture should probably be reevaluated at least annually while the culture is undergoing modification in order to reinforce the successes and to identify and correct the failures.

In the case of Bank B, the culture is extremely negative in virtually every area, with the work force crying out for direction and enlightened leadership. As indicated earlier, in severe cases such as these I am compelled to agree with the conclusions reached by Desmond Graves: "This example leads us to the somewhat radical conclusion that if you want to change the value system you have to change the people at the top, whose value system permeates the culture."[22]

Because Bank B appears to be incapable of breaking with the past, its chances for survival may be poor unless a change lf leadership occurs.

Bank A is a top-performing bank with a strong positive culture. However, improvements can be made in several areas, especially those dealing with "marketing and sales culture." The marketing strategies that have been successful in the past for Bank A will not be nearly as effective in the 1990s, given: (a) the proliferation of aggressive, sophisticated, and strategically focused competitors entering Bank A's market, (b) changing demographic characteristics, and (c) the strong possibility of an economic downturn early in the decade. Therefore, even though the culture has been positive in the past, significant ongoing cultural modification will become increasingly important in the future.

Ironically, as Bank A's management attempted to structure a culture modification plan, the organization's past successes represented one of the major impediments to implementation. Feelings of complacency and satisfaction caused many to question the need for strategic and/or cultural change, and the potential for resistance in several areas was extremely high, especially in the branch system where new sales and marketing accountabilities were to be installed. When cultural change becomes necessary, it is often the strong culture company that is most resistant.

However, by (a) reinforcing his Strategic Vision and focus, (b) communicating openly and honestly the reasons for the changes, (c) soliciting the active participation of employees at all levels in the process, and (d) leading the way through example, the bank's CEO has been successful thus far in initiating and reinforcing the process or strategic and cultural change. While the Bank A that enters the corporate battlefield in the 1990s will be considerably different from the one which fared so well in the 1980s, I am confident that it will continue to compete successfully and create value for its shareholders. The keys to its success have not changed: dynamic and enlightened leadership, vision, focus, commitment, accountability, discipline, and a strong, positive, corporate culture which has the ability to adapt to changing market conditions.

Why Cultural Change Intervention Often Fails

1. The strategic vision is never defined and the strategic focus never established.
2. The CEO lacks commitment, leadership ability, and/or power.
3. The board backs down and withdraws its support.
4. The absolute need for change is not communicated or is communicated poorly.
5. Management is not open and honest regarding the implications of change, therefore, mutual trust never develops.
6. Resistance, hostility, and negativism are never confronted constructively and are allowed to subvert the process.
7. Senior managers and/or middle managers and/or staff are never integrated into the change process and remain protectors of the status quo, rather than agents of change.
8. Accountability for results is not established; therefore, no-one takes management seriously.
9. Systems to measure and monitor actual change are not put in place.
10. No sense of urgency is created; people are led to believe the process is long-term so "why act now?"
11. Expectations for improvement in certain areas are unrea-

listically high, and resulting disappointment turns into distrust and active resistance.

12. The initiatives address only some of the cultural weaknesses, resulting in key issues, such as rewards and punishments, virtually ignored.

CORPORATE CULTURE AND HUMAN RESOURCE MANAGEMENT AND DEVELOPMENT

Traditional banking attitudes and practices relating to the management and development of human resources are an integral part of the old cultural paradigm that enlightened bankers are attempting to change. *In my view, virtually every aspect of HRMD must be challenged, and ultimately upgraded, in order to bring about a successful strategic and cultural revolution.*

As shown in Exhibit 4–18, it is the strategic plan (encompassing the total of ongoing strategic initiatives designed to transform the bank from today's reality to tomorrow's Strategic Vision), which will identify the skills, experiences, attitudes, and psychological characteristics required by the organization going forward. Therefore, HRMD must be actively involved in the Strategic Management and Planning process. Otherwise, HRMD policies will be, at best, nonsupportive strategically or, as is more likely, at odds with strategic priorities.

The seven key issues in HRMD, each of which will be discussed below, are: (1) strategic human resource planning, (2) recruitment, (3) screening and hiring, (4) orientation, training and placement, (5) performance expectations, (6) performance review, and (7) consequences (positive and negative reinforcement).

Key Issues in HRMD

1. Strategic Human Resource Planning
The director of HRMD must be an active participant in the Strategic Management and Planning process. This individual, to be effective, needs to have a clear understanding of the organization's Strategic Vision, business definition (including key

EXHIBIT 4–18
Enlightened Human Resource Management and Development

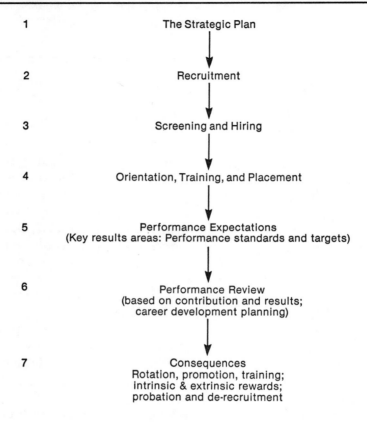

1	The Strategic Plan
2	Recruitment
3	Screening and Hiring
4	Orientation, Training, and Placement
5	Performance Expectations (Key results areas: Performance standards and targets)
6	Performance Review (based on contribution and results; career development planning)
7	Consequences Rotation, promotion, training; intrinsic & extrinsic rewards; probation and de-recruitment

lines of business), major strategic initiatives, profitability dynamics, and sources of competitive advantage. Only then can HRMD contribute meaningfully to the realization of the Strategic Vision. Because successful adaptation will require significant enhancement of every aspect of HRMD, the starting point in that transformation is the strategic plan, and HRMD's involvement in its creation.

2. Recruitment
Only when human resource managers have clear strategic direction can they develop a recruiting strategy which is supportive strategically, that is, which targets specific skills, experiences, and psychological profiles. For example, John Kanas,

President of North Fork Bancorp in Mattituck, New York, decided several years ago that his Strategic Vision for the company required a very special type of marketing director. His directive to the human resource manager was quite specific: find someone with a record of solid accomplishment at both Proctor & Gamble and Citicorp who would fit the North Fork culture. While it took several months, he eventually found the person he wanted, an exceptional marketing director who has validated the focus of Kanas's vision by playing a vital role in making North Fork a consistent high performer.

Going forward, banks must become more demanding in their hiring practices, and because the skills and experiences they seek are increasingly nontraditional, nontraditional recruiting methods will be required as well. In the 1990s, for example, an important recruiting strategy will be to create and reinforce an image of the bank as an extremely attractive and desirable place to work. In other words, public relations will not be limited to impressing customers, prospects, and the financial markets, but will be directed at prospective employees as well. Obviously, rhetoric will not be enough; the bank will have to make itself an exceptional place to work. Once it does, however, it will have to make sure that the word gets around.

3. Screening and Hiring

Testing procedures to identify specific types of competencies and skills, such as an aptitude for sales, are being used more and more in American business. Assumptions relative to an applicant's future success on the job, based solely on interviews, are practically worthless. In many banks filling the position is still the goal, not finding the individual with the greatest potential for contributing to a winning team.

When Mitsubishi of Japan and Chrysler formed a joint venture called Diamond-Star to produce automobiles in the United States, the rigorous screening practices of the Japanese were a revelation to their U.S. counterparts. Fully 24 percent of the applicants washed out almost immediately as a result of a series of written, medical, and drug tests. Of those who passed the initial testing, another 40 percent failed the subsequent screening and training procedures, including specialized testing designed to measure aptitudes for specific jobs. A heavy emphasis was placed on attitude, ability to integrate oneself effectively into a team, learning skills, and so forth.[23] Clearly, the Japanese understand the cost of hiring the wrong people.

Hiring, directly related to screening, is another area where traditional practices must change. David Spainhour, the incisive president of Santa Barbara Bank and Trust, a consistently high performing bank, involves himself personally in almost all recruiting, screening, and hiring decisions involving key leadership and management positions. Dave believes that it is one of his most important leadership priorities.

4. Orientation, Training, and Placement

Many high performing organizations, such as McDonald's, Disney, and IBM, devote attention to orienting their employees to the organization's culture and core values. By making sure that every new employee has a clear understanding of what the company stands for, its vision of the future, and what is expected of each employee in making that vision a reality, individual focus, commitment, and productivity are maximized.

In Japan, worker loyalty is only partly due to the Japanese character; in large measure it is a function of emphasis on hiring the right people, orienting them thoroughly to the organization's cultural values, and reinforcing consistently those values in meaningful ways. In my opinion, most organizations are devoting inadequate attention to the orientation process, a valuable and relatively low-cost tool for improving individual and organizational performance.

Another area where traditional attitudes must change is placement. Banks in the past have not evaluated thoroughly the specific skills, experiences, attitudes, and personality characteristics needed to excel at a specific job, nor have they devoted adequate attention to ensuring that people are placed where their background, experience, and aptitudes are most compatible with the position. The all too familiar occurrence of a person failing at a job, and then being assigned to a job where he or she can do less damage, can no longer be tolerated.

5. Performance Expectations

Too few managers do a satisfactory job of establishing and communicating performance expectations, yet this is one of the most powerful tools managers have for developing high performance people and for making a tangible and sustainable contribution to organizational excellence.

Stressing the relationship between the communication of high performance expectations, self-esteem, and productivity, J. Sterling Livingston writes: "Managers shape not only the expectations and productivity of their subordinates, but also influence their attitudes toward their jobs and themselves. If managers are unskilled, they leave scars on the careers of the young people, cut deeply into their self-esteem, and distort their image of themselves as human beings. But if they are skillful and have high expectations of their subordinates, their self-confidence will grow, their capabilities will develop, and their productivity will be high."[24] This is not an isolated view. The results of over 100 separate studies support the positive effects of establishing challenging, as opposed to easy, performance goals.[25]

Banking is one of the last major industries to establish quantifiable performance standards for all jobs. However, such standards can be established on the basis of quality, quantity, cost, and/or time. Many bankers are now realizing that the key to relating pay to performance is establishing and enforcing such standards. Furthermore, studies seem to reinforce the notion that most employees, especially high achievers, prefer to have compensation related to performance.[26]

For most banks, I believe that the establishment and reinforcement of high performance standards, and the linking of compensation to performance, represents one of the single greatest opportunities for improving individual and organizational performance, retaining quality employees, and dealing effectively and equitably with those who cannot or will not perform. I have yet to see a financial institution that could not enhance financial performance substantially through improvement in this area.

6. Performance Review

For many managers, performance appraisal is one of the most dreaded of all supervisory responsibilities. This results from several factors: (*a*) the lack of proper management training, especially as it relates to helping subordinates establish and meet goals, (b) vague and/or nonexistent job or position descriptions, (c) the failure to establish key results areas for each job which are compatible with the strategic plan, (d) the lack of quantifiable performance standards, (e) the use of appraisal documents which tend to be almost totally subjective, (f) fear of confronting substandard performers, and (g) compensation systems which practically guarantee mediocrity by failing to provide any significant difference in rewards between the best and worst performers.

According to Lawler, "A similarly grievous error can be the tendency to depend on completely subjective performance appraisals for the allocation of pay rewards. Considerable evidence exists to show that these performance appraisals are often biased and invalid and instead of contributing to positive motivation and a good work climate that improves superior subordinate relationships, they lead to just the opposite."[27]

Performance review in traditional bank cultures has been based on subjective and nonperformance-oriented criteria. However, according to H. Lon Adams and Kenneth Embley, "Senior management will merely be conducting a paper chase if its performance appraisal system is not synchronized with the organization's strategic plan and developed in harmony with each staff member's position description."[28]

Key Bank of Utah, where Embley is a Human Resources Vice President, has established one of the most sophisticated, comprehensive, and strategically focused performance management systems in the industry. The system links corporate goals, divisional and departmental strategies, and individual position descriptions in what is known throughout the company as individual "performance planning and review," or "PP and R." Quantifiable performance standards and goals are established for each accountability detailed in the employee's position statement. In this way, performance expectations are clearly defined, quantified, and communicated, and performance review is directly related to those expectations.

7. Consequences

Consequences, both positive and negative, must flow naturally from the previous steps, and be based on contribution to the

Strategic Vision. According to Kanter, "Status, not contribution, has traditionally been the basis for the numbers on employees' paychecks. Pay has reflected where jobs rank in the corporate hierarchy—not what comes out of them."[29] This will not be true of high performing banks in the 1990s.

Daniel Yankelovich concluded: "In principle, most Americans are willing to work harder and turn out a higher-quality product; indeed their self-esteem demands that they do so. That they are not doing it points directly to a serious flaw in management and in the reward system under which they perform their jobs. Why should workers make a greater effort if they don't have to and they believe that others will be the beneficiaries of such efforts?"[30]

If employees at all levels are expected to buy in to the Strategic Vision, become strategically focused, and commit themselves to the change process (and all the trauma and discomfort that goes along with it), the manner in which that commitment will be rewarded must change dramatically. Extrinsic rewards, such as salary, benefits, ownership, perks, bonuses, incentive plans, promotions, and training must be designed to meet the needs of today's workers while at the same time meeting the strategic needs of the company. Meanwhile, thoughtful and creative consideration must be given to the intrinsic rewards that are needed to motivate high performing people, including self-actualization, achievement, personal growth and development, pride, influence, and independence. The higher the individual rises in the organization, the more important these intrinsic rewards become.

If the organization is to be strategically focused on creating shareholder value, should not value enhancement influence the extrinsic rewards for at least some of the organization's human assets? Increasingly, organizations aspiring to excellence must elevate the extent to which a direct relationship exists between organizational performance, individual contribution, and the manner in which rewards are distributed. It is within this context that incentive plans continue to grow in popularity. Numerous studies have established a strong relationship between pay for performance and productivity and output, which will be discussed further in Chapter 6.

EXHIBIT 4–19
A Model for Human Motivation and Commitment

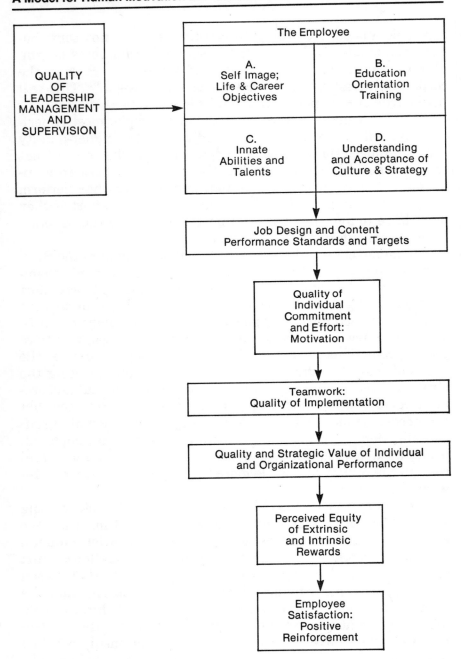

Corporate Culture and Employee Motivation

Exhibit 4–19 is a model which relates human motivation to various aspects of the organization's corporate culture, including rewards and punishments. Key elements in the model include: (1) the employee (self-esteem; innate abilities and talents; education, orientation, and training; and acceptance of the corporate culture), (2) quality of management and supervision, (3) job content and design, (4) quality of commitment and effort (motivation), (5) quality of implementation and teamwork, (6) quality and strategic value of individual and organizational performance, (7) satisfaction with extrinsic and intrinsic rewards, and (8) motivational reinforcement. Each of these issues will be discussed in Chapter 6.

SUMMARY

Every organization has a culture, the sum total of beliefs, values, attitudes, ideologies, and behavior patterns and norms shared and adhered to by a group. Because the existing culture exerts such a powerful influence on individual and group behavior, more and more studies find a direct relationship between an organization's culture and its financial performance.

Having worked with banks throughout the United States over the past decade to achieve and/or sustain high performance, I am convinced that nothing is more important to an organization's success than its ability to create and nurture a corporate culture which is strong, positive, adaptive, and strategically supportive. Furthermore, in my view, no leadership role is more important than fostering such a culture.

In order to ensure that the organization's culture is strategically appropriate, a four step process is necessary:

1. The existing culture must be subjected to an in-depth assessment which focuses on the culture's strengths and weaknesses in key areas. The author has identified seven key component areas and uses a survey instrument, designed specifically for financial institutions, to quantify strengths and weaknesses. Other diagnostic tools are available from a variety of sources.

In addition, personal interviews can provide invaluable insights into the cultural patterns and norms of an organization.

2. Given the organization's Strategic Vision and focus; financial performance and marketing objectives and strategies; and the nature of change affecting the business(es) in which the bank competes, the characteristics of the desired culture must be clearly defined, including the core values on which individual and group behavior will be evaluated.

3. Those areas where cultural modification is required (the cultural gap) must be prioritized and all potential impediments to cultural change identified. Next, specific cultural modification strategies must be developed, along with strategies to deal effectively with each impediment. Each strategy must have clearly assigned accountability.

4. A system must be established and implemented to monitor the results of each culture modification strategy. In cases of extreme cultural weakness, monthly review may be necessary; in other cases, quarterly, semiannual, or annual monitoring may suffice.

Directly related to an organization's culture is its approach to the management and development of human resources. Given the pervasive change which has impacted the financial services industry, and resultant industry overcapacity, survival is far from inevitable. Virtually every aspect of HRMD must be upgraded, from recruitment, screening, and hiring to performance review and intrinsic and extrinsic rewards.

As an integral component of the Strategic Management and Planning concept, leadership and corporate culture must be fine-tuned continuously in order to make sure that the needs of the organization, and its various constituencies, are being met. Therefore, as change occurs, and as offensive and defensive opportunities present themselves, strategic action plans in each of the seven key cultural components may be created and/or modified as an integral part of the process of Strategic Management and Planning. In my experience, nothing has greater power to contribute to enhanced financial performance than comprehensive and properly executed cultural analysis and reform.

CHAPTER 5

MARKET POSITIONING STRATEGY: CREATING SUSTAINABLE COMPETITIVE ADVANTAGE

There can be no corporate strategy that is not in some fundamental fashion a marketing strategy.

—Ted Leavitt

Improving banks' marketing capabilities will be the single most important key to growth and profitability during the next decade.

—Alex Sheshunoff

If any aspect of traditional banking practice is out of sync with the realities of the 1990s, and in need of strategic and cultural change, it is certainly marketing.

In light of severe industry overcapacity, changing demographic patterns, and the proliferation of aggressive and highly focused competitors, banks must not only find ways to protect and enhance their most valuable customer relationships but, in order to grow, must also take quality business away from their competitors. In the 1990s, higher levels of professionalism will be mandatory in all functional areas and lines of business. However, the one area where superior talent and experience will most distinguish the top performers from everyone else will surely be marketing and sales. In addition, most strategies in support of increased interest and noninterest income, as well as those designed to reduce funding costs, will be marketing and sales driven. Therefore, once an organization's leadership has initiated successfully the strategic and cultural revolution, defined clearly its business(es), conceptualized its Strategic Vision, and prioritized its opportunities for optimizing financial performance and shareholder value, supportive marketing and sales strategies must be created, implemented, and managed. These strategies, to be effective, must be consistent with, and supportive of, the strategic and cultural revolution itself.

WHAT IS MARKETING?

Prior to attempting to develop a marketing strategy or plan, it is critically important that the senior management team share a common understanding of what marketing is and how it contributes to enhancing the economic value of the firm.

I have previously defined "marketing" as follows: Marketing is . . . that function of the organization charged with converting corporate objectives to bottom-line reality through:

1. Determining, in a rational, informed, and strategic manner, the desired customer base.
2. Identifying and prioritizing specific current and future needs of desired customer and customer prospect segments.
3. Creating superior needs-satisfying benefits which respond profitably to customer and prospect needs and which differentiate positively the organization from its competitors.
4. Promoting and delivering those benefits effectively and efficiently to the market segments being targeted.
5. Converting the organization and everyone in it into a strategically focused, competitive, disciplined, and professional sales force committed to the organization's vision, cultural values, financial objectives, and customer satisfaction strategies.[1]

DEVELOPING THE MARKETING PLAN

Within the context of this definition a bank may wish to consider the matrix shown in Exhibit 5–1 as it develops its marketing plan.

EXHIBIT 5–1
Marketing Matrix

	FUNDING	EARNING ASSETS	FEE-BASED SERVICES
MISSION: FINANCIAL OBJECTIVES			
1. TARGET SEGMENTS			
2. SEGMENT NEEDS; SELF-PERCEPTION			
3. BENEFITS PACKAGE; COMPETITIVE ADVANTAGE			
4. DELIVERY AND PROMOTION			
5. SALES MANAGEMENT AND CULTURE			

In Chapter 2, it was suggested that a bank's business, in general terms, is "enhancing shareholder value through the creation and management of earning assets and fee-based services," and that a related function, funding, while extremely important, is not the business banks are in because it represents costs rather than earnings. It is, therefore, ironic that 60 percent or more of the typical bank's marketing budget is devoted to funding, rather than to the areas where earnings are generated. Furthermore, much of the funding related advertising is price oriented even when the bank cannot possibly hope to compete on that basis. The traditional allocation of marketing resources will come under increased scrutiny in the 1990s as banks (*a*) give greater attention to capital allocation and management, (*b*) attempt to define their businesses more strategically and to give greater emphasis to revenue producing activities, and (*c*) shift from price oriented to benefit-oriented marketing and sales strategies.

In support of the organization's strategic plan, I advocate that each of the three functions, funding, the creation and management of earning assets, and the creation and management of fee-based services, should have its individual mission, strategic focus, financial performance objectives, and accountability for results. Strategies must then be developed in each area by which those objectives will be realized. Because all such strategies will be marketing and sales driven, this requires an in-depth understanding of each of the key points in the definition provided above.

MARKETING AND THE BOTTOM LINE

> "Marketing is . . . that function of the organization charged with converting corporate objectives to bottom-line reality. . . ."

To be effective, those responsible for marketing research, strategy, implementation, and results must be focused strategically on the organization's financial objectives, and on the specific financial performance optimization opportunities discussed in Chapter 3. In my experience, few bank marketing directors enjoy a high level of credibility with their CEOs; all too often they are perceived to be far better at spending money than making money. Because many marketing directors lack a thorough understanding of the profitability dynamics of the business, their strategies are not structured, presented, and defended based on their ability to contribute to the attainment of key financial objectives. As a result, the true strategic value of marketing is not understood or appreciated by senior management. To be fair, the marketing director is not always at fault; in all too many cases he or she does not receive adequate direction or focus from the CEO, often because clear financial objectives have simply not been established and/or because the CEO has a superficial exposure to marketing as a discipline. Also, marketing, in many cases, has been relegated to such a low position in the organization structure that no one takes it seriously. Finally, many marketing directors have been promoted to positions for which they simply do not have the skills and experience that is required in today's highly competitive environment.

For marketing strategy to be effective, the marketing director position must have senior management status and be filled with a full-time marketing professional who participates actively in the Strategic Management and Planning process, has clear strategic direction and focus from the CEO, and realizes that strategy, to be of value, must be designed to support financial objectives. To be credible, he or she must have an in-depth understanding of the profitability dynamics of the firm and the industry. Marketing strategy must then be designed accordingly. Finally, marketing directors must be prepared to be evaluated on tangible and measurable results.

As indicated in Chapter 2, "strategic" is defined as "giving an advantage"; therefore, planning which fails to create an advantage for the institution vis-à-vis competitors is not strategic. Competitive advantage, in turn, results from creating superior needs-satisfying benefits packages which are properly positioned, promoted, priced, and delivered to strategically appropriate markets. This is what marketing is really all about. In other words, it is marketing which puts the *strategic* in planning and which bears the responsibility for "converting corporate objectives to bottom-line reality."[2]

Marketing initiatives that are not designed to support specific financial objectives are generally a waste of valuable resources, whether they be related to funding, earning assets, or fee-based services. They usually increase costs, not earnings.

Marketing Focus: Segmentation

"1. Determining, in a rational, informed, and strategic manner, the desired customer base."

According to Henderson, "Most dramatically successful business strategies are based on market segmentation and concentration of resources in that segment."[3] Segmentation strategy is generally based on geographic, demographic, and/or psychographic criteria.

The decision to pursue a segmentation or niche strategy,

whether it be related to funding, earning assets, or fee-based services, follows logically from the realization that:

a. Resources are scarce and must be managed strategically in order to maximize returns,

b. An overall market is comprised of numerous distinguishable subgroups or segments, each characterized by a certain homogeneity of (1) self-image, (2) needs (and wants disguised as needs), (3) buying styles and behavior patterns, (4) values and lifestyles, and (5) responses to offer variations,

c. A certain segment may have values which differ markedly from those of another segment; therefore, it may be extremely difficult and costly to position the bank positively in each,

d. Competitors are becoming much more focused and are targeting specific segments,

e. Many segments have already been lost to a dominant competitor,

f. The resource commitment needed to dominate varies from segment to segment,

g. Segments vary considerably in profit potential,

h. While a bank may enjoy a competitive advantage, for whatever reason, in certain segments, it will also suffer from a competitive disadvantage in others,

i. It is usually easier to maintain dominance than it is to dislodge a entrenched competitor.

Segmentation strategy should not be limited to noncustomers. As a bank attempts to define its "desired customer base," attention must be given to (a) those customers and/or customer groups which are most valuable to the bank based on clearly defined criteria; (b) noncustomer and/or noncustomer groups which are most attractive (given demographic factors, the segment's profit potential, risk considerations, the bank's Strategic Vision, business definition, relative competitive advantage, and capital allocation priorities); and (c) existing customers and/or customer groups, and noncustomers and noncustomer groups, which may *not* be desirable, given the same considerations.

Pareto's law (the 80/20 rule) should always be kept in mind: 20 percent of the bank's customers probably account for some 80 percent of the bank's profits. Many customers and customer groups, even though profitable, may not provide a return sufficient to create shareholder value. Others may be unprofitable altogether. Many banks, for example, have exited businesses such as credit cards; commercial, mortgage, agricultural, international or consumer lending; automobile leasing; upscale or private banking; data processing; and/or correspondent banking. Other banks have upgraded or reconceptualized their lending standards, thereby disqualifying from consideration specific borrowers, business types, and/or industries. In other cases retail service charges have been established to discourage accounts below a certain deposit level, effectively segmenting on an economic (demographic) basis.

In other words, while many banks have been content to let their customer base simply evolve, others have determined, based on strategic considerations, to restructure their customer mix to conform with their strategic vision. According to Patrick J. Leemputte of Price Waterhouse: "Based on our study, we believe restructuring can significantly increase the wealth of bank shareholders. But restructuring means getting out of some of the more traditional bank businesses and moving away from offering all services to all customers—an admission that past strategies may no longer work in today's competitive marketplace. Restructuring also means building from existing strengths in product, service and customer markets where the bank has—or can develop—a clear competitive advantage."[4]

Protecting and Enhancing the "Best" Customer Relationships

The first priority is to identify the bank's "best" customers, based on carefully defined criteria. Several excellent software programs are now available that enable a bank to use its customer data base as a strategic marketing tool, thereby facilitating this effort. Often referred to as integrated or data base marketing, the objective is to take the countless pieces of data regarding customer needs, habits, behaviors, and so forth, and organize them in a variety of ways which will provide the raw intelligence needed to develop sound and coherent strategy. Customer Insight, for example, is a PC-driven system used by several major banks to download relevant information from the bank's central data base, thereby allowing the bank to conduct market segmentation, targeted direct mail, and automated promotional tracking.

Once the most valuable customer list is compiled, strategies must be developed to protect and enhance those relationships, perhaps beginning with surveys and/or focus groups to determine the perceptions held by these customers regarding the bank and its products and services vis-à-vis competitors. Given the value these customers represent, it is simply unacceptable to make assumptions relative to their satisfaction level.

Once a baseline is established, programs can be developed and implemented to improve those relationships, and to measure and monitor success. Focus groups can also contribute greatly to this effort. There are literally an infinite number of cost-effective ways through which a bank can improve customer satisfaction, thereby enhancing and protecting valuable relationships. In the long run, if a bank's competitors want its best customers more than it does, they will surely prevail. Many banks today, in fact, are losing many of their most valuable customers and don't even know it!

Targeting Noncustomer Segments

The process by which desirable noncustomer market segments are selected involves two phases. In phase one a bank will identify as many distinct and accessible market segments as possible in each of the three areas previously mentioned: funding, earning assets, and fee-based services. The most attractive funding segments may be quite different from those representing opportunities for earning asset growth. Target segments for fee-based services will come from both lists and may include other segments as well. Therefore, each of these three areas must develop its own marketing strategy.

This first phase is best accomplished through no holds barred brainstorming sessions involving officers, employees, and directors. This phase is very much a right-hemisphere activity in that the objective is to go beyond the obvious, such as "affluent," "middle market," "small business," and so forth, the segments *everyone* is targeting. The key to effective segmentation is to look at the marketplace and see it differently than everyone else, thereby identifying homogenous groups which have not been recognized as market segments by the competition. These brainstorming sessions should be freewheeling, informal, and above all else, *fun!*

Demographic analysis is also extremely valuable at this stage, and helps to make the marketing strategist aware of certain broad categories which may be especially attractive. For example, *Fortune* reports: "Hispanics are a rapidly growing segment of the population, increasing 34 percent over 1980, four times the overall U.S. growth in that period. Their numbers may exceed 40 million by 2015, surpassing blacks as the nation's largest minority group. The market is not only expanding, it is also relatively inexpensive to reach. A 30-second spot on the top-rated Spanish TV show, 'Sabado Gigante', costs $11,500, compared with $360,000 for 'The Cosby Show.'"[5] Obviously, since 90 percent of the Hispanic population resides in just nine states, this information, like most demographic information, only has value for those who are positioned in those areas. However, a rapidly growing segment such as this, having $30 billion in purchasing power, cannot be ignored.

Another example at the macro level are baby boomers. According to *Bankers Monthly*, "There are 79 million baby boomers who were born between 1946 and 1964. The future of the country is in their hands and the future of retail banking is in their wallets."[6] This, of course, is a segment which many banks are targeting with great success. Still, in most markets no single bank has succeeded in staking out an unassailable position.

A less obvious market segment attracting attention from professional marketers is the 6 to 14 age group. Not only do these children receive approximately $5 million in spending money annually, they also have a significant influence on their parents' spending decisions. In addition, they provide fascinating insights into the buying habits and trends of the future. Selina Guker, president of Children's Market Research, Inc., publishes a newsletter called *Kid Trends* in which she presents these and other research findings. Among the recommendations: "Look for expanded opportunities in Financial Products and Services for children."[7] At least one group has already created a bank exclusively for children—Young Americans Bank in Denver, Colorado.

Other segmentation techniques focus on life-style and values patterns. One example is the VALs (values and lifestyles) Framework developed by Arnold Mitchell of SRI International and published in his book, *The Nine American Lifestyles*. Based on the responses of 2,713 respondents to 800 questions, Mitchell identified nine lifestyle groups: (1) survivors (4 percent), (2) sustainers (7 percent), (3) belongers (33 percent), (4) emulators (10 percent), (5) achievers (23 percent), (6) "I am me's" (5 percent), (7) experientials (7 percent), (8) societally conscious (23 percent), and (9) integrateds (2 percent).[8] Dozens of major U.S. corporations have made the VALs Framework a cornerstone of their market segmentation strategies.

Another popular lifestyle marketing approach is PRIZM (Potential Rating Index for Zip Markets), marketed by Claritas Corporation and based on a comprehensive analysis of census data by social rank, ethnicity, family life cycle, and housing style, all sorted according to zip codes. From the research, 40 distinct lifestyle/neighborhood "clusters" have been delineated and ranked by affluence, with names such as "Blue Blood Estates," "Young Influentials," "Money and Brains," "Blue Chip Blues," and "Furs and Station Wagons."[9]

Another product from Claritas is P$YCLE, a geodemographic segmentation system designed specifically for financial marketers. Using Federal Reserve data, Claritas isolated six key economic and demographic measures having exceptional relevance to consumer usage of financial products and services. Based on the six measures, eight primary P$YCLE segments and 23 P$YCLE subsegments were formed, thereby allowing bank marketers to target specific products to the most appropriate markets, thereby managing scarce resources more strategically.

More recently, promising segmentation techniques have even been developed based on attitudes and levels of self-esteem. According to Chester L. Kane, writing in *The Journal of Business Strategy:* "After conducting several studies segmenting consumers by self-esteem, we discovered that self-esteem is a new and meaningful segmentation method that does not correlate to demographics."[10]

Regardless of the segmentation model used, it is extremely important to make sure that the relationship between the model and the specific behaviors being targeted are thoroughly validated.

While larger banks may well define target segments in macro terms, such as baby boomers, Hispanics, young influentials, or achievers, many banks may find it advantageous to define their segments more narrowly so as not to compete directly with a much stronger opponent. For example, a typical brainstorming session might result in the delineation of segments such as pilots, sailing enthusiasts, professor/consultants, horse breeders, collectors, hot air balloonists, business owner/operators, franchisees, women professionals, and so forth. In my experience, it is not at all unusual to delineate from 50 to 100 distinct market segments in a typical brainstorming session. The only limitation is the creativity and insightfulness of the group.

While the typical bank will identify the most obvious segments, and will commit resources in competition with everyone else, including those with a decided competitive edge, the more creative and focused approach is to identify niches that no one else has thought of, thereby permitting product development, delivery, and promotion strategies which are truly unique, and which are recognized as such by the segment being targeted.

Segment Prioritization

The second phase is prioritization; from the lengthy list generated in phase one, the bank must now determine which segments are most appropriate strategically, based on clearly defined and relevant criteria. Key questions at this point might include the following:

1. Is the segment *large enough* to justify further research and an active marketing strategy? Can any segments be combined to better leverage marketing costs?

2. Does the segment have stable *growth potential* sufficient to justify the bank's interest?
3. Can the bank exploit or leverage existing or potential *competitive advantage;* that is, are the specific needs of the segment as perceived at this point compatible with the bank's relative strengths in the marketplace, as determined by market research?
4. Is the segment free from *domination* by any one competitor?
5. Does the segment have specific and *unique needs* that are not being met or that are being met poorly by the competition?
6. Are the specific needs of the target segment compatible with the *strategic objectives* of the organization?
7. Is the segment accessible at a *reasonable cost* and with a reasonable allocation of resources? and
8. How *price sensitive* is this segment vis-à-vis other segments?

Based on criteria such as these, the bank will select the segments which represent the greatest opportunity for creating competitive advantage. (See box, entitled "Market Segmentation Worksheet.") This does not mean that other segments will be ignored altogether or that the bank will not attempt to obtain quality business from other sources. It is merely an indication of where the bank's resources will be focused in order to obtain the most effective results.

Chase Manhattan Bank, for example, uses its elaborate geodemographic data base to target products to its wealthy and affluent customers. While this segment represents but 8.7 percent of households, it is growing faster than the market as a whole, accounts for 58 percent of all financial assets held by individuals, and is a segment where Chase clearly believes it has an exploitable competitive advantage.[11]

One of the most enlightening examples of sound market segmentation strategy is that of Miller Brewing Company.[12]

In 1971, Miller, the seventh largest U.S. brewer at the time, was purchased by Philip Morris, which was determined to leverage its superb marketing capabilities to boost Miller's sales.

Market Segmentation Worksheet

Segment _____

1. Is the segment large enough to justify your interest? _____
2. Does the segment have significant growth potential? _____
3. a) Is the segment free from domination by one or more competitors? _____
   b) If not "dominated," is there a clear "major competitor"? _____
   c) Who is this competitor and what specific weaknesses might (must) you successfully exploit? _____
   _____

4. How does this segment support your performance and profit objectives? (Be specific) _____
   _____
   _____
   _____

5. Are you satisfied that the definition of the segment is clear? That it is neither too broad nor too narrow? _____
6. a) Do the characteristics you have identified for this segment set it apart from other segments? _____
   b) What *specific* characteristics have you identified which segment participants themselves particularly value as setting them apart from other segments? _____
   _____

7. Are you satisfied that you have identified sufficient segment needs which rank high in importance—cost effectiveness—and differentiation value? (See needs analysis worksheet) _____
8. Have you done a thorough job of identifying "critical success factors" applicable to this segment? _____
9. Have you identified *specific* opportunities applicable to this segment which your bank is in an advantageous position to exploit? _____
   _____

10. Are you satisfied that you have identified *all threats* inherent in this market segment? _____

Market research revealed that Miller High Life, "the champagne of bottled beer," had been effectively positioned as a "country club beer." Unfortunately, research also indicated that the most attractive market segments, those consuming 80 percent of the total beer consumption, were blue-collar workers, young professionals, and college students, hardly the groups most likely to be country club members. Based on its research, Miller set out to position itself in these segments using the "Miller Time" campaign. Naturally, the advertising featured blue-collar workers and young professionals. Sales exploded and Miller began to outsell most other beers. Next, the marketers at Miller searched for a new and unique segment undiscovered by the competition. The result was the "fitness generation," those who were calorie conscious. In 1975, Miller Lite was introduced to penetrate this rapidly growing new segment and sales escalated even further. Subsequently, another segment was identified: drinkers of imported beer, essentially a subset of the young professional segment. Miller's answer was Lowenbrau, licensed by a German company but brewed in the United States. By 1981, brilliant segmentation and product development strategies had moved the company to the number two spot, right behind Anheuser-Busch.

Generic Marketing Alternatives

As banks develop their overall marketing strategy, it may be useful to consider the four generic approaches to marketing segmentation shown in Exhibit 5–2.[13]

Market penetration involves developing new marketing strategies to more effectively sell existing products and services to existing markets or market segments. An example might be a more sophisticated approach to cross-selling, including: (*a*) new recruiting, screening, and hiring standards to upgrade the sales staff; (*b*) branch redesign and/or better lobby displays; (*c*) ongoing product knowledge and sales training; (*d*) incentives; (*e*) sales tracking; and (*f*) sales management. Another example might be a direct mail/telemarketing campaign to sell home-equity loans to a select group of existing customers, as well as to prospects within an existing market. In almost all cases, a bank's best customers are also its best prospects.

Market development involves the marketing of existing products and services to new markets or market segments. This represents a classic market segmentation approach. A variant of this strategy involves packaging existing products in such a way as to create the perception of a "new" product, one which

EXHIBIT 5–2
Generic Marketing Alternatives

	Existing Products	New Products
Existing Markets or Segments	1. Market penetration	3. Product development
New Markets or Segments	2. Market development	4. Integration and diversification

appears to have been designed exclusively for the new segment. Another example might be to use direct mail and/or tele-marketing to market deposit products in areas where the bank does not have a physical presence. Still another is the development of loan production offices to market existing loan products to untapped geographic markets.

Product development refers to the creation of new products to better meet the needs of existing customers or existing markets. By leveraging the existing customer base, delivery systems and brand awareness, new opportunities can be created. Insurance products, discount brokerage, and mutual funds are perhaps the best examples of this strategy.

Integration and diversification requires the greatest expenditure of resources of the four strategies inasmuch as new markets and/or market segments must be penetrated using new products and services. An example might be the purchase of an insurance agency in a community where the bank is currently not active, or the development of remittance processing and lockbox capabilities to target utilities, mortgage lenders, and others who receive large volumes of payments on a regular basis.

Because Market penetration represents the most cost-effective of the four alternatives, it will be the initial focus of most marketing strategies. For those banks whose franchise and brand awareness are especially strong, product development may be the best way to leverage those strengths. This particular strategy, also called "franchise extension," has been used successfully by major companies in virtually every industry.[14] Banks that have developed unique products and services may wish to exploit that competitive advantage through a market development strategy. Integration and diversification makes sense strategically when a bank's existing markets are not growing and/or when the market for existing products is saturated and/or when the bank has a competitive advantage in new product development.

Market Research: Needs Analysis

> "2. Identifying and prioritizing specific current and future needs of desired customer and customer prospect segments."

Because a bank's best customers and prospects are being targeted aggressively by so many competitors, the advantage in the future will go to those who best understand the changing needs of customer and prospect segments. Excellence in analyzing the needs of the target segments is a prerequisite to a successful sales and marketing effort. However, according to a *Wall Street Journal* report based on extensive consumer research: "Thus, only 5 percent of the people in Mr. Hart's part of the study think that American business is listening to them and striving to do its best."[15] Clearly, a tremendous opportunity exists for banks who are willing to listen.

Fortunately, more and more bankers are realizing that they cannot make assumptions regarding changing customer and prospect needs and preferences, but must conduct sound market research, including the use of focus groups, in order to determine with confidence what the customer really wants. Because a great deal of skill and experience is needed to ensure that discriminating questions are asked, and that answers are

CEO's Perspective

Rick Parsons is President and CEO of First State Bank in Springdale, Arkansas.

Question:

Rick, you have made market research a cornerstone of your bank's competitive strategy and are achieving impressive results, especially considering the intensified competition in your market. What made you decide that market research was so important?

Answer:

Although our bank was performing well, we were still not reaching the goals we had set for ourselves. Frankly, we could not figure out why. Some of our people suggested that we advertise more, get our name out more, use television; in other words, throw more dollars at the problem.

But in my mind there was just too much uncertainty as to who and what our market was—and what it should be—and even less direction as to what our communication strategy should be. We simply weren't sure where we wanted to go, how to get there, or how to evaluate the success of our efforts. We needed more focus. Therefore, rather than simply spending a lot of money on new products and/or an expensive media campaign, we asked Alex Sheshunoff and Company to conduct comprehensive market research in our community. They targeted both retail and commercial markets; customers and noncustomers. And what they told us was surprising and hard to take. The results showed clearly that we had been paying too much attention to the "internal" side of the bank and not enough to the customer. And the customers noticed, giving us lower ratings than our major competitor on both service and expertise. They even had the perception that we were more expensive when in reality we were not.

As a result of the research, we knew exactly where we stood in the minds of our markets. We knew our strengths and, more importantly, we knew our perceived weaknesses, the specific things which had been preventing us from achieving our goals. By setting specific and measurable standards of performance, we were then able to determine where we wanted to be in the minds of the segments we elected to target, create strategies to get us there, and measure our success.

The professional market research, and the recommendations for action based on that research, gave us a cost-effective, quantifiable and focused plan for improving our performance. It may not be glamorous or glitzy, but we are convinced that corporate strategy must begin with sound market research. I simply won't spend any significant marketing dollars without it.

interpreted correctly, it is usually advisable to have this research conducted by professionals specializing in focus group research.

Questions to be explored might include: (1) What are their likes and dislikes, as well as their greatest frustrations, in dealing with financial institutions? (2) Is the quality of service they receive adequate? If not, why not? (3) Have they considered moving their account in the past six months and, if so, why? (4) If they elected not to, what changed their minds? (5) How important is quality versus price? (6) How do they define "quality"? (7) What best represents "value"? (8) What specific words and phrases do they use to describe that which represents quality and value to them? (9) In what services are they most interested? (10) Which specific services do they use most? (11) With how many financial institutions do they presently do business and why specifically did they choose each of them? (12) What are the principal factors that, in their minds, distinguish a mediocre bank from a good bank and a good bank from an excellent bank? (13) What specific characteristics, from their point of view, make them special or different as a group? That is, how do they perceive themselves? What is it specifically that makes this segment a segment? (14) If they were designing the bank and its products and services, what would *they* do differently? (15) What specific features and/or benefits would motivate them to move their relationship *now*?

More specific and focused questions will depend on the particular segment targeted, specific strategies the bank may have under consideration, and the responses to the more general questions. The objective is to end up knowing even more about the needs of the segment participants than they themselves know—to acquire knowledge that will allow the bank to differentiate its product offerings, and its promotion techniques, in ways that will prove irresistible to the target segment.

American Express provides a fascinating example of the value of focus groups. Despite an elaborate marketing campaign designed to make their card attractive to women, male cardholders continued to outnumber women four to one. Concerned, American Express executives listened to a group of Atlanta women who were selected to participate in a market

---

CEO's Perspective

Anthony S. Abbate is President of Interchange State Bank in Saddle Brook, New Jersey.

Question:

Tony, you compete with almost all the large New York and New Jersey banks. I can't imagine a more competitive market anywhere in the country, yet your growth and profitability have been excellent. On what has your marketing strategy been based?

Answer:

For years the philosophy that was practiced in our industry was to either give the customer what you *thought* he or she wanted or, if a larger bank in your area came up with a new product or service, then it must be a good idea so you would follow suit. Through a series of strategic planning meetings, we came to the conclusion that instead of playing defense, it was time to go on the offensive. Our decision was that we would become a market-driven organization. We began with a thorough market analysis, the purpose of which was threefold: to define our market; find the opportunities in that market; and exploit those opportunities.

This was done through extensive use of focus groups and an external survey encompassing customers and noncustomers. The results of this research enabled us to crystallize our strategy, concluding that we would not attempt to be the bank for all people. We would narrowly segment our market so we could implement sound marketing practices which would allow us to protect and advance our position in the marketplace.

Ongoing, we continue to utilize various forms of internal and external research methods. Research enables us to respond favorably and profitably to fluctuations in the marketplace and also helps to ensure the effectiveness of our marketing programs. It is impossible to respond to the needs of our customers and customer prospects, *as they define those needs,* if we are not constantly soliciting their input.

In order to become truly marketing driven requires a senior management team that is fully open-minded, supportive of one another, and respectful of one another's opinions. For example, our group, which meets weekly, consists of the functional heads of Finance, Loans, Operations, Branch Administration, Marketing and Human Resources. Bringing them all together and into the decision-making process cuts any communication problems to the quick and allows us to resolve any potential differences immediately. I think it is extremely effective to have the marketing and advertising executives become a part of top-management strategy meetings so that these individuals are not attempting to create programs in a vacuum. Furthermore, since people are the key to any successful business, there has to be representation from the Human Resources side so that staffing flows in support of strategy.

Because of this cooperative effort from conception to inception, we are able to implement the promotion of products faster, enabling us to respond to the needs of the marketplace on a timely basis. Our "Interchangeable CD" and "Interchangeable Mortgage" were highly successful products which resulted from our focus groups. We are now finalizing a new product called "Champ" (*ch*ecking, *as*set *m*anagement *p*lan), which has been developed in direct response to the needs of a market segment we are targeting.

This strategy has allowed us to achieve the levels of growth and profitability we have accomplished.

research panel. According to Jerry Walsh, the senior vice president in charge of marketing the card: "What absolutely floored me was the irony that they were so familiar with American Express and laudatory about it, yet they didn't see the American Express card as something for them."[16] As a result of insights gained in the focus groups, American Express commissioned a totally new advertising campaign that doubled the number of women applying for the card.

As a sidelight, the advertising firm Ogilvy and Mather in 1985 discovered that 76 percent of career women believed that most ads insult the average consumer's intelligence.[17] Clearly, more companies could learn a lesson from American Express on the value of market research.

Creating a Differentiated Benefits Package

"3. Creating superior needs-satisfying benefits which respond profitably to customer and prospect needs and which differentiate positively the organization from its competitors."

Once a bank has selected the most appropriate funding, earning asset, and fee-based segments, and has identified the specific needs, values, expectations, and behavior patterns of each, the next step is to create benefits packages that will enable the bank to gain a sustainable advantage over its competitors. Naturally, every effort should be made to develop benefits products that will appeal to multiple target segments. What the banker must not forget is that the bank is not selling "products," which are really nothing more than the vehicle by which benefits are delivered, but rather the benefits themselves. These benefits represent solutions to problems and/or the satisfaction of wants or needs. For example, consumers don't want IRA accounts— they want retirement security, a lifestyle that fulfills their dreams. The small-business owner wants more than a loan; among other things he or she wants a relationship with someone who understands his or her business, is sensitive to the psychology of entrepreneurship, has a solid understanding of business finance, can be relied on in a crisis, and won't be reassigned just when he or she finally has a real understanding of the business.

As discussed in Chapter 2, banks offer three basic types of products and services: (1) funding products and services, those which generate deposits used to fund earning assets, (2) earning asset products and services, those which produce a revenue stream and/or a fee if sold to a third party, and (3) fee-based products and services, those which produce fee income. Funding products, such as deposit accounts (demand or time), aid profitability to the extent that their total cost, net of related fee income, allows them to be invested in earning assets at a spread which will meet target returns. Earning asset products contribute to profitability when their earnings streams, net of all costs, meet ROE targets. Fee-income products enhance profitability when their volume covers fixed and variable costs and generates acceptable profit margins.

In each of these three areas, the individual bank must vie for market attention with a host of regulatory, cost, and tax-advantaged competitors. As is true in developing marketing strategy in any industry, the overriding requirement is to differentiate successfully the institution and its benefits package from the competitive mass—to position somehow the organization uniquely in the minds of the target markets in ways which are attractive, appealing, and which encourage and motivate action.

Solman and Friedman, in *Life and Death on the Corporate Battlefield*, write: "Size is not necessarily the key to success and survival on the corporate battlefield—the key to competition. Difference is."[18] David Ogilvy warns: "More often new products fail because they are not new *enough*. They do not offer any perceptible point of difference—like better quality, better flavor, better value, more convenience, or better solutions to problems."[19]

Financial service providers traditionally have done a marvelous job of convincing the marketplace that they are all the same; they have similar names, essentially the same product and service menus, look alike, have advertising messages that are almost impossible to distinguish one from the other, and insist on competing primarily on price—because it is easier. Price, however, is rarely the answer.

Customer Satisfaction: The Overriding High Performance Strategy

As banks attempt to dominate specific targeted market segments, the key to success is to be widely perceived within each as doing a better job of satisfying the customers' unique needs than anyone else. Therefore, while creating shareholder value must be a bank's overriding objective, it's overriding strategy must be *"to satisfy customer needs."* The former is no more important than the latter, nor should they be perceived as mutually exclusive. Essentially, all bank profits flow ultimately from direct or indirect customer relationships. Because customer satisfaction is a prerequisite to the retention and growth of quality customer relationships, it is also the only way to enhance the value of the company for its shareholders. Consequently, the enlightened organization seeking to create shareholder value will be driven to excel in satisfying the customer in ways which are compatible with its financial performance objectives.

Companies which are successful in creating, communicating, and delivering added value in exchange for a price premium benefit in two primary ways. First, higher profit margins result that can provide immediate term enhancement of shareholder value and/or can be used to fund additional market research, product development, and/or promotion. Second, over the longer term, the increased growth in market share, if managed properly, has the potential to produce significant scale economies which can provide competitive advantages on the cost side. In fact, a study by Phillips, Chang, and Buzzell establishes that, in most cases, superior quality, large market share, and lower costs, rather than being incompatible, actually go together.[20]

In product development and delivery, therefore, it is important to keep in mind what I call the Customer Satisfaction formula:

$$\text{Customer Satisfaction} = \text{Benefits} - \text{Costs}$$

Regardless of the product or service, customers will evaluate the decision to purchase products *rationally*, based on their particular values and priorities. What may not be rational in a strict economic sense is the relative value a customer or customer segment attributes to a specific benefit or package of benefits. Value, like quality, is highly subjective; emotion and ego are powerful factors. A major error made by many marketers is to impose their own perception of value on a customer or customer group. Successful strategy requires an acceptance of the target segment as rational in terms of what constitutes value to its members.

When a buyer chooses a Rolex watch for $10,000 over a Timex for $29.95, a Mercedes-Benz for $60,000 over a Ford for $20,000, or a CD at one bank paying 8 percent over CDs at competitor institutions paying 8.25 percent, it is clear that the perceived benefits somehow outweigh the difference in price in the buyer's mind. However, as soon as those perceived benefits no longer justify the price difference, for whatever reason, the customer will be motivated to go elsewhere, *no matter how good the product is*. This is, in fact, the dilemma facing many European manufacturers of luxury automobiles as they enter the 1990s, and a critically important lesson that marketers must never forget.

A company's competitive advantage in terms of relative perceived quality or value can deteriorate for one or more reasons: the company may, through complacency or some other reason, fail to maintain its previous standards of quality: a competitor may meet or exceed the firm's perceived levels of quality or value; and/or the perceived needs and/or values of the target segment may change. Therefore, a firm must view relative competitive advantage as dynamic rather than fixed, and must strive constantly to maintain or enhance its relative competitive superiority.

Marketing Strategy: Price or Benefits?

In developing marketing strategy, therefore, the banker can attempt to create customer satisfaction and increased sales based on price and/or based on benefits. Referring to Exhibit 2–1 in Chapter 2, lower costs and/or added value (benefits) may both result from (1) the manner in which resource inputs are acquired (phase one), (2) the process by which those resource inputs are converted into products and services (phase two), and/or (3) the manner in which the benefits packages (products and services) are designed, packaged, distributed, promoted, delivered to, and/or serviced for the end user or distributor (phase three). *Therefore, as bank marketers attempt to create "benefits packages," they must understand and evaluate everything that actually goes into the product or service, from the point at which the initial funding takes place to the point at which the earning asset is created.* In other words, the challenge of reducing costs and adding benefits is not exclusively an operations responsibility, even though operations and finance will play a vital role; it is essentially a marketing responsibility, which may challenge the traditional paradigm in many institutions. Divisional and functional barriers to effective strategic focus and teamwork must therefore be breached, as must the perception of marketing as strictly a staff responsibility. *Increasingly, as shown in Exhibit 5–3, the key to success in all line areas of responsibility is to find ways to reduce per-unit costs, and/or to*

EXHIBIT 5–3
Market Positioning Strategies

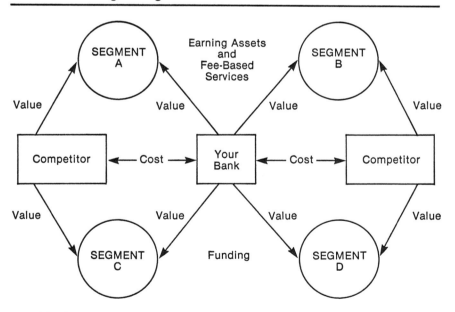

Key objectives

• Control per-unit costs, especially vis-a-vis key competitors.
• Create competitive advantages: added-value which transcends price and differentiates positively.

*add value, in all funding, earning asset, and fee-based products
and services, and to target specific competitors where these competitive advantages can best be created and exploited.*

This is the essence of any bank's competitive strategy and
an important key to prosperity in the 1990s. Therefore, bank
marketing directors must learn to work far more closely with
all functional areas of the organization in order to identify all
opportunities to add benefits and/or reduce per-unit costs. One
of the best examples of this approach is Interchange State Bank
in Saddle Brook, New Jersey where Tony Abbate, the bank's
dynamic and innovative President, has made the development,
implementation, and management of marketing strategy a
high level responsibility shared by the entire senior management team. As a result, the bank is sales and marketing driven
from the CEO to the front-line teller.

Competitive Advantage Based on Price

Banks attempting to create customer satisfaction based strictly
on price must have a sustainable cost advantage to be successful. This, in turn, will require superior performance in virtually
every phase of the product's creation, from raw material acquisition to sales, as well as volume levels sufficient to cover the
significant ongoing investment in new technology.

Because only one competitor in a given market can be *the*
low cost provider, most banks must consider a customer satisfaction strategy based primarily on benefits. This does not
mean, however, that costs do not need to be controlled carefully,
or that efficiencies will not be sought. Banks that pursue a
value-added competitive strategy must constantly seek more
cost-effective methods of enhancing customer satisfaction,
which requires a greater marketing and sales focus from all
functional areas, including operations and data processing.

Benefits-Oriented Marketing Strategy

Because each market segment is unique in terms of its needs,
values, and purchasing behaviors, benefits package design will
be based on the research done to this point, that is, the delineation of strategically appropriate segments and the needs assessment analysis for each. The benefits package for each segment,

in other words, must feature specific needs-satisfying benefits unique to that segment. The objective, of course, is to differentiate the benefits package in positive ways to the specific segment being targeted. In order for a differentiation strategy to be successful, the source of the differentiation must:

a. Represent value to the customer.
b. Attract the customer's attention, that is, be *recognized* by the customer as valuable.
c. Allow a price premium which exceeds its cost. (It also helps enormously if it cannot be easily duplicated by a competitor, which, admittedly, is extremely difficult in the financial services industry, especially for competition with limited resources.)

Therefore, during the needs assessment phase it is important to rank specific segment needs based on (a) their relative importance to segment members, (b) their cost-effectiveness to satisfy, and (c) their relative differentiation value, that is, the potential for contributing to product uniqueness (see box, "Needs Analysis Worksheet"). In addition, every effort should be made to preclude easy duplication by a competitor.

What Is a Value-Added Strategy?

Because bank products are essentially commodities (i.e., most financial institutions offer more or less the same products), there are those who believe that they cannot be differentiated successfully. However, such a point of view is not supported by experience in other industries. For example, many years ago United Fruit Co. made a strategic decision to differentiate its primary product, even though the prevailing wisdom insisted such a strategy would be unsuccessful. The strategy itself was a fairly simple one: put a sticker on it and advertise like crazy. The result? Within six months you could ask any man, woman, or child in America, "Who produces the best banana?" and the answer would be the same, "Chiquita!" Subsequently, Sunkist implemented with great success the same basic strategy with oranges and lemons.

Another fascinating example of successful differentiation was reported in *Forbes* in an article entitled "Hot Dogs with

Mustard and Glitz." Richard Portillo opened a small hot dog business in Villa Park, Illinois, in 1962. He now owns 11 Portillo's Hot Dogs restaurants (with over $20 million in annual sales and $2.5 million in pretax earnings), has plans for four more, and has been hired by a Japanese investment group to help establish a copycat chain in Asia. According to *Forbes:* "The lines at Portillo's outlets are often so long that employees with headsets radio orders ahead to the chef." What is Portillo's secret? "The hot dog business is characterized by low margins and little product differentiation. But Portillo doesn't sell just hot dogs. He sells fun."[21]

By understanding the market segment he is targeting, and creating "theme" restaurants that are highly unusual and "fun," Portillo has added considerable value to the generic product. He realizes, in fact, that he is not selling a product at all; he is selling *benefits*—"having fun," because it represents value to the segments to which Portillo has directed his marketing strategy, is an important benefit for which customers are willing to pay a premium.

Another interesting example is that of Alaska Airlines. According to *Traveler:* "Alaska Airlines, the top U.S. airline in our Second Annual Readers Choice Awards, is too small to compete route for route with the Uniteds or Deltas. Its operating costs are too high to carve out a niche as the next Peoples Express. So Alaska Airlines sells service and personality—and it's thriving."[22]

Lest the reader is still not convinced, consider what may be the least likely product of all to differentiate successfully—water! Not only is bottled water the fastest growing product in the beverage business in the United States, but over 500 firms are now competing for market share. Minalba is a fascinating case in point. Imported from Brazil, the product is being marketed as a "light" water, because it has fewer minerals and, allegedly, no "heavy" aftertaste. According to Helen Berry, Associate Director at Beverage Marketing Corp., an industry research group in New York City, "There's room for more people and there are plenty of niches."[23]

The lesson for bankers in these examples is that if you can differentiate bananas, oranges, hot dogs, air travel, and even

Needs Analysis Worksheet

Segment _____

List below each segment need and give a rating from 1 to 3 for each of the three evaluation criteria listed below. Also give a total needs rating. Rate as follows: 1 = low, 2 = moderate, 3 = extreme. You may also give 1.5 or 2.5 if necessary. The higher the total score (e.g., $3 \times 3 \times 3 = 9$) the more important it is to consider that need in developing the benefits package (product).

Need	Value to Segment Members	Cost Effectiveness to Communicate and Deliver	Differentiation Value	Total Rating
1.	×		×	=
2.	×		×	=
3.	×		×	=
4.	×		×	=
5.	×		×	=
6.	×		×	=
7.	×		×	=
8.	×		×	=
9.	×		×	=
10.	×		×	=
11.	×		×	=
12.	×		×	=
13.	×		×	=
14.	×		×	=
15.	×		×	=
16.	×		×	=
17.	×		×	=
18.	×		×	=
19.	×		×	=
20.	×		×	=

An Example of Successful Differentiation: First National Bank, Pulaski, Tennessee

One of the most daring examples of successful differentiation strategy is that of First National Bank in Pulaski, Tennessee, and its visionary CEO, Robert E. Curry. In 1985, Curry, who was killed tragically in October 1989, conceived the idea of building a dinner theater as part of the bank's main office. In Curry's vision, productions such as *Annie, Camelot,* and *Oklahoma* would be performed using the talented people of Giles County and the proceeds would go to community organizations. The theater would also be used for a variety of community events and would become the center of all civic and cultural activity for the county. As a result, the bank would score a marketing bonanza.

While those who knew the indefatigable Curry never questioned the ultimate success of the project, most bankers might consider a $1 million investment of this nature to be foolish and irresponsible. After all, it had never been done before! It didn't fit the banking paradigm.

Today, the program's success is measured in many ways. Dozens of local agencies have received thousands of dollars in badly needed assistance; hundreds of county residents have been able to develop and display their talents on stage; thousands have been able to enjoy over 25 productions, including a play written by Gregory McDonald (author of the *Fletch* series) especially for the Giles Heritage Theater; and First National has truly become *the* bank in Giles County. Not only has the bank received millions of dollars in new business but has also been awarded Bank Marketing's prestigious Golden Coin Award (which recognizes international excellence and innovation in bank marketing), *Forbes* magazine's Business in the Arts Award, the coveted Governor's Award in the arts, as well as the Tennessee Theater Association's Distinguished Achievement Award.

When one attends a function at the theater (which is often booked a year in advance) and observes the bank's officers serving dinner to several hundred appreciative and loyal customers, the vision and courage of Robert E. Curry become clear.

water, you can differentiate anything—even bank products and services. Leavitt argues the point persuasively: "The usual presumption about so-called undifferentiated commodities is that they are exceedingly price sensitive. A fractionally lower price gets the business. That's seldom true except in the imaginary world of economics textbooks. In the actual world of real markets, nothing is exempt from other considerations, even when price competition is virulent."[24]

Depending on the segment targeted, the relative strengths of competitors within that segment, and the bank's sources of exploitable and sustainable competitive advantage, the following are examples of benefits which might be used to differentiate or add value to a benefits package:

a. Stability—safety, soundness.

b. Responsiveness—fast turnaround.

c. Professionalism—expertise; well-trained, experienced personnel.

d. Specialization—for example, Merchant Banking, Investment Banking, Small Business Lending, Vendor Lease programs, Financial Planning, and so forth.

e. Extended hours—time convenience.

f. Size—"full-service"; resources.

g. Locations—place convenience.

h. Proprietary products—uniqueness.

i. Innovative—state of the art, modern.

j. Quality service—accurate, reliable, and friendly.

k. Flexibility—not constrained by rigid policies.

l. Financial engineering—expertise in corporate finance, creativity in meeting unusual financing needs.

m. Wealthbuilding—helping clients "get ahead," investment planning.

n. Simplicity—hassle-free, easily understood solutions (in contrast to increasingly complex, anxiety-producing alternatives).

While each of these are somewhat generic in nature, and will need to be further refined to reach the needs of a specific funding, earning asset, or fee-based segment, they represent several sources of differentiation corresponding to the needs of a variety of market segments.

When choosing a value-added strategy, the objective is to position the specific institution as the acknowledged leader in one or more key areas. Naturally, once a particular strategy is selected to target a segment valuing those specific benefits, ways must be found of making them as tangible and real as possible for segment members. Substantial investment in new technology, R&D, training, staffing, restructuring, fixed assets, and advertising may be required (all of which should have been factored into the analysis when the segment was selected initially).

Market Positioning Based on Product and/or Service "Quality"

Regardless of the segment targeted, the nature and composition of the benefits package, and the specific source(s) of differentiation, research indicates that it is extremely important for the institution to be perceived generally as delivering "quality." This is true in protecting existing customer relationships and in attracting and keeping new ones. According to a study by the Forum Corporation, which surveyed 2,374 customers of 14 different organizations, over 40 percent listed poor service as the main reason for moving to a competitor while only 8 percent listed price.[25]

The issue of customer dissatisfaction was researched and reported by the Washington, D.C.-based TARP (Technical Assistance Research Programs) which concluded:

a. On average, one in four customers is unhappy enough with service to leave.
b. 90 percent actually will leave.
c. Less than 3 percent of dissatisfied customers will actually file a complaint (for every complaint filed, 26 never report their dissatisfaction).
d. It costs five times as much to get a new customer as to keep an existing customer.[26]

In light of the formidable body of research supporting perceived superior service quality as a prerequisite for superior performance, the results of two recent studies should be of interest to commercial bankers. According to the annual consumer survey published by *American Banker*, credit unions have outranked banks for the sixth consecutive year in customer satisfaction. Of all types of financial institutions, they were the only ones to pick up a significant number of new loyal customers. Even thrifts did better than their bank counterparts in spite of their problems.[27] The thrift superiority was confirmed in another study conducted by Barry Leeds who reports that service quality at thrifts has "significantly surpassed" that of commercial banks. According to Leeds, the thrift customer representatives are better trained, listen better, and are more interactive with their customers. Whereas thrift employees have shown improved ratings for service since 1987, courtesy and friendliness by bank employees, according to the survey participants, have actually declined.[28] While some commercial bankers may prefer to blame irrational pricing and regulatory inequity for the loss of business to credit unions and thrifts, these studies seem to indicate that, for many, the issue is service quality—not price. Regardless, it seems clear that the overall perception of service quality at many commercial banks must be enhanced, which will not come about by making assumptions regarding consumer attitudes. Unquestionably, an absolute commitment to superior service quality must be established as a cultural norm, and supported, reinforced, and communicated successfully. However, it is also critical to realize that not everyone interprets quality in the same way. Each market segment's members will have fairly specific ideas as to what quality means to them, and what their expectations are in this regard. Therefore, banks must promote and deliver the specific benefits which represent value to those segments they are targeting.

Bankers, in other words, must determine their specific perceived strengths and weaknesses in the area of service quality, especially among their target segments, and must then work diligently to create, deliver, and reinforce those values that are meaningful to the customer—and that will alter market perceptions in their favor. Citibank, for example, discovered that what they believed constituted quality service was not always

CEO's Perspective

R. Carlos Carballada is President and Chief Executive Officer of Central Trust Company in Rochester, New York.

Question:

Carl, why did you chose a "quality service" marketing strategy to differentiate your bank and why has it been so successful?

Answer:

We selected a marketing strategy emphasizing quality service in 1985. As we began competing in a deregulated environment for the first time, we realized we needed to achieve differentiation on factors important to our customers. Differentiation would enable us to gain market share and increase earnings over the long term.

We analyzed what our customers wanted and what we felt we could do better than our competitors. As a relatively small bank in our market, but one with local decision making, we felt we had an advantage in being able to deliver a superior level of service. We also knew, from surveys we had conducted and other sources of information, that service was becoming increasingly important to our customers.

Once we realized we could deliver better service than our competitors, and that service was a key factor in an individual's choice of which bank to use, it was an easy decision to commit to a marketing strategy emphasizing quality service.

This strategy has succeeded at Central Trust for three reasons: commitment, focus, and continual service improvements.

A quality service strategy must have the total commitment of senior management if it is to be a success. At Central Trust, we've demonstrated that commitment publicly by having me serve as the spokesman for the bank in all of our advertising on this subject. We've also provided the direct phone numbers of all senior officers, including myself, to our customers so that they can call and discuss service problems. When I tell people in our TV ads to call me if there is a problem, it is more than just rhetoric. I really mean it.

Constant focus on the quality service strategy is another essential component of success. The strategy must be constantly emphasized in employee meetings and through internal communications. The strategy must also be built into the bank's performance evaluation system and reinforced through employee award programs. The strategy must become an integral part of the bank's culture, and all employees must have an understanding of the importance of the strategy.

Another reason that the strategy has been successful at Central Trust is the continual addition of service improvements. We are constantly examining our service, soliciting customer input, and asking, how could we be doing this better? The strategy has evolved and changed as the expectations and desires of our customers have changed.

consistent with the views of customers.[29] This invaluable information greatly enhanced their ability to design and promote new product offerings.

Service businesses, such as banking, have an additional challenge in using quality as a source of differentiation. According to Stanley M. Davis: "Because products are 'things,' whereas services are acts and interactions that must be participated in and experienced to become real, it is useful to think of the production and consumption of a service as a social event. Emotions, values, perceptions, attitudes, expectations, and other human traits of both the customer and the employee come into play more than they do with products. And there are more opportunities not only to manage, but to mismanage the exchange. Quality and value are all largely subjective."[30]

Therefore, as bankers design benefits packages in response to the unique needs of particular segments, it must be understood that a key component of the product is the ongoing interaction the customer has with each and every bank employee. *The employee is, in fact, an essential part of the product, in many ways the most important part. Even the finest product becomes mediocre when delivered by mediocre people.* Each "moment of truth," to use Jan Carlzon's terminology for an employee-customer interaction, will therefore serve to differentiate the institution for better or for worse in the mind of the customer. Because customer satisfaction, in other words, is highly influenced by the most recent "moment of truth," quality control does not end at the point of production or delivery but is an ongoing, never ending process. A customer's perception of quality is no better than his or her last encounter with a bank employee. Because most banks are not monitoring and measuring the consistency and quality of these interactions (and might be shocked if they did) they have not made a true commitment to customer satisfaction.

Measuring and Monitoring Customer Satisfaction

Perhaps the most telling indicator of a company's true commitment to customer satisfaction is the extent to which customer satisfaction is measured, monitored, and managed.

There are seven key requirements for the successful creation, implementation, and management of a customer satisfaction strategy.

First, the commitment of senior management to customer satisfaction must transcend rhetoric and catchy but empty slogans. The organization's leadership must be prepared to listen to what the customer has to say, even if it departs radically from existing perceptions and beliefs. The values and purchasing patterns of bank leaders may prove to be highly unrepresentative of the markets which the bank is targeting, and prior assumptions regarding needs and expectations may prove to be false.

Leadership commitment must include a willingness to question every aspect of how the bank conducts its business in order to identify all inherent obstacles to customer satisfaction, whether they be related to culture, architecture, hours, hiring and staffing practices, performance review, organization structure, use of technology, policies and procedures, product and service mix, and so forth.

Second, the bank must conduct ongoing professional market research to make sure that it maintains a superior degree of insight into the changing needs and perceptions of its most valuable customers and target market segments.

Third, the bank must determine the baseline level of customer satisfaction by segment vis-à-vis the competition, especially in those areas that best represent value and in which the bank seeks to differentiate itself.

Fourth, the bank must conduct ongoing intelligence gathering to determine what each major competitor is doing to improve customer satisfaction, and where the bank may have competitive disadvantages which must be overcome.

Fifth, strategic action plans to improve absolute and relative satisfaction in key areas must be created, implemented, and reinforced.

Sixth, decisions must be made with respect to what specific indicators of customer satisfaction will be measured, how often, and by whom. A variety of customer satisfaction measurement scales are currently used in businesses. Federal Express, for example, uses a 101-point scale where 101 signifies complete satisfaction while 0 represents complete dissatisfaction. General Electric uses a 10-point scale ranging from 1 (poor) to 10 (excellent). GE also ranks each customer satisfaction factor (benefit) from 1 (not important) to 10 (extremely important). A 5-point scale is used by IBM: 5 = very satisfied, 4 = satisfied, 3 = neutral, 2 = dissatisfied, and 1 = very dissatisfied.[31]

Seventh, accountability for customer satisfaction must be clearly delineated, and specific consequences established and reinforced for various levels of performance. For those who excel, liberal use of the three Rs (recognition, rituals, and rewards) must become a cultural norm. On the other hand, true commitment to customer satisfaction will demand that those whose attitudes and behaviors are nonsupportive of the bank's strategy, and who fail to respond positively to reorientation and training, be terminated or placed in a noncustomer contact position. However, as the battle for market share becomes a battle for survival, and as banks become more market and customer driven, everyone in the organization will have to play a vital role in delivering the highest possible quality of customer service. Under such circumstances, no position within an organization will accommodate those who cannot or will not play a positive role in delivering on that promise.

Promotion and Delivery

"4. Promoting and delivering those benefits effectively and efficiently to the market segments being targeted."

A bank's overall promotion effort includes every message sent to its markets and constituencies, whether they be intentional or unintentional, positive or negative.

In other words, the bank's official promotion strategy, which will most likely include advertising, public relations, personal selling, and sales promotion,[32] must be supported by a number of other important factors. For example, the exterior and interior appearance of the bank's facilities, its choice of signage, its logo, the attitudes, dress and grooming standards of its work force, its brochures and how they are displayed, the quality of all written communications, the quality of phone service, and the timeliness and accuracy of its statements all convey powerful messages to the marketplace—messages that may, in fact, be inconsistent with its official promotion strategy. Bank exteriors, for example, are often imposing and uninviting, and may nullify official statements promoting the bank as a warm and friendly place to do business. Banks typically design their structures with little or no consideration given to the specific impact they might have on the market segments being targeted. Meanwhile, rude and/or disinterested telephone operators may totally negate even the best marketing campaign extolling friendliness and service quality as cultural norms. Therefore, once a bank determines which specific segments it wishes to target, how it will differentiate itself, the benefits packages it wishes to promote, and the basis for its customer satisfaction strategy, it must assess and monitor regularly every conceivable message that is being sent to make sure that they are all supportive and consistent.

Promotion is communication, and communication, to be effective, requires that the symbols chosen by the communicator be easily recognizable and understood by the target audience. Therefore, promotion strategy must be designed to match the values, needs, and communication patterns of the specific segments being targeted. One of the great benefits of focus group research is the identification of language structure and usage unique to members of specific market segments. In this way they can be incorporated into future promotion efforts.

Promotion strategy has essentially five purposes: (1) to attract attention, (2) to inform and arouse interest, (3) to persuade, (4) to motivate to action, and (5) to remind and reinforce.

A. To Attract Attention

To be effective, promotion strategies must first gain the attention of those being targeted. Not only must the message be designed to appeal to the specific segment, but the medium itself must be carefully evaluated, as must alternative choices within the medium. A product designed for national distribution to professional women, for example, might be better received by readers of *Working Woman* than by readers of *Ladies Home Journal*. On the other hand, the best medium might not be a "woman's" periodical at all but rather *Forbes, Business Week, The Economist,* or an industry trade publication. Regardless, it is clear that the message will be evaluated in part on how it is packaged, that is, by the medium selected for its delivery. By matching the geodemographic and psychographic characteristics of its target markets with those of a periodical's reader base, a radio station's listener base, or a TV program's viewer base, scarce marketing resources can be utilized more strategically.

To attract the attention of the target market, the bank's promotion message must be (*a*) "different" and (*b*) appropriate. To be different requires creativity and the willingness to experiment with nontraditional symbols, both verbal and visual, and to depart from the mainstream. To create messages that are appropriate, in that they touch a nerve with the target market, requires sound market research. The more immediate the recognition of the bank's message as representing needs-satisfaction, the more likely it will be that interest will be aroused. Because the target segment members will be bombarded by dozens of competing messages, and may only allocate one or two seconds to each before making a decision to reject the message outright or to devote additional attention, *nothing is more critical to promotion success than the uniqueness and needs-satisfying properties inherent in the message.* Again, focus groups represent an excellent and relatively low-cost way to evaluate alternative promotion messages prior to implementation.

B. To Inform and Arouse Interest

Once the attention of the target market participant has been gained, the promotion message must inform, clearly and persuasively, how the benefits will meet his or her needs in a superior fashion. In so doing, the promotion message must arouse the target's interest to explore further the needs-satisfying benefits that are being proposed, and how they might be acquired.

As mentioned earlier, one of the keys at this stage is to use language that is appropriate to the specific segment, and to emphasize benefits rather than product features. In addition, the message should be focused, simple, and devoid of distracting and complex submessages which are not central to the promotional purpose.

C. To Persuade

Promotion strategy, to be effective, must persuade the target that his or her needs will, in fact, be satisfied more completely and appropriately by the benefits which are proposed, and that he or she would be sufficiently better off by responding in a positive manner to the offering to justify whatever effort is required.

In this regard it is possible to position a bank positively against a specific competitor without mentioning that competitor's name if you know the specific perceived weaknesses of that competitor in the marketplace. By making that competitor's customers even more aware of what they are not getting, and by offering a desirable and credible alternative, a bank can enhance its relative market position.

D. To Motivate to Action

It is not generally sufficient merely to persuade target segment members that the benefits being presented are valuable and desirable. Regardless of the segment being targeted, its members will have many conflicting pressures and priorities, and limited excess time or energy with which to respond. Therefore, the promotion message(s) should suggest a course of action that can be initiated with a minimum of inconvenience or effort; the easier it is for the individual to initiate action, the better. In addition, it helps if a sense of urgency can somehow be created, a valid reason for acting quickly. This is especially true for more traditional banking products since the market for these products is highly saturated and generally involves making a change—not just trying something new. An incentive is required. Switching a banking relationship is perceived as extraordinarily cumbersome and complex, and not at all urgent, and this fact goes a long way toward explaining the inertia which pervades the industry. By the same token, that inertia is breaking down rapidly. The reason is simple: more and more financial service providers, especially nonbanks, are making it easier and more convenient for consumers and businesses to move entire relationships, or profitable portions thereof, and are providing incentives to those who act quickly.

E. To Remind and Reinforce
It is far easier and much more economical to keep an existing customer than it is to get a new one. Therefore, promotion messages must also be designed to reinforce to existing customers that they have made a wise and prudent decision. Again, research is critical to success. The promotional messages should reflect (a) insight as to the specific needs of a particular segment, (b) the specific, superior benefits they are currently enjoying, and (c) a solid understanding of the strategies of competitors within the same segments.

One of the greatest untapped opportunities for most banks is to do a far more effective job of communicating promotional messages to existing customers, by customer segment, which reinforce the decision they have already made to do business with that institution. Such reinforcement, in addition to being highly cost-effective, also contributes to an effective cross-selling effort.

Promotion strategies are generally of two distinct yet related types: (a) institutional or image and (b) product and/or segment.

Institutional promotion involves positioning the institution in a particular manner vis-à-vis competitors. For example, the "Quality Is Job One" theme used by Ford Motor Company is a mass-market institutional advertising message designed to position Ford as a higher quality product vis-à-vis domestic and foreign competition. On the other hand, advertising for the turbo-charged Probe GT appearing in *Road & Track*, or the Lincoln Continental appearing in *Gourmet*, is designed to promote the benefits of specific products to specific segments.

Promotion Mix

Once the target segments have been selected, needs identified and prioritized, benefits packages created, and appropriate promotion messages conceptualized, the promotion mix becomes extremely important. For certain segments, the emphasis may be on outdoor advertising, direct mail, and personal selling; for others, print and radio advertising, supported by lobby displays, might be more effective. The important point here is that the most appropriate promotion strategy will be a function of several factors, and experimentation might be required to determine which mix produces the best results. The key factors determining the choice of promotional alternatives include: (a) size, homogeneity, and characteristics of the geographic area to be covered, (b) target segment media habits, (c) the demographic and psychographic characteristics of the segment being targeted, (d) the nature and focus of the competition, (e) the sources of differentiation (benefits), (f) available resources, (g) costs of promotion alternatives, and (h) specialized expertise available internally, for example direct mail, telemarketing, sales, and so forth.

Distribution

According to Friars, Gregor, and Reid of the MAC Group: "Distribution is more than a facility. It is the complete range of distribution activities involved in acquiring and maintaining customers. It includes the sum of people, technology, and outlets involved in a firm's efforts to acquire customers and maintain a customer franchise."[33]

Naturally, different distribution or delivery systems will be more appropriate for different segments and/or types of products. When greater value is added, thereby creating a more customized product, a more personal and higher-cost distribution alternative may be required. For commodity products (offering little added value) directed to a mass market, a low cost delivery alternative may be called for. Therefore, to the extent that a bank has a greater variety of distribution alternatives available, its overall strategic options are expanded as well.

Traditionally, each bank performed the roles of manufacturer, distributor, and retailer of financial products. In the early days banks even printed their own currency!

Because bank *product development* was a function of what regulators would allow, and what data processors would support, rather than a creative response to market needs, few banks ever really developed an expertise as innovative and market responsive product developers.

Distribution in the traditional bank related almost exclusively to the number and quality of locations from which a narrow product line was made available. Again, latitude in this area was constrained by regulation.

Sales, of course, in the true sense of the word, was virtually nonexistent in that bankers, for the most part, were order takers waiting patiently for new customers to walk through the front door.

In other words, although banks performed all three functions, they weren't really very good at any of them; under the old paradigm they didn't have to be.

Distribution Involving Bank/Third-Party Relationships

In the 1990s, however, for all the reasons discussed in Chapters 1 and 2, bankers are finding that growth and profitability are impossible without sustainable competitive advantage, which in turn will result from superior expertise in one or more of the three key areas: product development, distribution, and/or sales. In recognition of their limitations, and of the specialized expertise which is increasingly available from third parties, many banks are forming strategic alliances designed to make them more competitive.

As illustrated below (Exhibit 5–4), I have identified seven potential bank/third-party relationships, each of which may justify creative brainstorming sessions in order to evaluate its relative strategic merits. For each of the three roles (product developer or manufacturer, distributor, or retailer) the bank may select a third-party partner. Also shown in the diagram are the potential sources of competitive advantage the bank will probably need in each relationship to make its contribution meaningful.

A. In what might be characterized as a *sales dominant* bank, an exceptional level of sales and sales management expertise will have been developed, thereby giving the bank a

EXHIBIT 5–4

Alternative Potential Bank/Third-Party Relationships

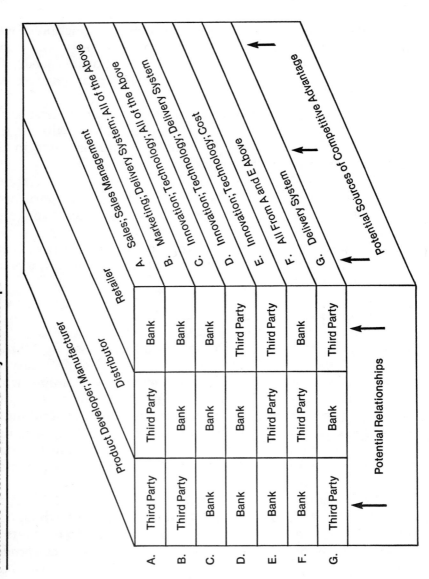

competitive advantage in sales and sales management. Theoretically, this expertise might be leveraged by placing a sales force in someone else's distribution network, selling products developed by a third party. In many cases these may be products which the bank also distributes through its own delivery system.

B. For those banks developing a competitive advantage in distribution and sales (perhaps via technology), the strategic opportunities inherent in a relationship such as this (linkage with exceptional product developers and suppliers) are endless. No longer constrained by the product development limitations of its own organization, these marketing-driven banks will be able to leverage their existing fixed costs and competitive advantages far more effectively. (This may offer the greatest potential of the seven scenarios.)

C. The *traditional bank*, which only distributes and sells those products which are created internally—and only develops those products that it is capable of distributing and selling—will have imposed considerable constraints on its ability to grow and profit, given the specialized competition with which it must do battle each day.

D. *Wholesalers* are those banks that manufacture and distribute products that are then sold by an outside sales force, perhaps on a door-to-door basis and/or during hours when the bank is not open, and/or to markets where that sales force has a competitive advantage. Another possibility might exist in conjunction with scenario *G*, where the bank allows its distribution network to be used by an outside sales force selling its own products. In such cases the bank may develop products and/or services which might more appropriately be sold by that sales force rather than its own.

E. In what might be called the *franchisee* relationship, a bank will leverage its considerable products development and technological expertise by making products available to non-competitor, marketing-driven banks (letter *B*, above), and non-banks, often creating a franchisor/franchisee relationship. Examples of such a relationship might also include the development of products which are distributed and sold through law firms, accounting firms, freight forwarders, consulting firms, mortgage firms, and so forth.

This type of relationship represents a tremendous potential source of competitive advantage for both parties. Another example might be the use of a large telemarketer to distribute and sell products or services generated internally. The relationships established by major credit card companies with airlines, hotel chains, and rental car companies represents an example of this strategy.

F. The most obvious application of this strategy is the growing popularity of placing low-cost banking outlets in supermarkets. Another scenario might result when a bank develops a specialized system for its internal use, such as a program for administering cafeteria benefit plans, and then places one or more salespersons in a third party's distribution network to sell that technology, thereby reaching attractive customers who might otherwise be inaccessible. In such cases, the more technologically complex the product, the greater the potential will be for the bank to use its own sales force. Another example might be a bank that has developed a competitive advantage in the leasing business and that might arrange with other financial institutions anywhere in the world to place its leasing officers in their distribution system on an income-sharing basis.

G. Distribution-oriented banks will be those who leverage their existing delivery system to present product offerings from third parties to their existing customer base. An example of such a strategy is the multitude of third-party product offerings included in monthly statements from oil companies, department stores, and credit card companies. Other examples include discount brokerage services, investment centers in banks operated by third parties, and a variety of space and fee-sharing arrangements. GNA, for example, was developed in 1980 specifically to market a wide range of investment products through the existing distribution network represented by financial institutions. The company custom tailors its services to the needs of each financial institution client.

Creating, Implementing, and Managing a Sales Culture

"5. Converting the organization and everyone in it into a strategically focused, competitive, disciplined, and professional sales force committed to the organization's vision, cultural values, financial objectives, and customer satisfaction strategies."

As discussed in Chapter 4, comprehensive corporate culture analysis will help to quantify both strengths and weaknesses relating to the bank's sales and marketing orientation. Specific relevant issues should include:

a. The degree to which the organization is strategically focused on financial performance and shareholder value objectives.

b. The perceived relationship between financial strategies and marketing strategies.

c. The level of commitment throughout the organization to superior performance and customer satisfaction.

d. Awareness of marketing focus, that is, consensus throughout the organization regarding target market segments.

e. The degree to which employees consider their jobs to be related to either sales or sales support.

f. The level of belief throughout the organization that the bank and its products and services are perceived as unique and superior by its target markets.

g. The extent to which employees believe that the bank is "the best bank" in its market.

h. The degree of consensus throughout the company that the bank is customer driven as opposed to product driven.

i. Commitment to, satisfaction with, and effectiveness of, both product knowledge training and sales training.

j. The degree to which both policies and procedures and operations and data processing support sales and marketing objectives.

k. Whether measurable performance standards exist for all employees relative to sales and sales support.

l. The relationship between sales and sales support performance and performance review and compensation.

m. Whether or not superior salespersons are recognized as "heroes" in the bank's culture.

n. Whether meaningful rituals exist to reinforce excellence in sales and sales support.

Once the bank's leadership has a clear understanding of the bank's strengths and weaknesses in each of these sales culture areas, a comprehensive plan can be created, integrating all functional areas of the organization to create the type of culture which will allow the bank to take quality business away from the competition in an aggressive and systematic manner. *Remember, you don't just create a sales culture. You must modify*

Industry Specialist's Perspective

Michael T. Higgins is President of Mike Higgins & Associates, Inc., and the author of *Beyond Survival.*

Question:

Mike, you specialize in helping banks implement and manage sales cultures. How are sales-driven banks different and what advice do you have for a CEO who wants a sales culture in his or her bank?

Answer:

Those banks that have created and sustained a successful sales-driven organization have:

1. Implemented and continually reinforced nine prerequisite disciplines necessary to sustain a successful sales culture.
2. A senior management team which has previously reached a consensus on the responsibility, activity, and time frames on how each of those disciplines had to be implemented; who was to be responsible; and how each of the disciplines would be continually reinforced.
3. A recognition among all senior officers and their subordinates that sales culture is not the theme of a successful sales-driven organization; *accountability* is the theme.

Organizational change to create a successful sales culture does not happen by decree. There are at least 10 major conditions that must be established in the organizational infrastructure to create the collective accountability necessary for producing the organizational change required to maximize an organization's potential. The conditions that must exist are:

1. Senior management is committed to the organizational mission.
2. Managers agree about the organization's vision and focus.
3. Organizational and individual success is defined in terms of critical results.
4. Managers have accepted individual accountability for producing specific, critical results.
5. Managers are empowered with sufficient authority and resources, and they are backed by an effective organizational structure necessary to support their accountability and to achieve results.
6. Coworkers follow through on commitments to support each other's work.
7. Managers set, and team members agree on, their performance expectations and goals.
8. Performance critical to achieving results is regularly measured.
9. Everyone receives timely feedback on his or her performance.
10. Successful achievement of results earns significant rewards.

The more immediate challenges, however, are to establish and manage the critical performance of each senior manager and thereby sustain the change necessary to make a difference. The challenge is really one of defining new expectations and behaviors that must replace old habits. The importance and difficulty of this challenge cannot be underestimated.

Successful CEOs have established a market-driven sales and service quality culture by explicitly identifying their expectations, setting specific goals, and measuring what the cultural change would produce in terms of bottom-line results. Successful managers have worked with their staffs to measure and manage the critical performance that must be consistently executed to achieve the necessary results. *It must all begin with senior manager accountability.*

Microcomputers have lent a new meaning to measurement. Systems are now readily available to target and measure senior- and middle-management accountability for all aspects of every job responsibility. It is now quite easy to measure, both quantitatively and qualitatively, sales, referrals, work flow, quality, and productivity. Everything can be and must be measured.

Accountability must be the focal point. The critical challenge lies in creating individual accountability through performance management throughout the entire organization. Each individual in the organization must be able to clearly identify the performance changes he or she must make on the job and understand how certain behavioral changes will produce measurable results that have both personal and organization benefits. When that is experienced, the organization will achieve the individual accountability required to compete successfully in a very competitive marketplace.

the culture you already have to make it sales and marketing oriented. Such a process must begin with a comprehensive analysis of the strengths and weaknesses of the existing culture.

There are at least three key requirements to becoming a true sales-driven organization.

First, the organization's leadership must be fully committed to making the transition, and willing to endure the pain, discomfort, and stress that will be inevitable in bringing about meaningful change. The transition will not be an easy one. In fact, in many ways this conversion will be a vital cornerstone of the cultural revolution discussed in Chapter 4. The impetus for cultural change, as well as constant unwavering reinforcement, must come from the top.

Second, every aspect of Human Resource Management and Development must be modified and upgraded to support the needs of a sales-driven organization. Recruitment, screening, hiring, and orientation must all reflect the intensified demands of the new environment. All job positions or descriptions must reflect key results areas and performance standards and targets relative to either sales or sales support. Ongoing sales training and product knowledge training must become a cultural norm throughout the company. Tracking and measurement systems must be installed to monitor sales, sales support, and customer satisfaction, and absolute accountability for performance in these areas must be established at all levels. Finally, there must be a direct and meaningful relationship between sales performance and intrinsic and extrinsic rewards. Compensation systems must be redesigned to be truly strategic in helping meet the sales objectives of the organization. In addition, sales management must, in my opinion, be viewed as a line responsibility. One of the greatest problems banks are having in becoming truly sales-driven is that line managers are refusing to become sales managers. Therefore, that responsibility is often assigned to a staff position within the marketing department. As a result, officers and employees at all levels do not feel accountable to the sales manager since he or she is not their immediate supervisor. The problem is often exacerbated by line managers who then resent the perceived incursion of the marketing department into their territory. *Bank leaders who refuse to make line managers responsible for measurable performance results in the areas of sales and sales support are simply not committed to a sales culture.*

Third, the bank must make a commitment to full-time professional marketing, as detailed above, including continuous market research. The success of the sales effort will be directly related to the bank's success in targeting strategically appropriate segments, ascertaining their needs, and creating needs-satisfying benefits packages which are perceived as superior to those offered by the competition. When professional marketing is in place, the sales effort is enhanced tremendously.

Conversely, weak and unprofessional marketing will make successful selling virtually impossible. Banking, in this respect, is no different from any other industry.

SUMMARY

Professional marketing is at least as important to a bank's ability to achieve and sustain excellence in the 1990s as are professional lending, investment management, the management of data processing and technology, and the management and development of human resources.

It is becoming increasingly clear to enlightened bankers that financial performance objectives can only be achieved with a supportive corporate culture and with a total commitment to marketing and sales strategies which create sustainable competitive advantage in (*a*) the creation and management of earning assets and fee-based services and (*b*) funding.

The first step in any successful marketing program is to have a clear Strategic Vision on which to build strategy. Specific objectives relative to the creation of shareholder value must be established along with underlying profitability and growth objectives. *Once the dynamics of profitability are thoroughly analyzed, and opportunities for performance enhancement identified, prioritized, and quantified, then—and only then—can appropriate marketing strategies be created.*

The position of marketing director must be a senior level position, staffed by a full-time professional who understands thoroughly the profitability dynamics of the business. In my view, *the single greatest failing in most banks attempting to become truly marketing and sales driven is the unwillingness to make the commitment to find and hire a true marketing professional.*

Once clear strategic direction is established, and the marketing position staffed properly, the first step is to identify the desired customer base. This process begins with the delineation of carefully defined criteria enabling the bank to identify and prioritize its: (*a*) best customers, (*b*) nondesirable customers and customer groups, (*c*) most attractive market segments, and (*d*) least attractive market segments. This process can be greatly facilitated through the use of data base marketing programs.

The next step is to identify the needs of target market segments. This is accomplished using proven research methodologies, including focus groups. Specific attitudes, opinions, preferences, needs, wants, and language patterns must be identified for each segment being targeted, including the bank's best customers.

Next, customized benefits packages must be created for each segment that differentiate the bank in positive ways from its competitors, contribute to profitable performance, leverage the bank's competitive advantages, and are perceived as meeting the unique needs of the target segment *better* than those offered by the competition.

Once the most appropriate benefits packages have been

created, they must be promoted and delivered effectively and efficiently to the segments being targeted. Promotion and delivery strategies, therefore, must be designed in response to the unique characteristics of each segment, not on some preconceived notion of what promotion and delivery may have meant in the past, or by some contrived formula presented by an advertising agency.

Finally, in order to become truly marketing and sales driven, the entire organization, and everyone in it, must be converted into a strategically focused, competitive, disciplined, and professional sales force which is fully committed to the organization's vision, cultural values, financial objectives, and customer satisfaction strategies. Everyone in the bank must perceive their jobs to be oriented around sales or sales support. Sales management, to be effective, must become a line responsibility, and the effectiveness of sales and/or sales support must become a key element in the performance appraisal of each officer in the organization.

CHAPTER 6

A MODEL FOR CREATING AND SUSTAINING HIGH PERFORMANCE

The art of progress is to preserve order amid change and to preserve change amid order.
> *—Alfred North Whitehead*

In a world buffeted by change, faced daily with new threats to its safety, the only way to conserve is by innovating. The only stability possible is stability in motion.
> *—Peter Drucker*
> *Landmarks of Tomorrow*

Having been privileged to work with literally hundreds of America's top bank CEOs throughout the decade of the 1980s, I am convinced that almost any bank, regardless of size or location, is capable of achieving and sustaining high performance, which I define as follows:

The High Performance Company

1. Creates value for its shareholders by performing consistently in the top 25 percent of its peer group.
2. Creates value for its employees through a strong, positive corporate culture and enlightened leadership.
3. Creates value for its customers and prospective customers through an uncompromising commitment to professional marketing, continuous innovation, and total customer satisfaction.
4. Integrates all of the above through mastery of the process of strategic and cultural change.

EXHIBIT 6–1
The Bettinger Model for Creating and Sustaining High Performance

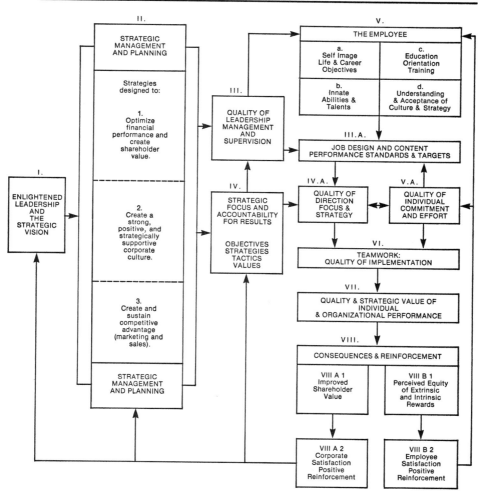

There are at least eight fundamental keys to creating and sustaining high performance. These specific issues are the focus of this book and comprise the model shown as Exhibit 6–1. *Shortcomings in organizational and/or individual performance, at any level, can invariably be traced to weaknesses in one or more of these areas.* Therefore, as I work with organizations to bring about strategic and cultural change leading to superior performance (even when the organization is already performing in the top quartile of its peer group). This model provides the methodology by which (a) specific opportunities for improved performance are identified and prioritized, (b) strategies and tactics are created and implemented, (c) results are measured, monitored, managed, and reinforced, and (d) continuous improvement is achieved.

Using the model, and beginning with Enlightened Leadership and the Strategic Vision, a systematic and comprehensive analysis must be performed on a regular basis to determine precisely where and how performance enhancement might be achieved. This approach to continuous improvement (which the Japanese call *Kaizen*) in each of the eight areas provides the basic foundation for ongoing Strategic Management and Planning and the methodology by which high performance is achieved and sustained.

A discussion of each of the eight key components of the model will comprise the focus of this chapter.

ENLIGHTENED LEADERSHIP AND THE STRATEGIC VISION

High performance, in any competitive endeavor, begins with enlightened leadership that refuses to tolerate anything less, has the power and courage to enforce that commitment, and will not be held captive by obsolete perceptions of reality and prior successes.

When such leadership is in place, a Strategic Vision can be conceptualized which represents a positive and strategically realistic response to the forces of change, a vision which meets the needs of each of the organization's various constituencies; shareholders, employees, customers, regulators, and the communities in which the firm operates.

Conversely, when an organization's leadership lacks commitment, power, the will to fight and overcome resistance to change, and/or the intellectual and emotional courage to break the bonds of tradition, the likelihood of a realistic and dynamic vision of the future being conceptualized, let alone realized, is practically nil.

The need for strategic and cultural change, and for the enlightened leadership which will make the Strategic Vision a reality, is not limited to poor or mediocre performers. Even those organizations that excelled in the 1980s must adapt strategically and culturally to the structural changes and intensified demands of the 1990s. In fact, satisfaction with past success can easily blind an organization's leadership to the fact that the paradigm upon which prior success was based may no longer be valid. Lacking the required sense of urgency, many of yesterday's top performers may underestimate the pervasiveness of change, in the process leaving themselves vulnerable to more adaptive and strategically focused competitors.

However, for those whose foresight has compelled them to make an absolute commitment to master the change process, via the six steps outlined in Chapter 2, the resulting Strategic Vision will serve as a compelling target toward which the organization's resources and energies can be directed. As such, it will illuminate clearly the specific areas where change is required.

For example, if the Strategic Vision, among other things, projects a $3 billion institution serving a tri-state area, generating 22.5 percent ROE, with a corporate culture in the positive range and a customer satisfaction rating of 9.0, we can compare that vision to today's reality (as shown in Exhibit 6–2) and easily identify the key strategic priorities in these areas.

By applying the methodologies discussed in Section II, critical success factors, key opportunities, and strategic action plans can then be established and integrated in the areas of (a) financial performance optimization (Chapter 3), (b) leadership and corporate culture modification (Chapter 4), and (c) market positioning and competitive advantage (Chapter 5). (The process by which these strategies are created, integrated, implemented, and managed represents the second component of the model, Strategic Management and Planning.)

A bank's Strategic Vision should also reflect its innovative

EXHIBIT 6–2
Formulating the Strategic Vision

	Today's Reality	Strategic Vision
ROE	15.0%	22.5%
Geographic Area	statewide	tri-state area
Size	$1.5 billion	$3.0 billion
Corporate Culture	weak positive 1.50	positive 3.00
Customer Satisfaction Rating	7.5	9.0

responses to the five key strategic initiatives or critical success factors discussed in Chapter 2:

1. Banks must develop new fee-based lines of business, thereby reducing their vulnerability to disintermediation.
2. Banks must reconceptualize their relationship with funds users and create, promote, sell, and deliver added value that transcends price.
3. Banks must reconceptualize the entire concept of funding and their relationship with funds providers and create, promote, sell, and deliver added value that transcends price.
4. Banks must reduce substantially the costs associated with performing the intermediary function.
5. The traditional "pooled-capital" concept must give way to capital allocation and management based on return on equity and shareholder value considerations.

The first prerequisite for sustained high performance, therefore, is enlightened leadership and the conceptualization and articulation of a Strategic Vision which (*a*) is based on a thorough understanding of the industry in which the firm operates, (*b*) results from paradigm-challenging lateral thinking at all levels of the organization (i.e., is not the product of obsolete perceptions of reality), (*c*) addresses the five key strategic initiatives listed above, and (*d*) specifies how the organization will be *fundamentally different* in the areas of profitability and shareholder value, leadership and corporate culture, and market positioning based on sustainable competitive advantage.

When the Strategic Vision is well conceptualized, in tune with new realities, and clearly outlines where strategic and cultural change is required, a solid basis for high performance will have been established. When the Strategic Vision is nonexistent, based on an obsolete paradigm, unrealistic, and/or poorly communicated, mediocre performance and strategic confusion are all but assured. In addition, the resultant lack of proper focus and direction will tend to affect adversely individual performance at all levels.

STRATEGIC MANAGEMENT AND PLANNING

Once the Strategic Vision has been developed (generally through one or more senior management retreats) and communicated, and the gap between that vision and the existing reality clearly defined, the next critical step is to establish a comprehensive and all encompassing system (discipline) by which the entire organization, and everyone in it, becomes focused on, and accountable for, the ongoing implementation and management of the process by which that gap will be eliminated. Traditionally, the process through which organizations have attempted to translate visions into reality have been referred to as strategic planning. However, in recent years the value and effectiveness of strategic planning has come under attack from many quarters. Writing in *Economic Review*, Whitehead and Gup assess the effectiveness of strategic planning in the financial services industry: "Even so, our results yield no consistent statistical evidence that strategic planning increases the profitability of the organizations studied."[1] Kenneth Anderson writes in the *McKinsey Quarterly:* "As with all enthusiasms that have swept the management community, a backlash has developed against strategic planning."[2] Porter, in *The Economist*, writes: "Today, strategic planning has fallen out of fashion."[3]

In my view, strategic planning, as typically practiced in the financial services industry, has proved to be ineffective in most cases in enhancing financial performance and shareholder value. There are several reasons for this:

First, as stated earlier, strategic planning is generally viewed by a majority of the organization's managers as a disruptive annual event; a bureaucratic exercise conducted by the comptroller or CFO. As such, it is perceived as an end, not the means to an end. Accordingly, ongoing implementation and management is not taken seriously. As soon as the planning frenzy is over, everyone goes back to doing the same old things.

Second, in many cases strategic planning is a top-down process by which planning assumptions are imposed on managers, forcing them to operate within parameters and constraints to which they have provided little or no input and which they are rarely allowed to challenge. Most first level supervisors, customer contact personnel, and lower level workers have limited involvement in the process. As a result, real ownership in the plan is limited to a handful of individuals at the top of the organization structure.

Third, all too often strategic planning, and the strategic thinking that is its essence, is viewed as a staff responsibility—even by many CEOs—and line managers have minimal creative and strategic involvement—which further limits their sense of ownership and accountability for results. *The bank's leader must be its top strategic thinker and planner, regardless of who else may be involved in the process.*

Fourth, in many banks strategic planning, for all but a few top managers, is almost exclusively numbers oriented and is actually budgeting masquerading as planning.

Fifth, reinforcing its budgetary orientation, the plan often becomes a control document by which the performance of operating units is rigidly measured, regardless of any fundamental structural changes that might materialize in the interim. The objective becomes "meeting plan"—not responding strategically to new opportunities, defensive as well as offensive.

Sixth, because the starting point is generally last year's plan, strategic planning tends to be viewed as a "logical" extension of the past and is therefore constrained by traditional paradigms and outdated realities. Lateral thinking that threatens to create conflict and disturb the organization's comfort level is discouraged and, all too often, punished.

Seventh, because strategic planning is typically an annual event, critical assumptions, once accepted, are often not challenged until the subsequent planning session, even though the dramatic acceleration in the pace and pervasiveness of change demands that an organization become more responsive at all levels to emerging offensive and defensive opportunities, and more willing to recognize and amend those strategies which are clearly not working.

Finally, marketing, corporate culture, and HRMD considerations are all too frequently not viewed as central to the strategic plan or to the planning process itself. To be honest, the selection of leaders for these areas (marketing and human resource management) is rarely based on the same standards as lending or trust, and human resource and marketing issues are deemed by many institutions to be far less strategic than are financial issues. Leaders may say that marketing and HRMD are important but all too often fail to support the rhetoric with meaningful action.

Furthermore, when the critically important interdependence between financial performance optimization, corporate culture, and market positioning strategy is not understood, financial objectives are established without the required supportive changes in corporate culture, HRMD, and marketing.

For these reasons, as discussed earlier, I advocate strongly that annual strategic planning be integrated into a process that I call Strategic Management and Planning. Such a system (*a*) places equal emphasis on creative strategy development (the planning component) and ongoing implementation, management, and accountability for results; (*b*) makes the entire organization more sensitive and adaptive to the implications of external change throughout the planning horizon; (*c*) gives everyone a sense of personal ownership and participation; (*d*) firmly establishes, monitors, and reinforces accountability for results; and (*e*) makes strategic thinking a natural and integral function of ongoing leadership and management rather than an unnatural annual disruption.

As seen in Exhibits 6–3 through 6–6, there are four phases in the process of Strategic Management and Planning.

Opportunity Identification and Prioritization

Phase one, Opportunity Identification and Prioritization, represents the process by which opportunities are identified and prioritized. As shown, and as discussed in Section II, key opportunities to create, enhance, and/or sustain competitive advantage must be prioritized in the areas of financial performance optimization, leadership and corporate culture, and market positioning. Whereas changes in the external dynamics are uncontrollable by the individual firm, its leadership does control change in each of the internal dynamics. In fact, strategic planning may be defined as "the process by which the firm's internal dynamics, which are controllable, are managed to best exploit changes in the external dynamics, which are not, in order to create, enhance and/or sustain competitive advantage leading to increased value for shareholders, customers, and employees."

Because the objective is constant improvement and adaptation to new external realities (technological, competitive, sociodemographic, geopolitical, legislative, and macroeconomic), innovative strategic initiatives will be required *continuously* from every level of the organization. Inherent in such an approach is the need to discard outdated strategies and tactics as changing conditions undermine their effectiveness. In the area of financial performance optimization, for example, the organization must *constantly* seek new opportunities, based on changing realities, to:

1. Allocate and manage capital more effectively.
2. Reduce the organization's vulnerability to disintermediation.

EXHIBIT 6–3
Strategic Management and Planning

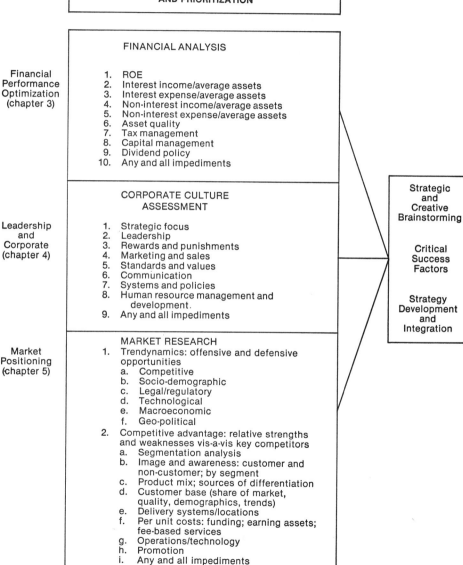

PHASE ONE
OPPORTUNITY IDENTIFICATION
AND PRIORITIZATION

FINANCIAL ANALYSIS

Financial
Performance
Optimization
(chapter 3)

1. ROE
2. Interest income/average assets
3. Interest expense/average assets
4. Non-interest income/average assets
5. Non-interest expense/average assets
6. Asset quality
7. Tax management
8. Capital management
9. Dividend policy
10. Any and all impediments

CORPORATE CULTURE
ASSESSMENT

Leadership
and
Corporate
(chapter 4)

1. Strategic focus
2. Leadership
3. Rewards and punishments
4. Marketing and sales
5. Standards and values
6. Communication
7. Systems and policies
8. Human resource management and
   development.
9. Any and all impediments

MARKET RESEARCH

Market
Positioning
(chapter 5)

1. Trendynamics: offensive and defensive
   opportunities
   a. Competitive
   b. Socio-demographic
   c. Legal/regulatory
   d. Technological
   e. Macroeconomic
   f. Geo-political
2. Competitive advantage: relative strengths
   and weaknesses vis-a-vis key competitors
   a. Segmentation analysis
   b. Image and awareness: customer and
      non-customer; by segment
   c. Product mix; sources of differentiation
   d. Customer base (share of market,
      quality, demographics, trends)
   e. Delivery systems/locations
   f. Per unit costs: funding; earning assets;
      fee-based services
   g. Operations/technology
   h. Promotion
   i. Any and all impediments

Strategic
and
Creative
Brainstorming

Critical
Success
Factors

Strategy
Development
and
Integration

EXHIBIT 6–4
Strategic Management and Planning

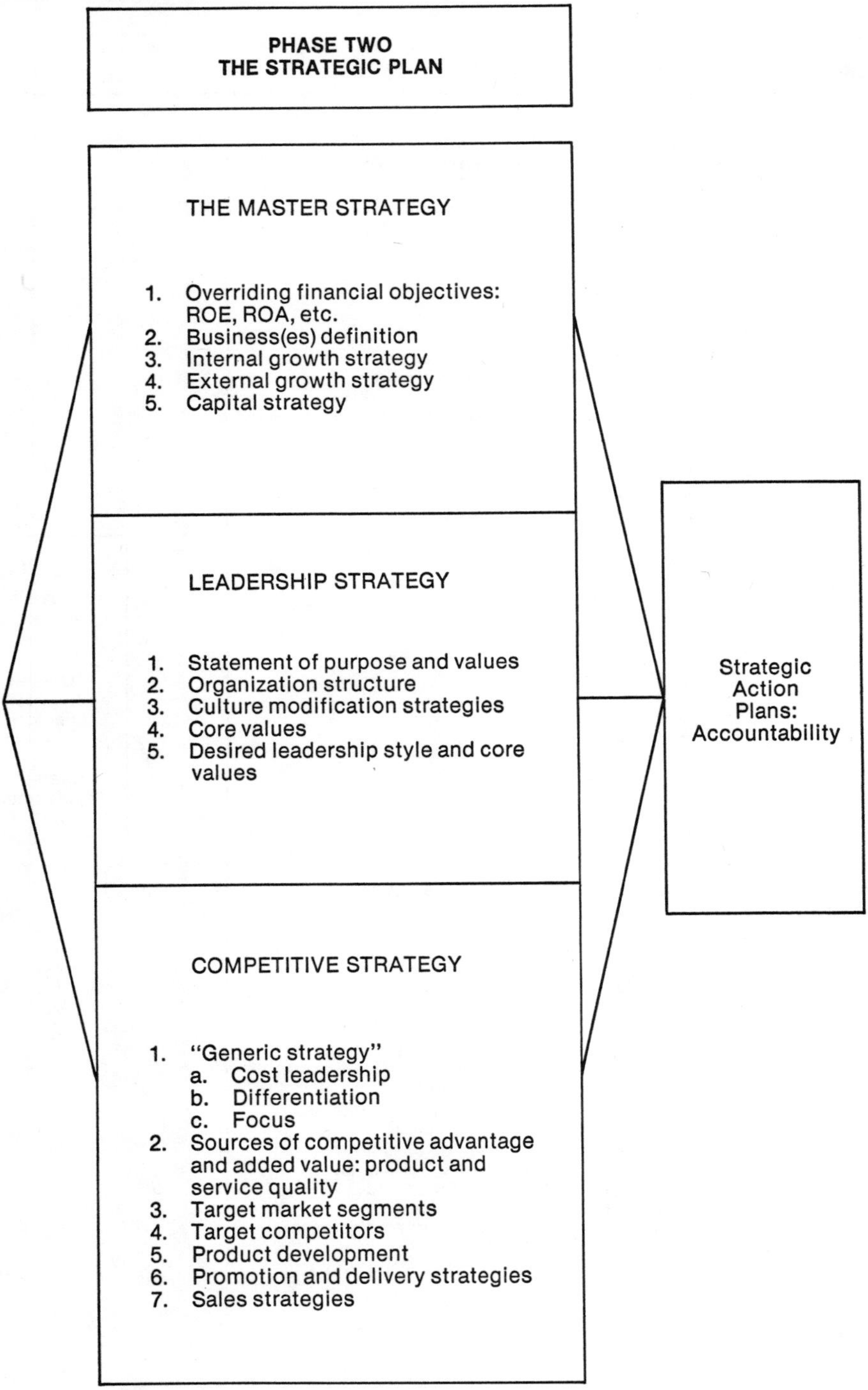

PHASE TWO
THE STRATEGIC PLAN

THE MASTER STRATEGY

1. Overriding financial objectives: ROE, ROA, etc.
2. Business(es) definition
3. Internal growth strategy
4. External growth strategy
5. Capital strategy

LEADERSHIP STRATEGY

1. Statement of purpose and values
2. Organization structure
3. Culture modification strategies
4. Core values
5. Desired leadership style and core values

COMPETITIVE STRATEGY

1. "Generic strategy"
   a. Cost leadership
   b. Differentiation
   c. Focus
2. Sources of competitive advantage and added value: product and service quality
3. Target market segments
4. Target competitors
5. Product development
6. Promotion and delivery strategies
7. Sales strategies

Strategic
Action
Plans:
Accountability

EXHIBIT 6–5
Strategic Management and Planning

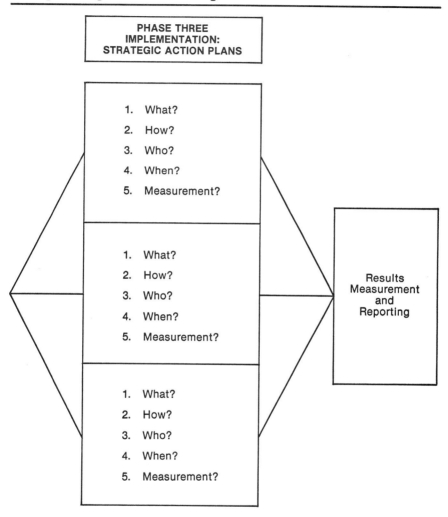

3. Reduce the costs associated with performing the intermediary function.
4. Increase interest income/average assets.
5. Reconceptualize the relationship with funds users and create added value which transcends price.

EXHIBIT 6–6
Strategic Management and Planning

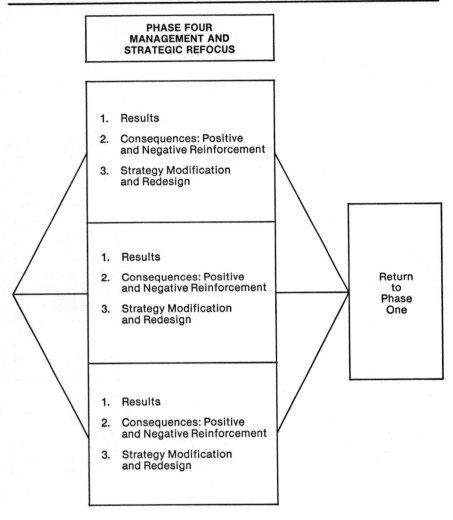

6. Become less product driven (the lending paradigm) and more market and customer needs driven (the financing paradigm).
7. Reduce *total* funding costs.
8. Improve asset quality.

9. Minimize taxes paid.
10. Increase noninterest income/average assets.
11. Identify and exploit specific competitor weaknesses.

In the area of market positioning, new marketing strategies must also be created *continuously* that will take advantage of the opportunities (defensive as well as offensive) brought about by change. Specifically, opportunities must be identified to provide the strategic support needed to accomplish the financial performance optimization opportunities listed above.

A market's competitive equilibrium is constantly being altered by external change in each of the areas previously mentioned, (technological, competitive, sociodemographic, geopolitical, legislative, and macroeconomic). Every competitive change creates new opportunities, both offensive and defensive, and the strategically astute organization will constantly seek ways to turn such changes to its advantage. For example, new technology is made available almost daily. In many cases the creative application of that technology may represent an opportunity to somehow reposition the bank more favorably vis-à-vis competitors. In other cases, new technology may alter the competitive equilibrium in a competitor's favor, especially when that competitor is larger and can more effectively leverage the fixed costs over a larger customer base. This represents a defensive opportunity (threat) and may require that the bank alter its strategy accordingly. One thing is certain: to do nothing in such cases, or to wait nine months until the next planning session prior to evaluating alternate strategic responses, is a prescription for mediocrity and failure in the highly competitive and rapidly changing environment of the 1990s. Banks fail to recognize and take seriously the competitive challenges and threats inherent in the strategic initiatives of competitors. Increasingly, in this era of Darwinian banking, such initiatives represent a direct attack on a specific institution that, for whatever reason, is considered vulnerable. To survive and prosper in the 1990s, banks must be sensitive to such challenges and respond accordingly, that is, *they must become much more competitive.*

On the one hand, a bank must be far more sensitive to, and

critical of, its own vulnerabilities. As internal weaknesses are identified, steps must be taken to limit the organization's exposure. On the other hand, banks must identify more timely and aggressively any competitor weaknesses that might be exploited successfully.

Often, shifts in a market's competitive equilibrium represent windows of opportunity of limited duration. For example, in one market with which I am familiar, two of the four largest banks have recently been purchased by out-of-state holding companies. In one case the new owner replaced an excellent data processing system, designed to create added value for the customer and productivity and pride for the employees, with a system that was not only inferior but that represented a clear disadvantage vis-à-vis competitors. The result has been a severe decline in customer satisfaction, a rash of closed accounts (many of which were among the bank's best customers), and an extremely high level of frustration at all customer contact positions. One branch manager noted: "I hate seeing my good customers walk in the bank because I just know they're here to close their accounts, and the people in _____ just don't seem to give a damn!" Clearly, those in charge of the acquisition seem to be more interested in cutting expenses than in enhancing earnings.

In the second case, the bank's mediocre financial performance over many years was due to an unacceptably high level of overhead expense. This was primarily attributable to severe overstaffing, weak performance standards and accountability for results ("country club" management), a corporate culture that stressed "warm, fuzzy" relationships over performance, and a number of branches that could not be justified economically. The acquiror's initiatives, though implemented poorly, were predictable and tactically correct: reduce excessive overhead expense, primarily through branch closings and personnel cuts—especially of those who persisted in fighting change in an effort to preserve the status quo.

In each of these examples, arrogance on the part of the out-of-state acquiror and a lack of sensitivity to corporate culture considerations resulted in a serious deterioration in morale. This, in turn, adversely affected the quality of customer service, caused many top performers to question their continued loyalty, and left customers concerned and bewildered as to what might happen next. For the competitor sensitive to strategic opportunity, a window was opened to launch an intelligent assault on the customers of each of these banks, especially those with whom the challenger might have a competitive advantage. An opportunity also presented itself to "pirate" the top performers of each institution.

Opportunities such as these may appear at any time—and must be exploited quickly. What are required in such cases include: (a) the intelligence network to detect and evaluate opportunities in a timely fashion, (b) leadership that can respond decisively, (c) a corporate culture that promotes competitive spirit as a core value, (d) professional marketing, and (e) exceptional sales and sales support.

Continuous improvement is also mandatory with respect to leadership and corporate culture. It is critically important in my view that leader-manager effectiveness be constantly enhanced in order to cope with the increased challenges which lie ahead. The upgrading of recruitment, screening, and hiring practices is mandatory, as is a greater commitment to ongoing training which is more strategically relevant.

Because an organization's culture is dynamic, it is imperative that change be managed and controlled in such a way as to make the culture stronger, more positive, and more strategically supportive and adaptive. High performing banks in the 1990s will be those that have created high performance cultures vastly different from those that prevailed in the past, and that are undergoing constant upgrading to cope with the new century which is almost upon us.

More specifically, cultural values must be established and reinforced that support the financial performance optimization and market positioning imperatives listed above. An almost perfect harmony must be created between financial, cultural, and marketing strategies.

Bank leaders who are not consciously and strategically managing their corporate cultures have little chance of surviving the 1990s.

Another important requirement in phase one is the identification of any impediments to the successful implementation of strategy. Many banks make the tragic error of attempting to implement strategy without giving adequate attention to those impediments (people, culture, technology, market image, competitive disadvantage, resources, etc.) that may make successful implementation difficult if not impossible. All such impediments *must* be identified in phase one and added to the list of opportunities so that strategies can be created to deal with them *prior* to implementation. Also, when it is determined that a particular impediment cannot be overcome, for whatever reason, the organization will be less inclined to waste scarce resources in an effort which is doomed from the start.

When Strategic Management and Planning is first implemented, the time frame for generating the basic raw intelligence (key opportunities) in the areas of financial performance and leadership and corporate culture will generally be 30 to 60 days. Market research will typically take longer, depending on the information required and the bank's commitment to research. Meanwhile, decisions must be made relative to the specific information needed on an ongoing basis in order to evaluate both external changes and internal performance in search of exploitable opportunities. For example:

- If a true commitment is to be made to quality service and customer satisfaction, how will each be measured, with what frequency, and under whose accountability?
- What process will be used to evaluate leader-manager effectiveness, how will development needs be identified, what remedial actions will be put in place, and how often will development progress be evaluated?
- How will a bank assess its current standing and position within its key target markets (funding, earning asset, and fee-based services), and how, and with what frequency, will the effectiveness of positioning improvement strategies be evaluated?
- Once core values have been established and communicated, how will overall support for those values be measured and with what frequency?
- How will the overall corporate culture be assessed and,

once culture modification strategies have been implemented, how, and how often, will success be measured?

- How will the bank attempt to stay abreast of new technological developments and how will their potential value to the bank be evaluated?
- How will the bank ensure that all potential benefits inherent in its existing hardware and software are fully exploited in order to reduce per-unit costs, create added value for the customer, enhance job content, and maximize sales effectiveness?
- How will the bank stay on top of competitor initiatives or weaknesses, legislative developments, and macroeconomic conditions on an ongoing basis, in order to be in a position to exploit quickly new opportunities and/or to respond strategically to competitive challenges?

In summary, in phase one specific opportunities to move from today's reality to tomorrow's Strategic Vision will be identified and prioritized, impediments to the successful implementation of strategy will be listed, and an overall methodology will be developed by which ongoing opportunities, in any area, can be recognized timely.

Developing the Strategic Plan

Phase two, Developing the Strategic Plan, will rely on companywide strategic brainstorming to develop the actual strategic plan. The plan will articulate the Strategic Vision, the organization's mission, key objectives, and the strategies which are needed to exploit successfully all opportunities from phase one. The more involvement all departments in the bank have in this phase, the greater the likelihood of successful implementation.

Implementation and Execution

Phase three, Implementation and Execution, represents the implementation phase and is where many banks are experiencing the greatest difficulty. For each strategy, tactic, and critical success factor in the strategic plan, one or more specific strategic action plans must be articulated. As discussed earlier, each will fix clear accountability for results, set forth an appropriate implementation timetable, and provide the methodology by which results will be evaluated. In other words, each strategic action plan will answer the key questions, what, how, who, and when, as well as the specific ways by which success (or failure) will be measured. While some action plans may have a final implementation date which is less than 90 days away, the ongoing measurement of success (or failure) may extend indefinitely into the future. Other action plans may have several implementation stages extending over several years. Key steps in the process, however, will have specific target dates so that implementation progress can be evaluated at each stage.

As leader-managers throughout the organization interact with their subordinates, the primary focus should be the strategic action plans for which each subordinate is accountable. *Therefore, it should be expected that leader-manager/subordinate interactions will be more frequent, more focused, and far more beneficial to both the employee and the organization.*

Management and Strategic Refocus

Phase four, Management and Strategic Refocus, represents the constant evaluation of results and the determination and distribution of appropriate consequences. Exceptional performance should produce exceptional recognition and rewards, as well as continuing support for the strategic initiatives themselves. Less desirable performance should trigger critical reassessment of (a) the strategy itself and/or (b) the effectiveness of the person accountable. If the strategy is flawed, strategic refocus and/or redesign may be called for. If the individual is simply not performing, the reasons must be determined and remedial action taken (see component V of the model). Consequences in such cases may range from dismissal to additional support in one form or another.

The product of phase four will invariably be the identification of additional opportunities to improve individual and organizational performance—which brings us back to phase one. In other words, at every level of the organization it will be expected that opportunities for performance enhancement will be continuously identified and acted upon. *Strategic action plans can originate anywhere—at any time.* Naturally, those individuals and business units that prove to be most effective in identifying new opportunities and/or in producing innovative strategic solutions should receive immediate and powerful positive reinforcement. In this way, strategically focused innovation and competitive spirit become meaningful cultural norms and values throughout the company.

QUALITY OF LEADERSHIP, MANAGEMENT, AND SUPERVISION

Several writers have argued that leaders "do the right things" while managers "do things right." Such a view is simplistic, naive, and just plain wrong. Doing things right is every bit as critical to success as is doing the right things and both are essentials of high performance leadership *and* management. Being a leader is certainly no excuse for not doing things right—nor is not being a leader (just a manager) an excuse for not doing the right things.

From the CEO to the proof department supervisor, the successful execution of every leader-manager responsibility in the high performance company requires (*a*) a clear understanding of, and commitment to, the Strategic Vision, (*b*) a firm grasp of the profitability dynamics of the business, (*c*) an absolute comprehension of how his or her job and area of responsibility relate to both (*a*) and (*b*) above, (*d*) clearly defined key results areas, performance standards, and performance goals or targets against which performance is measured, (*e*) an unshakable dedication to meaningful results, (*f*) mastery of the complex dynamics of human motivation and (*g*) genuine concern for the development and success of each and every subordinate. Weaknesses in these areas are no less common at the CEO or senior management level than at the supervisor level, and the high performance entity, regardless of the endeavor, requires excellence at each position. Furthermore, because the quality of leadership, management, and supervision is the bridge between

EXHIBIT 6–7
Evaluating Management Effectiveness

Manager or Supervisor Name _____   Date _____

Department _____

I. Direction and Focus

1. My supervisor keeps me informed to my satisfaction regarding:
   a. The organization's "mission" and strategic vision.
   b. Financial performance goals.
   c. How my job affects profits.
   d. Our competitive strategy.
   e. How we are doing.

	Strongly Agree	Agree	No Opinion	Disagree	Strongly Disagree
1a					
1b					
1c					
1d					
1e					

II. Performance Standards

2. My supervisor communicates clearly to me:
   a. The "key results areas" for my job; those which have the greatest impact on the organization's success.
   b. His or her *specific* performance expectations.
   c. How my performance is measured.
   d. Deadlines for all projects and tasks.
   e. Work priorities.
   f. Solicits my input in setting performance goals; and
   g. Is firm, consistent, and timely in monitoring and managing my performance.

	Strongly Agree	Agree	No Opinion	Disagree	Strongly Disagree
2a					
2b					
2c					
2d					
2e					
2f					
2g					

III. Conflict Resolution and Positive Reinforcement

3. My supervisor:

a. Confronts performance shortcomings positively.				3a
b. Listens to what I have to say.				3b
c. Seeks a "win-win" solution.				3c
d. Openly recognizes exceptional performance.				3d
e. Shares the credit when the team "wins."				3e
f. Is fair and consistent in formal performance appraisal.				3f
g. Motivates me to perform to the best of my abilities.				3g

IV. Management of Meetings

4. My supervisor effectively:

a. Plans the frequency and duration of meetings.				4a
b. Communicates and sticks to an agenda.				4b
c. Encourages input from all attendees when appropriate.				4c
d. Provides information which is useful and valuable.				4d

5. My supervisor could be even more effective by: _____

the Strategic Vision and the performance quality of the organization's human resources, it is essential to measure and monitor leader-manager effectiveness on a regular basis. Only in this way can meaningful expectations be established, shortcomings identified, remedies applied, and improvement monitored. Therefore, in addition to reviewing actual results in key results areas vis-à-vis standards and targets for all managers, I also recommend the use of a management effectiveness measurement tool similar to that shown as Exhibit 6–7. The use of this evaluation tool is highly successful when used in conjunction with ongoing leadership and management training designed to focus development efforts on the specific areas of weakness unique to each individual. Improvement, or lack thereof, can then be readily measured and monitored annually. In addition, such a system enables each manager to be considerably more effective and focused as a coach to those managers whom he or she supervises.

With the multitude of excellent management assessment and development programs currently available, there is no reason why management and supervisory effectiveness cannot be enhanced tremendously. Those organizations that are not attempting to upgrade continuously the skills of their leader-managers and are not measuring and monitoring their success in doing so are simply not committed to superior performance.

One of the most comprehensive studies ever conducted on high performance leadership and management involved over 16,000 high, medium, and low achieving managers from over 50 corporations. The methodology itself was based on work done by Benjamin Rhodes (the "Managerial Achievement Quotient") and Robert R. Blake and Jane S. Mouton ("the Managerial Grid").

Among other things, the study revealed the following: High performing leader-managers:

    a. Have an optimistic and positive attitude toward subordinates and expect superior results from them.

    b. Involve subordinates extensively in planning and foster open and honest communication.

    c. Attempt to structure the work situation in ways that allow subordinates to derive high levels of personal fulfillment.

d. Are highly focused on meeting performance objectives and goals *and* on the needs of their subordinates, which they do not view as mutually exclusive.

e. Are highly receptive to innovation and readily seek out new and better ways to achieve positive results.

f. Produce high achievers.

On the other hand, low or average performing leader-managers:

a. View their subordinates with pessimism and distrust.

b. Are less concerned with personal fulfillment, for themselves and for their subordinates, and more concerned with status and job security.

c. Do not involve subordinates in planning and foster an atmosphere devoid of honest and open communication.

d. Are concerned with production, not people (average performers) or neither production nor people (low performers).[4]

Successful leader-managers, therefore, are those who practice a management style that meets the needs of the individual *and* the needs of the organization.

Even when the Strategic Vision is sound, and the system of Strategic Management and Planning comprehensive and properly structured, weaknesses in the quality of leadership, management, and supervision, at any level, will adversely affect not only the performance of those managed but of the organization as a whole. As such, it is clearly one of the key dynamics of high performance, an area of significant opportunity for most banks, and one requiring continuous evaluation and upgrading.

JOB DESIGN AND CONTENT

One key manifestation of superior management is the ability to structure and organize work and to design and redesign jobs so as to meet the changing needs of both the organization and its members. Therefore, job design and content (component IIIA) is an extremely important factor in achieving and sustaining superior performance. Regardless of the quality of the employee, if he or she is in the wrong job, for whatever reason, performance is likely to be substandard. Each job, for example, has specific requirements regarding technical, interpersonal, and/or conceptual skills as well as its own inherent potential for contributing to a jobholder's feelings of achievement and self-actualization (Maslow's higher order needs). At the same time, each individual has inherent strengths and weaknesses in each of these areas (technical, interpersonal, and/or conceptual) as well as specific needs regarding feelings of achievement and self-worth. The challenge, of course, is to match individuals as closely as possible to job requirements, recognizing that both are changing over time and that certain constraints will always be present.

In cases where an individual performs extremely well in a position but, outgrowing the job, is ready and anxious to accept new challenges and responsibilities, the failure of the organization to meet those needs, either through advancement, job rotation, or job enlargement and redesign (horizontal or vertical) can result in disillusionment, frustration, weakened self-esteem, deteriorating performance, and all too often the loss of a quality employee. Horizontal job enlargement refers to the number and variety of specific operations or functions inherent in the job. Vertical job enlargement relates to the latitude the jobholder is given to participate in the planning and execution of issues associated with the job.

Research seems to support the notion that job content, in order to meet the needs of today's workers for achievement and self-actualization, must (a) allow meaningful feedback with respect to performance, (b) be perceived as requiring abilities and skills that the employee values and considers important, and (c) include a high level of control to the job holder in setting goals and creating the strategies and tactics to achieve those goals.[5] Based on the results of such research, every effort should be made to design jobs accordingly. This represents a significant opportunity for most, if not all, companies, including commercial banks.

Of course, promoting an individual to a position which requires skills and abilities the individual does not possess and cannot acquire also tends to result in substandard performance, frustration, and a lessening of self-esteem. According to research done by Kornhauser, job content can have a substantial impact on the mental health of the jobholder as measured not only by self-esteem, but by (*a*) manifest anxiety and emotional tension, (*b*) hostility versus trust and acceptance, (*c*) sociability and friendship versus withdrawal, (*d*) overall satisfaction with life, and (*e*) personal morale versus despair and social alienation.[6]

Because job design and content can influence tremendously the emotional well-being of the jobholder, which correlates directly with the quality of the individual's performance on the job, there is an ongoing need in any company aspiring to superior performance to monitor and manage the appropriateness of job design and content. Failure to do so can cause the loss of quality employees who are ambitious and committed to personal development but have outgrown the jobs they are in, or who have been placed in jobs which are incompatible with their abilities. At the same time, those who are in jobs which do not meet their needs for achievement and self-actualization will tend to experience a deterioration in self-esteem, emotional wellness, and work quality. Quite often, job enlargement can meet both the needs of the employee and those of the organization at a modest cost in terms of time and effort. The key is having leader-managers who are sensitive and well trained relative to this issue. Here again, this represents a tremendous opportunity for any firm.

According to one researcher, "If there is one confirmed finding in all the studies of worker morale and satisfaction, it is the correlation between the variety and challenge of the job and the gratifications which accrue to workers."[7] Because few banks have given proper attention to job design and content, it is an issue which represents an important opportunity for enhanced performance.

STRATEGIC FOCUS AND ACCOUNTABILITY

Much of this book has already been devoted to the importance of strategic focus and accountability. Weakness in this area, as shown by the relationships in the model, can almost invariably be traced to (*a*) weak or nonexistent Strategic Vision (component I), (*b*) the lack of a comprehensive system of Strategic Management and Planning with which to translate the vision into meaningful and realistic strategic action plans (component II), and/or (*c*) weak leadership, management, and supervision (component III). However, the stronger the organization is in each of these areas, the more strategically focused it will be. In addition, with proper attention to job design and leader-manager excellence, key results areas and performance standards and targets will have been established for each position in the company based on organizational priorities. Therefore, everyone should know exactly job criteria, expectations, how he or she are doing at any point in time, and what consequences are most likely to result. This, in turn, will contribute greatly to a high Quality of Direction, Focus and Strategy (component IV.A.), one of the two key factors affecting Teamwork and the Quality of Implementation (component VI).

THE EMPLOYEE

Inasmuch as every organization is composed of people, and because organizational performance represents the sum total of individual performances, the first step in any model dealing with employee motivation is to identify the key factors affecting individual performance. After all, *one cannot expect realistically to change organizational performance without first changing the performance of people.* Furthermore, ample evidence exists to support the idea that substantial room for improvement exists. The oft-quoted Public Agenda Foundation Study, for example, reports that fewer than one out of five Americans say they work at full potential. Seventy-five percent admit they could "significantly increase their performance."[8]

Every employee is unique and brings a special mix of skills, experiences, aspirations, and values to an organization. Furthermore, as circumstances change, both within the organization, and within the individual, the relationship between the employee and the organization changes as well.

In an attempt over many years to identify what makes an

individual employee successful and productive, I have come to focus on four key component areas. In my view, recruitment, screening, and hiring practices must be upgraded to better match organizational needs with a prospective employee's strengths and weaknesses in each of these areas. The first component, "self-image and life and career objectives," is an extremely powerful factor. According to Ferguson, "High intention cannot exist with a low self-image. Only those who are awake, connected, and motivated can add to the energy of an organization. Everyone else adds to entropy, randomness."[9] Joe D. Batten writes: "Lack of self-esteem is at the bottom of the majority of business problems."[10]

As banks initiate the process of strategic and cultural change, individual self-esteem, especially at key positions (including *all* customer contact positions) becomes an increasingly important critical success factor. Those whose self-image is weak, for whatever reason, will tend to be more resistant to change initiatives and far less likely to become willing and active participants in the strategic and cultural revolution. Poor self-image, regardless of the cause, adversely affects an employee's attitude and behavior toward customers, co-workers, subordinates, and supervisors. Lacking a positive outlook toward the future, such a person rarely sets goals and objectives, has a difficult time following through on projects, and can have a negative impact on the performance of others. Furthermore, weak self-esteem at the supervisory level can be especially detrimental to an organization's effectiveness. For these reasons, when evaluating individual performance, especially at the manager-supervisor level, it is my practice to first focus on self-esteem in an effort to identify possible weaknesses, their causes, and workable solutions. (In seeking solutions for severely damaged self-esteem, outside professional intervention is frequently required.)

The second component of the individual affecting performance is "innate abilities and talents." Examples, which vary from person to person, include intelligence, creativity, interpersonal skills, charisma, digital or manual dexterity, the ability to handle stress, and a variety of other specific, inherent attributes. The importance of innate abilities to success in the financial services industry is increasing as more intense competition imposes ever greater demands on employees at all levels. Furthermore, the specific types of skills needed are changing in response to competitive, demographic, and technological change.

Naturally, if an individual's innate abilities are well matched to the demands of a particular job, one might expect to observe a direct relationship between the degree of ability and the quality of individual performance, all other things being equal. Conversely, when performance does not meet expectations, the cause is often the lack of the specific, innate skills and abilities which are needed for that particular job. This realization can be especially disappointing when the individual has been successful in previous assignments. The practice of promoting someone to a job requiring different skills from those that made the person successful in the past is common and often leads to frustration and failure—a classic lose-lose situation. Such practices, in fact, are a major contributing factor to what has come to be known as the Peter Principle.

The third component affecting individual performance is "education, orientation, and training." Again, the more appropriate an individual's education (including experience) and training, and the more fully the individual has been oriented to the vision, mission, objectives, and values of the organization, the better the expected performance, all other things being equal. Conversely, a leading cause of substandard performance in the banking industry is inadequate training, the lack of relevant experience, inappropriate educational background, and/or the lack of a comprehensive and focused orientation program.

In the 1990s, as banks attempt to deal effectively with the five key strategic initiatives discussed earlier, the demands on each employee to deliver a superior level of performance will escalate substantially. Meeting the needs of both the organization and its members will therefore require a much greater commitment to professional and strategically focused training than has existed in the past. Nonbanks, such as insurance companies and brokerage firms, have made a major financial commitment to training, an area where they perceive bank competitors to be vulnerable. Aetna Life and Casualty provides an interesting example. Ranked first in revenues and fourth in

assets among Fortune 500 service companies, Aetna, which received the corporate award for 1989 from the American Society
for Training and Development, invests $40 million annually in
training and education, including a major emphasis on technology. Aetna's management openly acknowledges its conviction
that the key to productivity and growth in the financial services industry is training and development and has backed the
rhetoric with the resources needed to get the job done properly.[11]
Aetna's financial performance speaks for itself.

As banks seek opportunities for improving individual performance, education, training, and development are being recognized as critical success factors warranting far greater resource commitments.

The fourth component, "understanding and acceptance of
corporate culture and strategy," is extremely important and
generally overlooked. Even the best educated, most gifted, and
highly self-confident individuals may perform dismally if they
do not understand or accept the organization's business philosophy, culture, values, and/or strategies. One of the more salient
revelations of the famous Hawthorne studies was the direct relationship between productivity and productivity improvement
and the extent to which the goals of individuals and work
groups are perceived to be in sync with those of management.
The weaker the perceived correlation, the more likely it is that
productivity will remain at low levels or decline further.[12]

When an individual's personal philosophy and values are
not compatible with those of the company (as perceived by the
employee), commitment will be low or nonexistent and performance will suffer. The more adamant one's opposition to organizational values, the more destructive and dysfunctional his or
her behavior is likely to be. Conversely, the greater the perceived "fit" between organizational and personal values, the
greater the level of commitment and effort one might expect, all
other things being equal. Therefore, one of the key issues in
corporate culture analysis should be the extent to which the
organization's employees understand and accept the organization's cultural values and business philosophy and strategy.
Weaknesses in this area must be identified and quantified in
order that meaningful corrective action might be taken.

One of the seven key culture components, as discussed in

Chapter 4, and one which has an especially powerful impact on an employee's acceptance of the prevailing culture, is the organization's approach to rewards and punishments, a major factor influencing the quality of individual commitment and effort (component V.A.). More specifically, when employees accept the organization's philosophy regarding rewards and punishments, and believe that delivering the performance the organization wants will result in the rewards the employee wants, motivation will tend to be high.[13]

To summarize, as leader-managers attempt to initiate and direct the process of strategic and cultural change, a period of disorientation will generally occur as employees are asked to discard old values, behavior patterns, and work priorities, and to embrace new ones. The degree to which the natural process from denial to commitment can be accelerated will have a powerful influence on individual performance at all levels. This, in turn, will be facilitated when highly focused and dedicated managers identify in advance those who are most likely to resist change initiatives and make special efforts to communicate with them as openly, honestly, and forcefully as possible. In many cases, these individuals will be those who (a) have low self-esteem, and/or (b) lack the specific inherent skills and abilities needed for success in the new environment, and/or (c) have been inadequately trained, educated, and/or oriented, and/or (d) do not understand and/or accept the organization's cultural values and business strategy. Therefore, the ability of leader-managers to identify and correct weaknesses in these key areas will have a powerful impact on individual and organizational performance, and, in my view, will be a key management and supervisory responsibility in the 1990s.

V.A. QUALITY OF INDIVIDUAL COMMITMENT AND EFFORT

Assuming that the employee has (a) a strong, positive self-image and job-relevant innate abilities, (b) is appropriately educated, oriented, and trained, (c) understands and accepts the corporate culture (component V), (d) is in the right job (component III.A.) and (*e*) benefits from quality of leadership, management, and supervision (component III), one might expect that motivation, or the quality of individual commitment and effort (component V.A.), will be high. Conversely, individual weaknesses and/or shortcomings in commitment and/or effort (a lack of motivation) can almost invariably be traced to problems in one or more of these five key areas (*a* through *e* above), thereby allowing corrective action which is properly focused. Therefore, regular assessment of the existing strengths and weaknesses in each must become a major focus of Strategic Management and Planning. This is the only way that constant and measurable improvement in each area can be realized. In this regard, a properly structured assessment of corporate culture, supported by focused and nonthreatening interviews, should provide a wealth of valuable information regarding the organization's strengths and weaknesses in each of the five areas already mentioned, as well as in each of the other three components of the model. It will also provide the bench mark against which improvement strategies can be measured and monitored.

TEAMWORK: QUALITY OF IMPLEMENTATION

Naturally, motivation or the quality of individual commitment and effort (component V.A.) will have a powerful impact on the overall quality of implementation and teamwork (component VI). Strategies are simply implemented more effectively when people are highly motivated—which, in turn, encourages a more powerful sense of teamwork in order to ensure success.

At the same time, individual commitment and effort, to be supportive of organizational priorities, must be directed and focused properly. It doesn't accomplish much to have people, regardless of how motivated they may be, running off in different directions, yet this is exactly what is happening in many organizations. Naturally, the larger the organization, the greater the ongoing effort that is needed to maintain proper strategic focus.

Many bankers believe their strategic plans to be sound;

they just never seem to get implemented properly—
and they're not sure why. In my experience, the problem can
almost invariably be traced to weak motivation (component
V.A.) and/or focus (component IV.A.), which in turn results
from weaknesses in components I through V of the model, as
discussed above. In such cases, the path to improved implementation begins with a systematic assessment of strengths and
weaknesses, beginning with Strategic Vision and enlightened
leadership and continuing with each of the other seven components.

As long as an organization's leadership remains committed
absolutely to continuous improvement in support of sustainable
high performance, the model, if used properly, will provide the
framework which will make it possible.

QUALITY AND STRATEGIC VALUE OF INDIVIDUAL AND ORGANIZATIONAL PERFORMANCE

One cannot evaluate the quality and strategic value of an individual's performance, or that of an organization as a whole, unless specific and measurable goals are in place against which
performance can be assessed. As has been discussed, required
levels of organizational performance are becoming increasingly
clear as the financial markets punish those institutions which
fail to create shareholder value and as enlightened leaders
more clearly articulate a Strategic Vision for their organizations' futures. On the individual level, as well, banks have
made considerable progress in developing more objective and
relevant criteria on which to evaluate performance.

This model, therefore, is based on the notion that to
achieve and sustain high performance, (a) a Strategic Vision
must be created which establishes clear and meaningful objectives against which organizational performance can be measured and (b) a process of Strategic Management and Planning
must be in place by which every individual becomes accountable personally for specific and quantifiable contributions to
the realization of that vision.

CONSEQUENCES AND REINFORCEMENT

A critical success factor in effective organizational functioning, human motivation, and superior performance, and one of the seven key components of corporate culture, is the relationship between results and their consequences. In this regard I am reminded of a cartoon I saw recently which shows a football coach in the locker room with his team prior to a big game. On the chalkboard he has written: "Winners share $25,000; losers share $5,000." His message to the team: "So much for motivation. Now let's discuss strategy."

In the case of the organization, the consequences of superior performance will, by definition, be Improved Shareholder Value (component VIIIA1). This, in turn, will produce Corporate Satisfaction and Positive Reinforcement (component VIIIA2) for the Strategic Vision, the Strategic Management and Planning process, and the organization's leadership and strategic focus. Financial, corporate culture, and market positioning strategies, and the process by which they are conceptualized, implemented, and managed, will all receive ongoing support.

With respect to the individual employee, the issue is considerably more complex and raises several key questions. First, what assumptions and expectations exist, organizationally and individually, relative to the cause and effect relationships between performance on the one hand, and rewards and punishments on the other? Second, what mix of intrinsic and extrinsic rewards and punishments might be made available and on what basis might they be distributed? Third, how will the success of compensation strategies be measured?

It is beyond the scope of this book to review and evaluate the full range of research in the areas of human motivation and compensation. However, my research and experience convince me that (a) banks aspiring to high performance in the 1990s must adopt systems which link, as closely as possible, individual and/or group performance to rewards and punishments, (b) a wide range of intrinsic and extrinsic rewards should be used to help achieve the organization's objectives, and (c) the full motivational potential available from strategic management of rewards and punishments is not being realized by most organizations.

In addition, because satisfied workers are not necessarily productive workers,[14] I believe that banks must resist the temptation of attempting to satisfy everyone. Rather, the objective should be to satisfy those whose needs can best be met via meaningful contribution to the needs of the organization. Just as a bank cannot be all things to all people in a marketing sense, it cannot reasonably expect to meet the diverse needs of every type of worker. *It must therefore select, reward, and retain those for whom value is created through creating value for shareholders and customers.* Furthermore, those whose contribution is greatest should receive the largest rewards. Ample evidence exists to support the notion that greater levels of positive consequences encourage enhanced levels of performance.[15] Most banks pay their top performers too little and the worst performers too much, and, by so doing, unconsciously encourage and promote mediocrity. The lack of a clear relationship between performance and compensation is especially acute at the CEO level. In fact, perhaps my greatest frustration as a consultant is the infrequency with which top bank CEOs throughout the country are adequately compensated for the *economic* value they create for their shareholders.

When superior performance results in extrinsic and intrinsic rewards which are perceived as fair, and consistent with expectations, the high performer will be satisfied, which will produce employee satisfaction (component VIIIB2) in two primary ways.

First, as the model indicates, the quality of individual commitment and effort will be reinforced, that is, the employee will be motivated to maintain or enhance the behavior and performance level which produced that satisfaction. Known as *expectancy theory,* the supposition is that people make choices based on expected returns—both extrinsic and intrinsic. According to Kopelman: "Because expectancy theory has typically demonstrated superior predictive validities in comparison to other theories, it is generally viewed as a dominant, if not predominant, theory of work motivation."[16] The greater the expectation that a particular behavior or energy expenditure will produce a desired result, the greater will be the motivation to deliver the performance needed to achieve that result. Of particular interest to the company committed to high performance is research that supports the notion that higher performers in particular are influenced by rewards linked directly to performance. In other words, high performers tend to respond to monetary and nonmonetary rewards which are administered contingently (according to performance) with expressions of personal satisfaction and a renewed commitment to excel. Conversely, rewards administered noncontingently have been shown to have a detrimental affect on the work attitudes of high achievers.[17] Furthermore, research indicates that managers who perceive that monetary compensation is a function of performance are rated more effective in their jobs.[18]

The second manner in which positive reinforcement takes place at the individual level relates to self-esteem, perhaps the single most powerful factor in job-related individual performance. To the extent that one feels the rewards for performance rendered have been equitable and satisfying, self-esteem will be reinforced positively, as will the individual's acceptance of, and support for, the organization's corporate culture and business philosophy. On the other hand, when one feels that his or her efforts have not produced the rewards which were warranted and/or promised, self-esteem will be adversely affected. Often, the only remedy is to go elsewhere. Organizations that give inadequate attention to this important issue will almost invariably lose their best performers.

As a final point relating high performers, self-esteem, and compensation policy, a Hay Group study, *Research for Management*, makes the important point that those who work in successful organizations are more satisfied with their pay, even when their pay is lower.[19] Therefore, there seems to exist a strong correlation between individual satisfaction and corporate satisfaction.

Performance Appraisal and the Distribution of Rewards and Punishments

Naturally, the quality of performance appraisal throughout a company is an important key to ensuring that the distribution of rewards (and punishments) provides the desired positive re-inforcement.

Performance appraisal systems, to be effective, need not be complex or elaborate. In fact, one simple yet effective approach is to require each employee, including officers, to complete a performance plan at the beginning of each review period which poses three questions: (1) What are the organization's vision, mission, objectives, and master strategy? (2) How, *specifically,*

Performance Appraisal Systems Should

1. Ensure that managers manage and supervisors supervise by making all managers and supervisors accountable for the measurable development and performance of their subordinates.
2. Relate each job, and the role of the employee in the job, in a meaningful way to the organization's vision, goals, and objectives.
3. Establish key results areas and performance standards (based on quality, quantity, cost, and/or time) for each job—and performance targets for each employee.
4. Facilitate frequent and meaningful supervisor/employee interaction.
5. Encourage each employee to contribute, without fear of ridicule or criticism, any ideas, including changes in job design and content and organization structure, which might enhance individual and/or organizational performance.
6. Allow all managers and supervisors to be as objective as possible in evaluating performance and in providing timely, constructive, and properly documented feedback.
7. Contribute to each employee's feelings of achievement and self-actualization.
8. Maximize compensation equity and employee satisfaction and motivation.
9. Identify, reward, develop, and retain the organization's "high potential" employees.
10. Reinforce the organization's cultural values.
11. Identify in a timely manner all individual and organizational training and development needs.
12. Assist in realistic career planning.

does the employee's job contribute to their realization? and (3) What *specifically* is the employee going to do during the review period to maximize that contribution, that is, what added value will he or she bring to the position, how will his or her contribution be measured, and what consequences might realistically be expected in return?

Such a document, once accepted by a supervisor, becomes, in essence, a performance contract which (a) focuses the employee clearly on the organization's strategic direction and priorities, (b) ensures that the employee understands how his or her job relates to those priorities, (c) establishes specific measurable criteria, agreed to in advance by employee and supervisor, on which performance will be evaluated, (d) allows the supervisor to make sure in advance that the rewards that will be made available have value to the employee and will therefore have the power to motivate, and (e) facilitates the most appropriate mix of extrinsic and intrinsic rewards.

A well-designed performance appraisal system should, in my view, accomplish at least 12 primary objectives. I generally recommend that an organization evaluate the existing system on a scale of 1 to 10 in each of these areas and then involve the entire work force in developing a plan which will allow performance appraisal to play a more meaningful and strategic role in helping the organization realize its Strategic Vision. Progress should then be evaluated on a regular basis in order to realize constant and consistent improvement.

Incentive Compensation

Incentive compensation, which is widely recognized as perhaps the most direct way of linking rewards to performance companywide, continues to be an emotional and controversial topic among bankers. Many resent providing additional compensation to people who are simply doing "what they are paid to do." Others consider incentives, combined with a freeze on salary increases, to be the only answer to the problem of escalating personnel costs. Still others would like to implement incentive plans but haven't yet found one that is "perfect," that is fair to everyone.

Regardless of one's opinion, research seems to establish beyond question that incentives do work. One well-published study encompassed over 4,700 specific instances of output-based compensation replacing time-based compensation. The study reported productivity increases ranging from 29 percent to 63 percent with the median increase an impressive 34.5 percent.[20] Another study reported increased output of 30 percent for individual incentive plans and 18 percent for group plans.[21] Still another study covering worker productivity for the period 1971 to 1975 reported performance increases ranging from 18 percent to 46 percent as a result of financial incentives.[22]

In a nationwide study conducted by the author in 1986 (with Sheshunoff and Company), of those banks using incentive compensation plans, 27 percent rated them highly effective, 36 percent effective, 28 percent moderately effective, and only 5 percent ineffective. (The remaining 4 percent failed to respond.)[23]

The main thing to bear in mind when evaluating incentives is that incentive compensation is a strategy and, like any strategy, must be evaluated on its relative ability to contribute to the achievement of specific corporate objectives. In this regard, many factors must be considered, such as (1) economic conditions, (2) the market's competitive equilibrium, (3) the existing corporate culture, (4) the quality of management and supervision, and (5) the extent to which the organization's leadership and management is trusted by the work force. However, once it has been established that incentive compensation makes sense for a *particular* institution at a *particular* point in time, there are several keys to making any incentive plan successful:

1. The plan must be strategic; therefore, it must also be flexible. For incentive compensation to be effective, it must be viewed as strategy, that is, it must be seen as a means to an end rather than an end in itself. The relationship between the incentives and the achievement of *specific* corporate objectives must be understood clearly in advance. Management needs to be satisfied that the objectives which are important *now* can best be facilitated through the use of incentives.

Since market realities are constantly changing, the performance objectives of the organization will most likely change as well. Therefore, all strategies, including incentives, must be flexible. When an incentive compensation plan is implemented, it should be made perfectly clear that the program is not permanent; that it has been designated and implemented to facilitate the accomplishment of a specific objective. If and when that objective is accomplished, or if and when priorities change, the incentive compensation plan may change as well.

2. The plan must be simple and easy to understand. Many incentive compensation plans fail because they are so complicated and unwieldy that no one understands them. It is important that individual employees have a clear understanding of the relationship between specific behaviors and accomplishments and related rewards. They must be able to see that doing 'A' results in 'B.' Complex mathematical formulas, in other words, may doom any plan to failure.

3. An ongoing communication strategy should be included as part of the overall incentive strategy. It is vitally important that a great deal of thought be devoted to the best way in which any incentive compensation plan might be communicated. Employees must be fully aware of the strategic justification for the plan, that is, how it relates to the vision, mission, and objectives of the firm. The communication process should help to keep the plan simple and easy to understand and reinforce core cultural values, while focusing the work force strategically.

Periodically, the organization's members need to be updated as to organizational performance vis-à-vis objectives. Individuals and work groups that have been particularly successful under the incentive plan should be used as examples to the rest of the organization as to what is desirable and possible. An effort should also be made periodically to solicit input from the work force as to how well the plan seems to be working and how they believe it might be made more effective. Like any other strategy, effectiveness can be enhanced dramatically by encouraging employee participation and involvement.

4. Rewards must be related objectively to desired performance; they must influence day-to-day behavior. In a Yankelovich poll of Japanese and American workers, the question was asked: "Who would benefit most from an increase in (worker) productivity?" While 93 percent of the Japanese workers believed that workers would benefit most, only 9 percent of the American workers felt the same.[24] Apparently, American workers perceive minimal relationship between personal success and organizational success, yet it is that relationship that is required for any compensation plan, including incentives, to be viable. The ability of workers to satisfy their needs for achievement, self-actualization, *and* monetary recognition must be linked to the realization of organizational objectives.

Many "bonus" plans, for example, are implemented in the mistaken belief that they are incentive plans. To the extent a bonus plan is consistent with expectancy theory, that is, actually motivates individuals to behave or perform differently, it qualifies as an incentive plan. However, bonus plans often have little or no meaningful impact because employees have difficulty relating their day-to-day performance with the organization's performance, that is, they do not feel they can affect the outcome. Most bonus plans end up being, in essence, a sort of "Christmas Club."

5. The plan must be perceived as reasonably fair. More importantly, management's intentions must be perceived as sincere. Many banks hesitate to implement incentive plans because they fear they will not be totally fair. Unfortunately, few plans, if any, are completely fair, nor do most people expect them to be. However, they do expect management to be totally honest and sincere, especially in the high performing company. Therefore, management's intentions must be perceived as sincere and aboveboard. There must exist within the corporate culture a general feeling that management is honorable and trustworthy; that there exists genuine management concern for the welfare and well-being of the employees. In fact, research has shown few negative side effects from the use of incentives except in cases where (*a*) trust is low and (*b*) subjective standards are used.[25] In those cases where the corporate culture reveals strong feelings of distrust for management, the implementation of incentive plans should be deferred until the problems can be adequately researched and defined and corrective measures designed, implemented, and validated as successful.

6. The plan must provide for the training necessary to

allow everyone to maximize their contribution and success. Incentive plans often fail because employees do not receive the training needed to make a positive and meaningful contribution. The first type of training needed relates to strategic focus; employees must understand the organization's objectives and why the incentive plan has been implemented. The second type of required training is technical. Many incentive plans are based on increased output, which often requires higher levels of technical expertise. Also, plans based on qualitative factors such as customer satisfaction often rely heavily on superior levels of technical competence and consistency. A third type of necessary training is management and supervisory. Incentive plans require somewhat unique supervisory skills, including more frequent supervisor/employee interaction and the ability to motivate and inspire subordinates when necessary. Fourth, for any incentive plans dealing with sales, ongoing product knowledge training becomes a critical success factor. With respect to each product or benefits package, the employee must have an in-depth understanding of the *market(s)* to which that product is directed, the specific *features* of the product, the *benefits* that the product delivers, the specific *needs* that the benefits are designed to satisfy, the *superiority* of the product to competitive products, *pricing*, the most commonly anticipated *objections* and how to deal with them, and how each product can be delivered to the customer in the most efficient way. A fifth essential need relates to sales training which, of course, is closely related to product knowledge training. Employees must have confidence in their ability to identify and develop prospects, ascertain their perceived needs, present product benefits in the most effective manner, adjust the sales delivery to each type of prospect, and close effectively. Sales training, like product knowledge training, must be ongoing.

As discussed in Chapter 5, a bank must develop a targeted market positioning strategy that prioritizes specific segments and segment members. Incentive plans are a good way to reinforce that prioritization.

7. Incentives must be meaningful enough to motivate increased levels of performance. Incentive compensation plans often fail because the workers do not consider the rewards to be sufficiently meaningful. Careful thought must be given to the value of specific products and/or customer relationships and the rewards must reflect that value. For example, with demand deposits increasingly hard to come by, and with increased pressure on net interest margin, the reward for demand deposit acquisition should be significant.

In this respect, I admit to another bias: I do not believe that incentive plans should have "caps." If a plan has been designed properly, the more the employee earns the more the organization benefits. Therefore, why would anyone want to put a limit on those benefits? "Caps," in my experience, tend to discourage and demotivate the high performer.

8. Rewards should be available within a reasonable time period. The motivational value of incentives is enhanced when the employee has access to the reward within a reasonably short time frame. When the payoff is within reach, the reward becomes that much more tangible. This is one reason why many banks pay incentives monthly or quarterly or on a "piece-by-piece" basis.

Still, there are two primary situations that warrant deferring the incentive payoff. The first is to retain superior performers; if a portion of an employee's incentive compensation is withheld until future time periods, those employees generating the most business will also have the most to lose should they elect to leave.

The second instance relates to commissions paid on the generation of loan business. Recognizing the fact that a potential conflict of interest is created whenever incentives are paid for loan generation and that credit quality may be compromised, many banks will defer a portion of the incentive compensation until a sufficient period has elapsed during which borrower performance can be evaluated. If the quality of the credit proves to be inferior, the incentives withheld are retained by the bank.

9. Some minimum or base level of expected performance must be communicated clearly to all participants. It is important that a corporate culture be cultivated wherein employees understand they must make a positive contribution on a daily basis to the attainment of the bank's performance goals, that is, performance *standards* must exist.

Quite often, a feeling is created in some organizations that employees only need excel when incentive plans are in effect. When the plans expire, for whatever reason, employees no longer put forth extra effort. A potentially serious weakness of incentive plans is the tendency for people to become driven by the rewards, not by contributing to the objectives which the rewards are designed to support. Therefore, performance standards in the organization must be high. Furthermore, they must be communicated and reinforced at all times. Incentives should then be perceived as rewarding performance exceeding that which is expected as "standard."

10. Care must be taken to ensure that emphasis on short-term goals is compatible with—rather than contrary to—the firm's long-term best interests. Numerous books and articles in recent years have criticized the tendency of American corporations to overemphasize short-term performance.[26] In an age of instant communication, extensive media reporting, and "knee-jerk" reaction in the financial markets, many managers focus far too heavily on short-term considerations to the detriment of longer term, more strategic, decision making. Incentives should not be allowed to encourage such shortsighted behavior. For example, incentive compensation that rewards ROA performance must not allow management to increase ROA by curtailing growth when to do so would be contrary to the firm's long-term interests. By the same token, incentives based on return on equity must not allow the target to be achieved through excessive and imprudent leverage. Also, growth objectives must not be achieved through acquisitions which dissipate shareholder value.

11. The plan should recognize that not everyone is motivated by the same things. While one should never underestimate the power of money as a motivator, it should also be recognized that not everyone is motivated by money. The highly creative individual, for example, often responds far more favorably to recognition, special projects, and increased creative independence. Employees at some levels of the organization may be more responsive to incentives that satisfy their longer-term needs, such as stock options or some form of deferred compensation. Other employees may be highly motivated by nonmonetary rewards such as extra days off or paid vacation.

The important thing is to be as creative as possible in identifying a variety of incentive compensation alternatives and then matching those alternatives to the needs and personality profiles of the employees. Sensitivity to the fact that not everyone is motivated in the same way can dramatically enhance the effectiveness of any incentive compensation plan.

12. Rituals should be used to reinforce desired performance. In order to promote pride, feelings of achievement and enhanced self-esteem, while at the same time sending a message to the entire organization reinforcing management priorities and values, rituals to recognize outstanding achievement can be an extremely important and low-cost component of any successful program.

13. Work force members at all levels should have a voice in designing incentive plans. The best way to achieve high levels of employee support for any strategy is to have the employees themselves help design the strategy. Incentives are no exception.

14. Management must be totally committed philosophically to the use of incentives, and must communicate and reinforce that commitment regularly. As with all strategy, successful results require management's full support and commitment. When commitment is weak, the work force will quickly realize that such is the case and lose interest.

Management's commitment to an incentive compensation plan will not be measured by verbal proclamations, but will be evaluated by the extent to which management supports the plan on a daily basis, leads by example, and recognizes in meaningful ways those who are most successful. Management's commitment to training and to an active communication process will also be interpreted positively.

SUMMARY AND CONCLUSIONS

There has always been something special about the last decade of a century; an extraordinary burst of creative energy, vision, and hope which has reshaped and redefined practically every aspect of man's existence.[27] It is almost as though the great minds in every discipline reject once and for all the failed theories of the previous 90 years and consolidate enthusiastically their collective genius and optimism toward developing the new conceptual breakthroughs which will propel and sustain mankind well into the following century.

The 1990s, therefore, may well prove to be the most tumultuous and dramatic decade in the history of the world, producing an unprecedented outpouring of creativity and new technology that will challenge virtually everything "known" to be true in every industry. The rate at which technological innovation is changing our lives is almost incomprehensible and will accelerate dramatically as the new century gets under way. Futurist Marvin Cetron and former *Omni* senior editor Owen Davies, for example, predict that: "All the technological knowledge we work with today will represent only 1 percent of the knowledge that will be available in 2050."[28]

Therefore, of all the transitions necessary for survival and superior performance in the 1990s, regardless of the industry, none is more compelling, in my view, than mastering the process of strategic and cultural change. The first step in such a process, as discussed in Chapter 2, is to eradicate the paradigm conforming mentality that pervades most organizations, replacing it with a state of mind which accepts and welcomes the inevitability of change, seeks constantly those innovative new perspectives that are in tune with emerging realities, and challenges aggressively and optimistically all the organization's norms and regularities. Until an organization liberates itself successfully from the obsolete and invalid paradigms of the past, and makes lateral thinking a cultural norm, it will be unable to conceptualize, implement, and sustain those strategies necessary to support a successful transition.

The initiator of the new mentality must be an enlightened leader who has the power, the intellect, and the courage to pay the price that successful strategic adaptation generally requires. Such a leader must mobilize and energize the board and senior management team to create, and commit themselves to, a Strategic Vision; a conceptualization of what the organization must look like at the end of a specific time frame. This is the second step in mastering the process of strategic and cultural change.

The third step is to define clearly those business(es) in

which the firm will compete, as well as the basis by which sustainable competitive advantage will be attained. Because many banks have failed to define their business(es) correctly, they are poorly focused strategically, are mismanaging scarce resources, and will have a difficult time surviving.

The fourth step requires that a discipline be established that not only ensures that the organization respond strategically to emerging opportunities, but that the resultant strategies and tactics are properly implemented and managed. In other words, strategic planning must be enhanced and incorporated into a system of Strategic Management and Planning. The process itself will involve four phases. First, opportunities will be identified and prioritized in the areas of shareholder value and financial performance optimization, leadership and corporate culture, and market positioning (sustainable competitive advantage); second, a strategic plan will be created to exploit the opportunities from phase one; third, strategic action plans must be designed for each strategy that establish clear accountability for results, determine how any perceived impediments will be overcome, and establish an implementation timetable; fourth, through a system of measuring and monitoring results, positive and negative reinforcement must be provided, including strategy refocus and redesign whenever necessary. Because new opportunities will constantly surface in this phase, it leads directly to the first phase as those opportunities are prioritized for future action. The Strategic Management and Planning process, therefore, focuses the entire organization relentlessly on the timely identification, prioritization, and exploitation of all emerging opportunities to move the organization closer to its Strategic Vision, or to reconceptualize that vision if necessary.

The fifth step in the process of strategic and cultural change involves focusing the entire organization strategically, that is, directors, senior and middle managers, and staff must all share a common understanding of the Strategic Vision, the strategic plan, and their individual roles and accountabilities in making it happen.

Finally, the organization's corporate culture must undergo considerable modification in order to purge itself of those characteristics and values that are no longer appropriate, and that may represent major impediments to the organization's ability to adapt, to create and implement the strategies and tactics necessary for survival.

Once an organization's leadership has initiated successfully the strategic and cultural revolution, the primary focus becomes one of continuous improvement directed toward the realization of the Strategic Vision. To facilitate the effective, ongoing management of this process, I have developed the model shown as Exhibit 6–1.

It is my belief that achieving and sustaining superior performance is a function of continuous improvement in eight key areas, each of which represents a component of the model. Shortcomings in organizational and/or individual performance can invariably be traced to specific weaknesses in one or more of these component areas. Through periodic assessment of an organization's relative strengths and weaknesses in each component, specific opportunities for performance enhancement can be readily identified, prioritized, and acted upon. In this way, the spirit of the strategic and cultural revolution can be sustained and reinforced indefinitely.

ENDNOTES

INTRODUCTION

1. Biehell, Richard R., and Scott Schaeffer. *A Day in the Country*. New York: Harry N. Abrams, 1984, p. 19.
2. Albrecht, Karl, and Ron Zemke. *Service America*. Homewood, Illinois: Dow Jones-Irwin, 1985, p. 54.
3. Toffler, Alvin. *The Adaptive Corporation*. New York: Bantam Books, 1985, p. 8.
4. Peters, Tom. *Thriving on Chaos*. New York: Harper & Row, 1987, p. 4.
5. Ferguson, Marilyn. *The Aquarian Conspiracy*. Los Angeles: J. P. Tarcher, 1980, p. 131.

CHAPTER ONE

1. Capra, Fritjof. *The Tao of Physics*. New York: Bantam Books, 1976, p. 42.
2. Drucker, Peter F. *Innovation and Entrepreneurship*. New York: Harper & Row, 1985, p. 53.
3. Kuhn, Thomas. *The Structure of Scientific Revolutions*. Chicago: Phoenix Books, University of Chicago Press, 1967.
4. Tuchman, Barbara W. *The March of Folly*. New York: Alfred A. Knopf, 1984, p. 7.
5. Janis, Irving L. "Groupthink." In *Organizations Close Up*, ed. J. L. Gibson, J. M. Ivanevich, and J. H. Donnelly, Jr. Plano, Tex.: Business Publications, 1985, p. 168.
6. McCoy, Charles. "First Interstate Bancorp Sheds Its Chairman But Not Its Problems." *The Wall Street Journal*, January 18, 1990, p. A8.

7. Bennis, Warren. *The Unconscious Conspiracy: Why Leaders Can't Lead.* New York: AMACOM, 1976, p. 40.
8. Foster, Richard. *Innovation.* New York: Summit Books, 1986, p. 36.
9. Roberts, Steven M. "Firrea: The $166 Billion Solution." *The Bankers Magazine,* January–February 1990, p. 7.
10. Allen, Paul H., and Dominic J. Casserley. "C&I Lending Turning the Corner on Economic Returns." *The Bankers Magazine,* January–February 1990, p. 39.
11. See "The Seduction of Senator Alan Cranston." *Business Week,* December 4, 1989; and "A Legal Bank Robbery." *Time,* November 27, 1989.
12. Kane, Edward J. "Defective Regulatory Incentives and the Bush Initiative." *Independent Banker,* November 1989, p. 32.
13. *Statistical Information on the Financial Services Industry.* Washington, D.C.: American Bankers Association, 1987, p. 1.
14. Barret, William P. "No Frills." *Forbes,* Nov. 14, 1988, p. 52.
15. Source of all S&L data in this section from Sheshunoff Information Services, Inc. *S&L Quarterly,* December 1988 ratings.
16. Porter, Michael E. *Competitive Advantage.* New York: Free Press, 1985; and *Competitive Strategy.* New York: Free Press, 1988.
17. *The Fidelity Catalogue,* Fidelity Investments, 1989.
18. *Statistical Information on the Financial Services Industry.* Washington, D.C.: American Bankers Association, 1987, p. 7.
19. Allen, Paul H., and Dominic J. Casserley. "C&I Lending Turning the Corner on Economic Returns." *The Bankers Magazine,* January–February 1990, p. 37.

CHAPTER TWO

1. Ferguson, Marilyn. *The Aquarian Conspiracy.* Los Angeles: J. P. Tarcher, 1980, p. 34.
2. Nadler, Gerald, UPI. "Gorbachev Pushes for a Party Purge." *Salt Lake Tribune,* July 22, 1989, p. 1.
3. Leavitt, Ted. "The Innovating Organization." *Harvard Business Review,* November–December 1989, p. 7.
4. Kanter, Rosabeth Moss. *The Change Masters.* New York: Touchstone Books, 1983, p. 27.
5. De Bono, Edward. *New Think.* New York: Avon Books, 1968, pp. 14–15.
6. See Ornstein, Robert E. *The Psychology of Consciousness.* New York: Harcourt Brace Jovanovich, 1977.

7. Pascale, Richard T., and Anthony G. Athos. *The Art of Japanese Management.* New York: Warner Books, 1982, p. 139.
8. Ferguson, Marilyn. *The Aquarian Conspiracy.* Los Angeles: J. P. Tarcher, 1980, p. 349.
9. Ohmae, Kenichi. *The Mind of the Strategist.* New York: McGraw-Hill, 1982, p. 4.
10. MacKinnon, Donald W. *In Search of Human Effectiveness.* Buffalo, N.Y.: Creative Education Foundation, 1978, p. 135.
11. Ogilvy, David. *Ogilvy on Advertising.* New York: Vintage Books, 1985, p. 49.
12. Naisbitt, John. *Megatrends.* New York: Warner Books, 1982, p. 92.
13. Drucker, Peter F. *Management.* New York: Harper & Row, 1974, p. 78.
14. Leavitt, Ted. "Marketing Myopia." *Harvard Business Review: On Management.* New York: Harper & Row, 1975, pp. 176–96.
15. Ohmae, Kenichi. *The Mind of the Strategist.* New York: McGraw-Hill, 1982, p. 2.
16. Von Oech, Roger. *A Whack on the Side of the Head.* Menlo Park, Calif.: Creative Think, 1983, p. 48.
17. Labich, Kenneth. "The Seven Keys to Business Leadership." *Fortune*, October 24, 1988, p. 60.
18. Labich, Kenneth. "Making Over Middle Managers." *Fortune*, May 8, 1989.
19. Henkoff, Ronald. "Cost Cutting: How to Do It Right." *Fortune*, April 9, 1990, p. 48.

CHAPTER THREE

1. Buzzell, Robert D., and Bradley T. Gale. *The PIMs Principles.* New York: Free Press, 1987, p. 9.
2. "The Next Samurai." *The Economist.* December 23, 1989, p. 71.
3. Ibid., p. 100.
4. Maddox, Jeffrey D. "Managing for Value: Can Banks Make the Transition." *The Bankers Magazine*, September–October 1989, p. 73.
5. Porter, Michael. "From Competitive Advantage to Corporate Strategy." *Harvard Business Review*, May–June 1987; see also H. Buckner, "Seeking New Sources of Earnings." In *The Corporate Planners Handbook 1974–1975*, ed. D. E. Hussey. London: Pergamon Press, 1974.

6. Weston, J. Fred, and Eugene F. Brigham. *Managerial Finance.* Hinsdale, Ill.: Dryden Press, 1975, p. 537.

7. Dreyfus, Patricia. "Go with the (Cash) Flow." *Institutional Investor*, August 1988, pp. 56, 57.

8. See Cates, David C. "Bank Analysis: Why Measures of Performance Don't Work." *Bank Accounting and Finance*, Fall 1987.

9. Rather, John. "A Banker Who Balances Development with Open Space." *The New York Times*, June 25, 1989.

10. Wonder, Jacquelyn, and Priscilla Donovan. *Whole Brain Thinking*. New York: William Morrow and Company, 1984, pp. 9, 10.

11. Hedges, Robert B. Jr. "Strategy and Shareholder Value." *Bank Accounting Finance*, Fall 1987, p. 62.

12. Osborn, Neil. "Breaking Up Is Hard to Do." *Euromoney*, June 1989, p. 5.

13. Bettinger, Cass. "A Sale-Leaseback Strategy Can Maximize Earnings and Capital Potential." *Banking Outlook*, Spring 1990, p. 10.

14. See Bettinger, Cass. "The Importance of Magic in Bank Marketing." *Bank Marketing*, December 1985.

15. See Bettinger, Cass. "Hyping Customer Satisfaction for the Wrong Reasons Can Sabotage Performance." *Banking Outlook*, Summer 1989.

16. Sheshunoff, Alex. "Boosting Fee Income: Waiver Management's the Wave of the Future." *High Performance Banking*, October 1989, p. 1.

17. "Expense Control Boosts Stock Prices 40 Percent." *ABA Bankers Weekly*, p. 12.

18. "Managing Now for the 1990s." *Fortune*, September 26, 1988, p. 52.

19. Drucker, Peter F. "The Coming of the New Organization." *Harvard Business Review*, January–February 1988, p. 46.

20. Hekhuis, Dale J., and Richard C. Raymond. "Productivity Imperative for Banks." *The Magazine of Bank Administration*, December 1985, p. 38.

21. Fuhrman, Peter. "Gianni Agnelli's Days in the Sun." *Forbes*, November 14, 1988, p. 130.

22. Fairlamb, David. "European Banks' Big Hi-Tech Bet." *Institutional Investor*, October 1989.

23. Swift, Clinton R. "Checking Out Image." *Bank Management*, May 1990, p. 32.

24. Stiller, Blake. "Are Banks Overdosing on Technology Buying?" *Bankers Monthly*, December 1988, p. 14.

25. Tracey, Brian. "Bank Systems Expenditures Slowing Down after Decade of Steady Growth." *Computers in Banking*, October 1989, p. 42.
26. Violano, Michael. "Can Micros Make It Big in Branch Automation?" *Bankers Monthly*, March 1990, p. 52.
27. Rizzi, Joseph V. "Investment Alternatives with High-Yield Bonds." *The Bankers Magazine*, January–February 1990, p. 67.
28. See Isom, T.; S. D. Halladay; S. P. Amembal; R. D. Leininger; and J. M. Ruga. *The Handbook of Equipment Leasing*. Salt Lake City: Amembal & Isom, 1988, chapter 3.
29. Dince, Robert R., and Don P. Holdren. "An Examination of the OCC's Report on Bank Failure." *Issues in Bank Regulation.* Spring 1989, p. 17.
30. See Bettinger, Cass. "Why Marketing Is the Key to Credit Quality." *Journal of Commercial Bank Lending*, March 1986.
31. See Bettinger, Cass. "What It Takes to Be a Professional Lender." *Journal of Commercial Bank Lending*, March 1988.
32. See Bettinger, Cass. "Five Keys to Improving Loan Quality." *Commercial Lending Review*, October 1986.
33. Taylor, John H. "Our Competitors Can't Touch Us." *Forbes*, March 20, 1989, p. 86.
34. Kreuzer, Therese. "At Hibernia, It's Mardi Gras All Year." *Bankers Monthly*, February 1990, p. 22.

CHAPTER FOUR

1. Hofstede, G. *Culture's Consequences*. Beverly Hills, Calif.: Sage Publications, 1980, p. 394.
2. Schwartz, Howard, and Stanley Davis. "Making Corporate Culture and Business Strategy." *Organizational Dynamics*, Summer 1981.
3. Machiavelli, Niccolo. *The Prince*. New York: Oxford University Press, 1984, p. 21.
4. Killman, Ralph H. "Corporate Culture." *Psychology Today*, April 1985, p. 64.
5. Schein, Edgar H. *Organizational Culture and Leadership*. San Francisco: Jossey-Bass, 1986, p. 2.
6. Bennis, Warren. *The Unconscious Conspiracy: Why Leaders Can't Lead*. New York: AMACON, 1976, p. 168.
7. Follett, Mary Parker. "Constructive Conflict." In *Dynamic Ad-*

ministration: The Collected Works of Mary Parker Follett, ed. H. C. Metcalf and L. Urwick. New York: Harper & Row, 1942.

8. See Lawrence, P. R., and J. W. Lorsch. *Organization and Environment*. Homewood, Ill.: Richard D. Irwin, 1969.

9. Labovitz, George H. "Managing Conflict." In *Organizations Close-Up*, ed. J. L. Gibson, S. M. Ivanovich, and J. H. Donnelly, Jr. Plano, Tex.: Business Publications, 1985.

10. Flint, Jerry. "It's a New World." *Forbes*, November 14, 1988, p. 172.

11. Sargent, Alice G., and Ronald J. Stupak. "Managing in the '90s: The Androgynous Manager." *Training & Development Journal*, December 1989, p. 31.

12. Mintzberg, Henry. *Power In and Around Organizations*. Englewood Cliffs, N. J.: Prentice-Hall, 1983, p. 172.

13. Lawler, Edward E. III. "The Strategic Design of Reward Systems." In *Readings in Personnel and Human Resource Management*, ed. R. S. Schuler and S. A. Youngblood. New York: West Publishing, 1984, p. 254.

14. Deal, Terrence C., and Allen A. Kennedy. *Corporate Cultures*. Reading, Mass.: Addison-Wesley Publishing, 1982, p. 63.

15. Schawdel, Francine. "Nordstrom's Push East Will Test Its Renown for the Best in Service." *The Wall Street Journal*, August 1, 1989, p. 1.

16. Carnevale, A. P.; L. J. Gainer; Ann S. Meltzer; and S. L. Holland. "Skills Employers Want." *Training and Development Journal*, October 1988, p. 1.

17. Beer, M.; B. Spector; P. R. Lawrence; D. Q. Mills; and R. E. Walton. *Managing Human Assets*. New York: Free Press, 1984, p. 79.

18. Peters, Thomas J., and Robert H. Waterman, Jr. *In Search of Excellence*. New York: Harper & Row, 1982, p. 280.

19. "Botching Up a Great Bank." *Fortune* (adapted from *Breaking the Bank* by Gary Hector), June 6, 1982, p. 280.

20. Webber, Alan M. "Red Auerbach on Management." *Harvard Business Review*, March–April 1987, p. 87.

21. Silverzweig, Stan, and Robert F. Allen. "Changing the Corporate Culture." *Sloan Management Review*, Spring 1976, p. 38.

22. Graves, Desmond. *Corporate Culture: Diagnosis and Change*. New York: St. Martin's Press, 1986, p. 131.

23. Hampton, William J. "How Does Japan Inc. Pick Its American Workers?" *Business Week*, October 3, 1988, p. 84.

24. Livingston, J. Sterling. "Pygmalion in Management." *Harvard Business Review*, July–August 1969, p. 81.

25. Kopelman, Richard E. "The Case for Merit Awards." In *Organizations Close Up*, ed. J. L. Gibson, J. M. Ivancovich, and J. H. Donnelly, Jr. Plano, Tex.: Business Publications, 1985, p. 116.
26. Beer, M.; B. Spector; P. R. Lawrence; D. Q. Mills; and R. E. Walton. *Managing Human Assets*. New York: Free Press, 1984, p. 260.
27. Lawler, Edward E. III. "The Strategic Design of Reward Systems." In *Readings in Personnel and Human Resource Management*, ed. R. S. Schuler and S. A. Youngblood. New York: West Publishing, 1984, p. 260.
28. Adams, J. Lon, and Kenneth Embley. "From Strategic Planning to Employee Productivity." *Personnel*, April 1988.
29. Kanter, Rosabeth Moss. "The Attack on Pay." *Harvard Business Review*, March–April 1987, p. 8.
30. Yankelovich, Daniel. "The Work Ethic Is Underemployed." *Psychology Today*, May 1987, p. 8.

CHAPTER FIVE

1. Bettinger, Cass. "Marketing: You Can't Do It If You Don't Know What It Is." *Bank Marketing*, August 1985.
2. Bettinger, Cass. "What Puts the *Strategic* in Planning?" *Bank Marketing*, February 1985.
3. Henderson, Bruce. *Henderson on Corporate Strategy*. New York: New American Library, 1979, p. 9.
4. Leemputte, Patrick J. "Strategic Repositioning for Shareholder Value." *Issues in Bank Regulation*, Spring 1989, p. 8.
5. Lieblich, Julia. "If You Want a Big, New Market. . . ." *Fortune*, November 21, 1988, p. 181.
6. Violano, Michael. "Baby Boomers Are Banking's Booming Market." *Bankers Monthly*, July 1989, p. 46.
7. Ward, Bernie. "Find It, Fill It." *Sky*, September 1989, p. 79.
8. Mitchell, Arnold. *The Nine American Lifestyles*. New York: Macmillan, 1983.
9. Weiss, Michael J. *The Clustering of America*. New York: Harper & Row, 1988.
10. Kane, Chester L. "Overcome the 'Me Too' Product Syndrome." *Journal of Business Strategy*, March–April 1989, p. 15.
11. Nolfarth, John H. "Technology Cuts Reaction Times." *Bankers Monthly*, September 1989, p. 65.
12. Solman, Paul, and Thomas Friedman. *Life and Death on the Cor-*

porate Battlefield. New York: Simon & Schuster, 1982, pp. 91–92.

13. Ansoff, H. Igor. "Strategies for Diversification." *Harvard Business Review*, September–October 1957, pp. 113–24.

14. See Abrams, Bill. "Exploiting Proven Brand Names Can Cut Risk of New Products." *The Wall Street Journal*, January 22, 1981.

15. Freedman, Alix M. "Most Consumers Shun Luxuries, Seek Few Frills But Better Service." *The Wall Street Journal*, September 19, 1989.

16. Abrams, Bill. "American Express Is Gearing New Ad Campaign to Women." *The Wall Street Journal*, August 4, 1983.

17. Alsop, Ronald. "Prisoners of the Past." *The Wall Street Journal*, March 24, 1986.

18. Solman, Paul, and Thomas Friedman. *Life and Death on the Corporate Battlefield.* New York: Simon & Schuster, 1982, p. 42.

19. Ogilvy, David. *Ogilvy on Advertising.* New York: Vintage Books, 1985, pp. 167–68.

20. Buzzell, Robert D., and Bradley T. Gale. *The PIMs Principles.* New York: Free Press, 1987, p. 86.

21. Bultman, Janis. "Hot Dogs with Mustard and Glitz." *Forbes*, December 12, 1988, p. 118.

22. Sugarman, Aaron. "Why Our Readers Voted Alaska Best U.S. Airline." *Traveler*, November 1989, p. 50.

23. Ramierz, Anthony. "Tired of Heavy Drinks? Light Water Hits U.S." *Salt Lake Tribune*, November 26, 1989, p. A-5.

24. Levitt, Theodore. *The Marketing Imagination.* New York: Free Press, p. 73.

25. Blume, Eric R. "Giving Companies the Competitive Edge." *Training and Development*, September 1988, p. 25.

26. Peters, Tom. *Thriving on Chaos.* New York: Harper & Row, 1987, p. 112.

27. "Voice of the Consumer: Fifth Annual Survey." *American Banker*, October 5, 1989.

28. Marshall, Jeffrey. "Thrifts Outperforming Banks on Service, Survey Finds." *Banking Week*, July 3, 1989.

29. Zemke, Ron, with Dick Shaaf. *The Service Edge.* New York: New American Library, 1989, p. 191.

30. Davis, Stanley M. *Future Perfect.* Reading, Mass.: Addison-Wesley Publishing, 1987, p. 105.

31. Hanan, Mack, and Peter Karp. *Customer Satisfaction.* New York: AMACOM, 1989, chapter 3.

32. Enis, Ben M. *Marketing Principles*. Santa Monica, Calif.: Goodyear Publishing, 1977, p. 359.
33. Friars, E. M.; W. T. Gregor; and M. L. Reid. "Market Focus: Key to Successful Distribution Strategies." *Texas Banking*, August 1986, p. 21.

CHAPTER SIX

1. Whitehead, David D., and Benton E. Gup. "Bank and Thrift Profitability: Does Strategic Planning Really Pay?" *Economic Review*, October 1985.
2. Anderson, Kenneth. "Corporate Strategy: The Essential Intangibles." *McKinsey Quarterly*, Autumn 1984, p. 3.
3. Porter, Michael E. "The State of Strategic Planning." *The Economist*, May 23, 1987, p. 17.
4. Zemke, Ron. "What Are High-Achieving Managers Really Like?" *Training/HRD*, February 1979, p. 35.
5. Lawler, Edward E. III. "Job Design and Employee Motivation." *Personnel Psychology* 22 (1969), p. 429.
6. Kornhauser, Arthur. "Job Satisfaction in Relation to Mental Health." In *Management and Motivation*, ed. Victor H. Broom and Edward L. Deci. New York: Penguin Books, 1983, p. 83.
7. Katz, Daniel. "The Motivational Basis of Organizational Behavior." *Behavioral Science* 9 (1964), p. 140.
8. Yankelovich, Daniel. "The Work Ethic Is Underemployed." *Psychology Today*, May 1987, p. 6.
9. Ferguson, Marilyn. *The Aquarian Conspiracy*. Los Angeles: J. P. Tarcher, 1980, p. 352.
10. Batten, Joe D. *Tough Minded Management*. New York: AMACOM, 1978, p. 40.
11. Galagan, Patricia A. "Underwriting Business with Training." *Training and Development Journal*, October 1989, p. 32.
12. Cohen, William A., and Nurit Cohen. *Top Executive Performance*. New York: John Wiley & Sons, 1984, p. 45.
13. Beer, M.; B. Spector; P. R. Lawrence; D. Q. Mills; and R. E. Walton. *Managing Human Assets*. New York: Free Press, 1984, p. 116; and Lawler, Edward E. III, and Lyman Porter. "Antecedent Attitudes of Effective Managerial Performance." *Organizational Behavior and Human Performance* 2 (1967), pp. 122–42.

14. Bragfield, Arthur H., and Walter H. Crockett. "Employee Attitudes and Employee Performance." *Psychological Bulletin* 52 (1955).
15. Vroom, Victor H. *Work and Motivation.* New York: John Wiley & Sons, 1964, p. 205.
16. Kopelman, Richard E. "The Case for Merit Awards." In *Organizations Close Up,* ed. J. L. Gibson, J. W. Ivancovich, and J. H. Donnelly, Jr. Plano, Tex.: Business Publications, 1985, p. 114.
17. Podsakoff, Philip M.; Charles N. Greene; and James M. McFillen. "Obstacles to the Effective Use of Reward Systems." In *Readings in Personnel and Human Resource Management,* ed. R. S. Schular and S. A. Youngblood. New York: West Publishing, 1981, p. 270.
18. Stogdill, Ralph M. *Handbook of Leadership.* New York: Free Press, 1974, p. 118.
19. Macher, Ken. "Empowerment and the Bureaucracy." *Training and Development Journal,* September 1988, p. 42.
20. Nash, A. N., and S. J. Carroll, Jr. *The Management of Compensation.* Monterey, Calif.: Brooks/Cole, 1975, pp. 199–202.
21. Locke, E. A.; D. B. Feren; V. M. McCaleb; K. N. Shaw; and A. T. Denny. "The Relative Effectiveness of Four Methods of Motivating Employee Performance." In *Changes in Working Life,* ed. K. D. Duncan, M. M. Grunebim, and D. Wallis. New York: John Wiley & Sons, 1980, pp. 363–88.
22. Katzell, R. A.; P. Bienstock; and P. H. Faerstein. *A Guide to Worker Productivity in the United States 1971–1975.* New York: New York University Press, 1977.
23. Bettinger, Cass. "Incentive Compensation Works Best with Established Guidelines." *American Banker,* December 10, 1986.
24. Peters, Tom. *Thriving on Chaos.* New York: Harper & Row, 1987, p. 399.
25. Lawler, Edward E. III. "The Strategic Design of Reward Systems." In *Readings in Personnel and Human Resource Management,* ed. R. S. Schuler and S. A. Youngblood. New York: West Publishing, 1984, p. 259.
26. See Hayes, Robert, and William F. Abernathy. "Managing Our Way to Economic Decline." *Harvard Business Review,* January–February 1979.
27. Cetron, Marvin, and Owen Davies. "100 Years of Attitude." *Omni,* October 1989, p. 18.
28. Cetron, Marvin, and Owen Davies. "Future Trends." *Omni,* October 1987, p. 116.

INDEX

A

Abbate, Anthony S., 211–12, 218
Accountability for results, 110–11
Adams, H. Lon, 187
Aetna Life and Casualty, 274
Alaska Airlines, 220
Albrecht, Karl, 3
Alex Sheshunoff & Co., 86, 97
Allen, Robert F., 170
Allied Bancshares, 8
American Express, 211
American National Bank, 62
Anderson, Kenneth, 252
Andrews, Suzanna, 1
Art of Japanese Management, 30
Asset quality, 119–20
"Attractiveness test," 72
Auerbach, Red, 167

B

Bank branches, and occupancy
    expense, 116–18
Banking
    business of, 38–39
    changes in, 17–19, 63
    cost reduction, importance of, 45
    and creative thinking, 31–34
    and discrimination, 156
    fee-based services, 43–44
    funding and funds acquisition, 41–
        43, 44

Banking—*Cont.*
    and revolutionary changes of
        1980s, 11
    and shareholder value, 16–17, 70–
        78
    strategic initiatives, 43–46
    survival in the 1990s, 2–4
    and third-party relationships, 235–
        38
    traditional role of, 17–18
Batten, Joe D., 273
Benefits package, creating, 213–29
Bennis, Warren, 9, 145
Berry, Hellen, 220
"Better off test," 72
Bettinger high performance model,
        247–93
    consequences and reinforcement,
        278
    employees, 272–77
    leadership, 248–51, 265–71
    performance, 278
    strategic focus and accountability,
        271–72
    strategic management and
        planning, 251–64
    teamwork, 277–78
Bitner, William L., III, 59
Board of directors, and strategic
        focus, 53–54
Borrowing power, increase by
        depositors of, 21
Brainstorming, 263
Breaking the Bank, 164

Brewer, Harold, 112–13
Burns, James E., 9

C

Capital composition and ratio, 79–80
Carballada, R. Carlos, 177, 226–27
Carlzon, Jan, 227
Cash flows, 75, 76
Cetron, Marvin, 291
Change, and paradigm paralysis, 6–
23
   savings and loan industry, as
     example of, 11–16
   technological discontinuity, 9–11
Claritas Corporation, 202
Clemens, John K., 127
Commercial paper market, 23
Commitment phase, 132–33
Communication, importance of, 26–
27, 169–70, 230
Competition, for banking business,
1–2
   competitive advantage, 37–38
   nontraditional financial institu-
     tions, 15
   savings and loans institutions, 12–
     13
Competitive advantage, 37–38, 218
Competitive Advantage, 20
"Competitive Analysis Report," 86
Competitive Strategy, 20
Comprehensive analysis of existing
     culture, 134, 136–74
   communication, 169–70
   leadership, 140–47, 150
   office politics, 149–50
   methodology, 136–38
   rewards and punishments, 151–53
   sales, 157–61
   standards and values, 161–69
   strategic focus, 138–40
   systems, policies, and procedures,
     170–74
   teamwork and workgroup cohe-
     siveness, 147–49

Conflict resolution, 145–47
Corporate culture
   changes in, 63, 104, 130–38, 177–
     82
   desired culture defined, 174–77
   explained, 128–30, 135
   and high performance leadership,
     127–91
   and human resource management
     and development, 182–90
   and managing interest expense,
     99–100
   and motivation, 189–90, 275
   standards and values, 161–69
"Cost of entry test," 72
Cost reduction, 45
"Cover-up or Speak-No-Evil Reflex,"
   15
Credit unions, 225
Cultural change; *see* Corporate
   culture
Culture's Consequences, 129
Curry, Robert E., 222
Customer base, identifying, 244
Customer satisfaction, 214–16, 228–
   29

D

Database marketing, 199
Davis, Owen, 291
Davis, Stanley, 129, 227
Deal, Terrence, 153
De Bono, Edward, 30
Decision making, 6–7
Defining business of organization,
     35–46
   mission statement, 61–63
"Denial or Trust Me Reflex," 45
Denial phase, 131–32
Deregulation, 10, 23
Discount rate, 75
Discrimination, 156
Dreyfus, Patricia, 76
Drucker, Peter, 7, 67, 108, 246
Duggan, Bob, 62
Durant, Ariel and Will, 6

E

Earning asset mix, 95–96
Earnings component, 74–78
Earnings measure of performance, 75–76
Earning versus nonearning assets, 91–93
Education and training, 59–60, 121, 154–56, 274
Einstein, Albert, 7
Embley, Kenneth, 187, 188
Employees
  motivation of, 272–77
  reaction to cultural change, 131–33
  recruiting and hiring, 123–24
  standards and values of, 164–69
European Economic Community, 3, 111
Expectancy theory, 280
Exploration phase, 132, 133

F

Fargen, Denny, 62
FASB 95 and FASB 104, 78, 120
Ferguson, Marilyn, 24
Finance companies, 23
Financial performance optimization, 258–59
First Interstate Bancorp, 8–9
First National Bank of McCook, 62
Flamson, Richard, III, 24
Focus groups, 210, 211
Follett, Mary Parker, 145
Ford, Henry, 1
Ford Motor Company, 147–48, 233
Foster, Richard, 9
Fractional pricing, 97–98, 102
Franchisee relationship, 237
Franchise extension, 208
Friedman, Thomas, 214
Funding and funds acquisition, 41–44

G

General Motors Acceptance Company (GMAC), 15
Goldman Sachs, 23
Gorbachev, Mikhail, 24–25
Graves, Desmond, 181
Groupthink, 8–9, 10, 65
Growth and profitability strategies, 70–78
"Guilt Redistribution or Weasel Reflex," 15
Gup, Benton E., 251

H

Hector, Gary, 164
Henderson, Bruce, 197
Hibernia Corporation, 123
Higgins, Michael T., 240–42
High performance, dynamics of, 90, 105, 119
High performance company, 246
High performance model; see Bettinger high performance model
"High Performance Planning Report," 86
High performance strategy, 4–5, 125
Hofstede, G., 129
Human resource management and development, 182–90, 242
  orientation and placement, 185–86
  motivation, 189
  performance, 186–88
  recruitment, 184
  screening and hiring, 184–85
  strategic planning, 183–84

I

Implementation phase, 263
Incentives, 283–90
Individual retirement accounts (IRAs), 21

Innate abilities and talents, 273–74
Innovation, 9
Integrated marketing, 199
Integration and diversification, 207
Integrative and segmentalist
    organizations, 29
Interchange State Bank, 218
Interest expense, 98–101
Interest income, 90–98
Investment policies, 120
IRAs, 21

J–K

Job design and content, 269–71
Junk bond market, 23
Kanas, John Adam, 79
Kane, Chester, 203
Kane, Edward J., 14
Kanter, Rosabeth Moss, 29, 188
Kennedy, Allen A., 153
Key Bank of Utah, 188
Killman, Ralph H., 131
Kopelman, Richard E., 280
Kornhauser, Arthur, 271
Kroc, Ray, 52, 61
Kuhn, Thomas, 8

L

Labich, Kenneth, 52
Lateral (right-handed) thinking, 30–
    34
Lawler, Edward E., III, 151, 187
Leadership during change, 26, 27,
    180, 242
    accountability, 60–61
    and corporate culture, 127, 130–
        31, 140–47
    developing a new state of mind,
        28–34
    management sensitivity, 150–51
    strategic focus, 53–63

Leadership during change—*Cont.*
    strategic management and
        planning, 46–49
    strategic vision, 34–35, 141, 248–
        51
Leadership quality, 265–69
Leavitt, Ted, 29, 36, 41, 67, 193, 223
Leeds, Barry, 225
Lending paradigm, 44
*Life and Death on the Corporate
    Battlefield*, 214
Lifestyle groups, 202
Livingston, J. Sterling, 186
Loans, 120, 122–24

M

MacKinnon, Donald, 31–32
Macro analysis, 122
Maddox, Jeffrey, 71
Management effectiveness, 266–67
Management quality, 265–69
Management sensitivity, 150
"Management and Strategic
    Refocus," 264
March of Folly, 8
Market development, 206
Marketing
    alternatives, generic, 206–8
    defined, 194
    focus and quality, 120–21
Marketing director, 244
Market penetration, 206, 207–8
Marketing plan, developing
    benefits package, creating, 213–
        29, 245
    bottom line, 196–97
    needs analysis, 208–13
    promotion and delivery, 229–38
    sales culture, 238–43
    segmentation focus, 197–208
Market positioning strategy, 193–
    243, 259
    based on quality, 224–28
    benefits oriented, 218–19

Market positioning strategy—*Cont.*
  competitive advantage, 218
  customer satisfaction, 228–29
  promotion and delivery, 229–38
  sales culture, 238–43
  sales increase, 216–18
  value-added, explained, 219–24
Megatrends, 35
Merger/acquisition, 97
Micro analysis, 122
Middle management, and strategic
  focus, 54–57, 60–61
Miller Brewing Company, 204–6
Minalba, 220
Mind of the Strategist, 31
Mintzberg, Henry, 149
Mission statement, 61–63
Mitchell, Arnold, 202
Morrow, Mike, 97
Motivation, 48, 142, 189–90, 276–77,
  289

N

Naisbitt, John, 35
Needs analysis, 208–13
Nelson, Roy, 61
Nonbanks, 15, 20–21, 23, 45
Noninterest income, profitability
  dynamics of, 101–2
Nontraditional financial institutions
  (nonbanks), 15
North Fork Bancorp, 79

O

OCC Failure Report, 119
Office politics, 149–50
Ogilvy, David, 32, 214
Ohmae, Kenichi, 30, 46
*100 Best Companies to Work for in
  America*, 148
*Organizational Culture and
  Leadership*, 140

Organizational Dynamics, 129
Organizational structure, 106–10,
  145
Orientation, 177, 185–86, 274
"Ostrich reflex," 14
Ouchi, William G., 127
Overhead expense, 105–15
  control through accountability,
    110–11
  and changes in organizational
    structure, 106–10
  occupancy expense, 116–18
  salary and benefits, 106
  technology, 111–15

P

Paradigm, challenging traditional,
  24–27, 64
Paradigm paralysis, 7
"Paradigm shift," 8, 10
Parsons, Rick, 209–10
P$YCLE, 202
Peoples Bancorp, 52
Performance appraisal, 281–83
Petersen, Donald, 147–48
Pinola, Joseph, 9
Pooled capital, 45
Portfolio risk, 123
Porter, Michael E., 20, 72, 252
Porter's Model of Industry
  Attractiveness, 20–23
Portillo, Richard, 220
Potential Rating Index for Zip
  Markets (PRIZM), 202
Pricing strategy, 57–59, 96–97
PRIZM, 202
Product development, 207
Profitability dynamics of asset
  quality, 119–20
Profitability dynamics of return on
  assets
  analyzing earning asset mix, 95–
    96

Profitability dynamics of return on assets—*Cont.*
  diversification and fee-income sources, 103–4
  earning versus nonearning assets, 91–93
  interest income, 90–91
  noninterest income, 101–2
  peer group analysis, 86–90
  pricing, 96–98
  sale-leaseback, 93–95
  waivers, managing, 103
Profitability dynamics of return on equity
  consensus on ROE target, 78–79
  desired capital ratio and allocation, 79–80, 83–85
  opportunity, 83–85
  required ROE and incremental earnings, 80–82
Promotion and delivery, 229–38
Public Agenda Foundation Study, 272
Pure growth strategy, 70
Pure profitability strategy, 70

Q–R

Quality, 265–69
Quality of Individual Commitment and Effort Component, 275–76
Rappaport, Alfred, 69
Regulation Q, 11, 17
Resistance phase, 132
Return on assets (ROA)
  profitability dynamics of, 86–98, 103, 105–15
  required, and incremental earnings, 80–82
  taxes, 124
Return on equity (ROE), 16
  management based on, 45
  profitability dynamics of, 78–90
Reward systems, 151–53, 275–76
Right-handed thinking, 30–34

Riley, Pat, 24
Rituals, to support values, 153–54, 290
Roach, Stephen, 113
Russell, O. C., Jr., 123
Ryan, Michael F., 32–34

S

Sale-leaseback, 93–95
Sales culture, 238–43
Sales dominant bank, 235, 236
Savings and loan industry, changes in, 11–16
Schein, Edgar H., 140
Schwartz, Howard, 129
Securitization, 118
Security Pacific Automation Company, 113
Segmentalist organizations, 29
Segmentation, as marketing focus, 200–206
Self-esteem, 273
"Sell the bank" strategy
Senior management, and strategic focus, 53
Shareholder value, 16–17, 43, 45, 52, 62, 244
  creating, 69, 81–82
  growth and profitability strategies, 70–78
Sheshunoff, Alex, 193
Sheshunoff and Company, 86, 284
Silverzweig, Stan, 170
Solman, Paul, 214
Statement of purpose and values, 61–63
Stiller, Blake, 113
Strategic action plans, 48, 90
Strategically supportive culture, 63
Strategic change process
  challenging tradition, 24–27
  communication, importance of, 26–27
  key steps in, 27–66

Strategic focus, 28, 49–63, 121
and accountability, 271–72
and analysis of existing culture,
138–40
attitude toward change, 139–40
enhancing, 59–63
example of weak, 55–58
and interest expense, 99–100
ROE target, consensus on, 78–79
Strategic initiatives, 43–46
Strategic management and planning,
251–64
Strategic planning, 27, 46–49, 251–
64
Strategic vision, 27, 34–35, 38
desired culture, identifying, 134,
174–77
leadership and, 248–51
and marketing, 244
mission statement, 61–63
strategic planning association, 46–
49
Structure of Scientific Revolutions, 8
Supervision quality, 265–69
Suppliers, and increase of borrowing
power, 21
Swatch watches, 10

T

Teamwork, 147–48
Technological advancement, and
paradigm shift, 10

Technological discontinuity, 9–11
Thrift institutions, 16
Titcomb, Woodbury C., 52
Toffler, Alvin, 3
Toynbee, Arnold, 4
Training, 59–60, 121, 154–56, 274,
286–87
Tuchman, Barbara, 8

U–V

United Fruit Company, 219
VAL's Framework, 202
Value, in financial theory, 74–75
Value-added, 219–24
Violano, Michael, 114
Von Oech, Roger, 46

W–Z

Walsh, Jerry, 212
Walters, Bob, 72–74
Whitehead, Alfred North, 246
Whitehead, David D., 251
Wholesalers (banks), 237
Wiley, D. Linn, 50–51, 62
Workgroups, 148–49, 175–76, 177
Yankelovich, Daniel, 188
Zemke, Ron, 3
Zullinger, Robert, 127–28